Beyond the
Latin Lover

8½. Courtesy of Photofest.

Beyond the
Latin Lover

Marcello Mastroianni,

Masculinity, and Italian Cinema

Jacqueline Reich

INDIANA UNIVERSITY PRESS

Bloomington and Indianapolis

This book is a publication of
Indiana University Press
601 North Morton Street
Bloomington, IN 47404-3797 USA

http://iupress.indiana.edu

Telephone orders 800-842-6796
Fax orders 812-855-7931
Orders by e-mail iuporder@indiana.edu

The paper used in this publication meets the minimum requirements of American National
Standard for Information Sciences—Permanence of Paper for Printed Library Materials,
ANSI Z39.48-1984.

Manufactured in the United States of America

An earlier version of chapter 2 appeared as "Undressing the Latin Lover: Marcello
Mastroianni, Fashion, and *La dolce vita*" in *Fashion Culture,* ed. Stella Bruzzi and Pamela
Church Gibson (London: Routledge, 2000): 209–20.

Library of Congress Cataloging-in-Publication Data

Reich, Jacqueline, date
Beyond the Latin lover : Marcello Mastroianni, masculinity, and Italian cinema /
Jacqueline Reich.
p. cm.
Includes bibliographical references and index.
ISBN 0-253-34351-8 (alk. paper) — ISBN 0-253-21644-3 (pbk. : alk. paper)
1. Mastroianni, Marcello, 1924—Criticism and interpretation. 2. Latin lovers in motion
pictures—Italy. 3. Masculinity in motion pictures. I. Title.
PN2688.M33R45 2004
791.43'028'092—dc22

2003017465

1 2 3 4 5   09 08 07 06 05 04

Contents

Acknowledgments

This project owes its completion to many people and institutions that have helped me over the course of the past several years. The generous junior research leave accorded me by my home institution of the State University of New York at Stony Brook gave me the large chunk of time needed to immerse myself in Mastroianni's films. A grant from my union, the United University Professionals, funded my trip to Italy to gather primary materials, and the staff of the Mediateca Regionale Toscana, in particular Umberta Brazzini and Donatella Aguglia, bent over backward to accommodate my needs, making me feel part of their family. Photofest allowed me access to their rich collection of film stills. The librarians of Stony Brook's interlibrary loan office also need to be acknowledged for their quick and persistent ability to locate the many obscure materials I requested.

I am indebted to many colleagues who patiently read the manuscript in various forms and provided unwavering support. At Stony Brook, Krin Gabbard and Louise Vasvari were there every step of the way, as mentors and editors. Mary Jo Bona, Helen Cooper, Fred Gardaphé, David Gilmore, Robert Harvey, Iza Kalinowska-Blackwood, Ann Kaplan, Shirley Lim, Adrienne Munich, and Lori Repetti at various times and in various ways helped both me and this project along. A very special thanks goes to Charles Franco, the chair of the Department of European Languages, whose steadfast defense and encouragement of all things pertaining to my academic career has been essential to my professional and personal well-being. In addition, the department's secretarial staff, especially Marie Sweatt and Joan Vogelle, imparted unconditional support for even ridiculous requests. My Cinema and Cultural Studies students, in particular those in the Marcello Mastroianni/ Sophia Loren seminar, helped me shape and articulate many of the ideas expressed herein.

I would like to thank many other colleagues and friends whose various fields of expertise helped shape my vision of Mastroianni's films: Stephen Gundle, for his time in reading major portions of the manuscript; and Mark Chu, Roberto Dainotto, John Eipper, Piero Garofalo, Meg Gallucci, James Hay, Norman Holland, James Mandrell, Toby Miller, and Eva Woods, for pointing me in the right direction when I found myself at a loss. Ellen Nerenberg and Ruth Ben-Ghiat invited me to present my work at Wesleyan University and the Columbia Modern Italian Studies Seminar, respectively, and the comments I received at these lectures proved invaluable to the book's development, as did my presentations at the Humanities Institute at Stony Brook and the University of California at Berkeley. The influence of three of my professors at the latter university—the late Gian Paolo Biasin, Gavriel Moses, and Steven Botterill—is felt throughout this study, and I owe them a great deal of gratitude.

At Indiana University Press, Michael Lundell's unwavering support and championing of this project, even during difficult times, means more than I can express. Richard Higgins also deserves much thanks for often thankless tasks. I also would like to express gratitude to the keen comments and strong support of the two anonymous readers, in particular the second reader, whose insights into the manuscript helped shape my own conclusions. The copyediting staff should be heartily congratulated for their careful corrections of my many mistakes.

The birth of this project coincided with the birth of my son Sean, and although he is too young to appreciate it, I am indebted to his patience during Mommy's many trips upstairs and "be right back"s. My family members, in particular my parents Barbara and Leo Reisner and Bob and Dale Reich, kept me going with constant words of encouragement and generous offers of babysitting. In that area, a special thanks goes to Stephanie Nelson, whose love and care of my son freed me from unnecessary worry during the time I needed to devote to this project. I would like to express my love and thanks to my sisters Alexandra and Lindsay Reich, my in-laws Edith and Martin Szold and Stuart and Stephanie de Ganon, my brother-in-law and bibliographic wiz Pieter de Ganon, and Elaine, Larry, and Allison Glickman, and to my extended family of good friends—Pam Metzger, Becky Devlin, Brian Downey,

Leslie and Dan Ilany, and Sandy Zabar. Finally, I can honestly say that this work never would have come about without the love, support, and devotion of Matthew de Ganon, to whom I dedicate it as well. He is my lover in all the word's meanings.

Introduction

This study was born, so to speak, on the day of Marcello Mastroianni's death, December 19, 1996. Mastroianni had not made his battle with pancreatic cancer public, so his demise came as a shock to many, including myself. In reading about his life, I began to notice a pattern in both American and Italian tributes. Almost all obituaries somehow referenced his star image as the consummate Latin lover, the most manly of European men, while at the same time introducing some antithetical element, be it "self-deprecation" (*New York Times*), "imperfection" (*Time*), or reluctance (the U.K.'s *Daily Telegraph*). I began to consider the contradictions inherent in these descriptions: that although Mastroianni, as commodity, was often marketed as the quintessential Italian man, his characters betrayed instead a much more conflicting image of Italian masculinity than the category of Latin lover allowed.

These notions of self-deprecation and imperfection led me to contemplate not only Mastroianni's life, work, and legacy but also the broader topic of Italian masculinity per se. Even the word itself—masculinity—is not easily translatable into Italian. *Mascolinità, maschilità,* and even to some extent *virilità* qualify as Italian equivalents.[1] Very little scholarship exists on the subject. The first Italian scholarly anthology to deal with the subject, *Genere e mascolinità* (Gender and Masculinity), edited by Sandro Bellassai and Maria Malatesta and published in 2000, makes great strides in tackling the issue of Italian masculinity from a multi-disciplinary, albeit materialist, perspective. A worthy predecessor is Simonetta Piccone Stella and Chiara Saraceno's *Genere* (Gender), which, although an anthology of mostly translated articles, also ad-

xi

dresses Italian scholarship's reluctance to turn the lens of gender studies onto itself.[2] In the United States, the anthropologist David Gilmore's work on Mediterranean masculinity opened the door for increased debate, and its influence looms large in this study.[3] Much work in Italian cultural studies has historicized Italian masculinity, particularly in its relationship to Fascism, or Italian-American ethnicity, with little attempt to theoretically anchor these cultural representations.[4]

My work redresses this gap in scholarship by taking an in-depth look at Marcello Mastroianni, one of Italian masculinity's quintessential icons. On an extra-national level, Italian masculinity has been widely seen as the sexual masculine ideal of Western civilization. What this study reveals, however, is that this image is misleading, and there is no better window into the image of contemporary Italian masculinity than its representation in Italian cinema.

Scholars of American masculinity have shown how cinema, stardom, and gender shape and reflect significant shifts in contemporary culture and society. Italy is no exception, and is in fact a unique case study, given the many social and political upheavals of the second half of the twentieth century: its fifty-eight post-war governments (at last count); the transition from the hardships of post-war reconstruction in the 1940s and the 1950s to the economic boom of the 1960s; the cultural, social, and sexual upheavals of the 1970s, in particular the feminist movement; and the aging of its population. Yet when one examines the "greatest hits" of post-war Italian cinema, the era for which it is most famous, one sees that underneath the façade of a presumed hyper-masculinity is really the anti-hero, the Italian *inetto* (the inept man), a man at odds with and out of place in a rapidly changing political, social, and sexual environment.

No actor came to personify this phenomenon better than Mastroianni. In the course of Mastroianni's long career, he appeared in diverse roles such as the sexually impotent protagonist of *Il bell'Antonio* (Mauro Bolognini, 1960), the gay anti-Fascist radio announcer in *Una giornata particolare* (A Special Day, Ettore Scola, 1977), and an older man who marries a young dwarf in Maria Luisa Bemberg's *De eso no se habla* (I Don't Want to Talk about It, 1993). Moreover, as anti-heroes rather than Latin lovers, his characters collide with important political, social, and economic changes in post-war Italy. In *I soliti ignoti* (Big Deal on Madonna Street, Mario Monicelli, 1958), the rapid growth of the Italian economy in the 1950s and the ensuing division between rich and poor form the backdrop for Mastroianni's unemployed photographer forced to care for his infant son while his wife serves jail time for black marketeering. The post-1960s malaise experienced by the characters in

Marco Ferreri's *La grande bouffe* (Blow-Out, 1973) leads them to eat themselves to death in a last hedonistic frenzy. Fellini's *La città delle donne* (City of Women, 1980) ridicules Mastroianni's middle-aged Don Giovanni within the context of the 1970s feminist movement.

This study does not pretend to be a comprehensive analysis of Mastroianni's cinematic career, a task ably managed by Donald Dewey's biography *Marcello Mastroianni: His Life and Art*.[5] Rather, it seeks to debunk the myth of the Latin lover in favor of that of the anti-hero through an analysis of some of Mastroianni's films, while at the same time situating the films within the context of the many transformations of post-war Italian society. Because Mastroianni made more than 150 films, I have chosen to concentrate on those which would be most familiar to an English-speaking audience and readily accessible to scholars and students who wish to compare the analyses with the actual texts. Moreover, because I have situated this study so heavily in post-war Italian culture (it draws on contemporary literature, history, theater, and anthropology), I have elected to deal mostly with Mastroianni's Italian films, despite the fact that, especially in the last stages of his career, he starred in many international productions. I do, however, break my own rules twice: first, in my discussion of some of his hard-to-find early films with Sophia Loren, for they establish a pattern in their work together; and second, in the last chapter's examination of Mastroianni's final years, a period in which he participated in relatively few Italian productions, due, in part, to a national industry decline.

The definition of masculinity I use in my project is grounded in the greater historical, cultural, political, and economic shifts of twentieth-century Italy. Michel Foucault has argued that sexuality and gender are constructions influenced by various institutions that contribute to the constitution of individual identity. The historian George Mosse has cited the growth of bourgeois respectability as one of the primary factors involved in this construction of both a twentieth-century European masculine ideal and the "deviant other." Thus, masculinity in general, and Italian masculinity in particular, can be seen as (to borrow David Halperin's terminology) "modern, Western, bourgeois productions," shifting over time and varying with respect to culture. In Italy, the many social and political changes of the second half of the twentieth century have produced unsteady and conflicting masculine roles, which found expression in the figure of the *inetto* in Mastroianni's films.[6]

The book's first chapter summarizes the main thesis: namely, that the roles Mastroianni played reflected an Italian masculinity in crisis in post-war Italy. It defines the dominant terms employed throughout the study: the star, Italian masculinity, and the *inetto*, and situates them within the context of twentieth-century Italy and Italian cinema. Chapter 2 turns its attention to Federico Fellini's *La dolce vita* (The Sweet Life, 1959), the film that made Mastroianni an international star and labeled him the quintessential Latin lover. Mastroianni's character (Marcello Rubini) is a classic *inetto*. Mired in mediocrity as a tabloid journalist and emotionally impotent in his relationships with women, he actively chooses passivity and alienation as a way of life as he joins a world of aristocratic decadence at the end of the film. Moreover, Marcello's ultimate failure in his search for meaning and spiritual redemption in an increasingly materialist world is directly affected by Italy's industrial rise to power after the devastation of World War II and its growing presence as cultural commodity. The Latin lover is above all a consumer icon offered up for consumption as a mass-marketed product. Mastroianni became a symbol for Italian style, for a national public experiencing greater prosperity after years of struggle, and for an international consumer market hungry for all things Italian, especially fashion.

Chapter 3 explores two of Mastroianni's most important post–*dolce vita* films: *Il bell'Antonio* and *Divorce—Italian Style* (*Divorzio all'italiana*, Pietro Germi, 1961), both of which directly engage traditional and contemporary notions of Sicilian masculinity. Through an examination of anthropological studies of Sicily done in the 1950s and 1960s as well as writings by important Sicilian authors such as Vitaliano Brancati and Leonardo Sciascia, this chapter reveals how these two seemingly very different films both demystify the rigid constructions of masculinity which came to dominate Sicilian life: the *gallo* (the Sicilian version of the Don Giovanni) and the *cornuto* (the cuckold). Both films expose the tendentious nature of those very masculine constructions with Mastroianni as *inetto*, the first through the melodramatic psychological examination of impotence, and the second through a satiric play on the Sicilian honor code against the backdrop of the politically charged issue of divorce.

Mastroianni's work with Federico Fellini, from *8½* (1962) to *Intervista* (Interview, 1987), the subject of chapter 4, reveals how the director self-consciously parodies Mastroianni's Latin lover image, particularly in his characters' usually unsuccessful encounters with women. In a different twist on Fellini studies, however, this chapter concentrates on the comic aspects of the Fellini/Mastroianni collaborations. Films such as *City of Women*, with Mastroianni as the inept Casanova who confronts the fervid feminist in a biting satire of both stereotypes, as well as his pseudo-documentary *Block-notes di un regista* (A Director's Notebook, 1970) give expression to many of the deep-seated anxieties surrounding

cultural constructions of Italian masculinity, allowing the male character to laugh at what he fears: his shortcomings in relation to the masculine ideal, and his ineptitude in dealing with increasingly challenging
models of femininity.

In chapter 5, I examine the figure of the *inetto* in Mastroianni's
twelve collaborations with Sophia Loren, from Alessandro Blasetti's
Peccato che sia una canaglia (Too Bad She's Bad, 1954) up through
Robert Altman's *Prêt-à-Porter* (Ready to Wear, 1994). There his characters meet their match in Loren's various incarnations of what Kathleen
Rowe has termed the "unruly woman," defined as a woman who disrupts the norms of femininity and social hierarchy of male over female through outrageousness and excess in their body, behavior, and
speech.[7] This chapter traces the history of the unruly woman in Italian history and culture from Medieval and Renaissance literature up
through twentieth-century variety theater and post–World War II cinema.
Loren's characters, with their exaggeratedly feminine body and calcu-
lated use of performative femininity, call into question traditional masculine gender constructions and at the same time redefine the feminine.
Mastroianni's inept counterparts, forced to deal both literally and figu-
ratively with the "woman on top," address the post-war conflicts of Italian masculinity in the face of a more independent femininity.

The book's final chapter deals with the representation of aging Italian masculinity as Mastroianni came to embody it on screen. Here I
argue that in Mastroianni's later films, including Fellini's *Ginger and
Fred* (1986) and *Intervista* and Giuseppe Tornatore's *Stanno tutti bene*
(Everybody's Fine, 1990), the now-aging *inetto* exhibits a nostalgic
longing for a world that has been altered by the dissolution of the traditional family structure and changing sexual codes and conventions.
Unlike Hollywood stars, who often attempt to mask the effects of aging
on their bodies or hide themselves from view, Mastroianni seemed to
embrace it, revealing a melancholic figure and a flaccid body that often
failed to live up to the evolving constructions of Italian masculinity. A
look into Mastroianni's last films also allows a glimpse at some of his
international productions, especially his American ones, and how they
negotiate the exigencies of the classical Hollywood narrative's denial of
aging with Mastroianni's in-your-face representations, even while confronting death.

There are several leitmotifs to this study. Certainly, the image of the
Latin lover reappears in almost every chapter: in its persistence as Mastroianni's extracinematic icon, as well as his consistent desire to take on
roles which would challenge that image. Luigi Pirandello's concept of
humor—what he called the "feeling of the opposite"—also proves es-

sential for all discussions of ineptitude, particularly in relation to the comic. Scholars have noted Pirandello's profound influence on twentieth-century Italian cultural representations, and film is no exception.[8] In this study, Pirandello's presence is especially felt in theorizing the *inetto* (chapter 1), in the role of humor in Fellini's films (chapter 4), and in the idea of youthfulness as masquerade (chapter 6).

Inevitably, in an examination of a career of Mastroianni's magnitude, many films fall by the wayside. Some notable, and often painfully felt, omissions in this study include Mario Monicelli's *Il Compagno* (The Organizer, 1963), Michelangelo Antonioni's *La notte* (The Night, 1961), and Nikita Mikalkov's *Oci Ciorne* (Dark Eyes, 1987). Some may also fault me for my failure to include detailed discussions of two other important Mastroianni collaborators: Marco Ferreri, with whom Mastroianni made *La grande bouffe* and *Ciao, maschio* (Bye, Bye Monkey, 1977); or his films with Catherine Deneuve, including *La cagna* (Liza, 1972) and *Touche pas à la femme blanche* (Don't Touch the White Woman, 1974), both directed by Ferreri as well, and *L'Événement le plus important depuis l'homme a marché sur la lune* (A Slightly Pregnant Man, Jacques Demy, 1973). My choices are due in part to editorial concerns (the length of the book and the desire to concentrate on Mastroianni's work with one director and one star) and personal preferences. Mostly, however, I decided to place my focus on Federico Fellini because of the profound impact he and Mastroianni had on world cinema, as well their shared status as national symbols. Along those lines, my decision to interrogate his work with Loren as opposed to Deneuve has to do with Loren's comparable status as international icon of Italian femininity. I also limited my analysis to films in which Mastroianni was the protagonist, and not a supporting actor. That excluded interesting works such as Agnès Varda's *Les Cent et une nuit de Simon Cinema* (One Hundred and One Nights, 1995) and *Al di là delle nuvole* (Beyond the Clouds, Michelangelo Antonioni and Wim Wenders, 1995). I leave these films for future scholars to pursue.

Beyond the
Latin Lover

1

In the Beginning

Mastroianni, Masculinity,

and Italian Cinema

> I don't like myself very much. You might think I'm just
> being modest. But I have skinny arms, skinny legs, very
> skinny, that have actually impeded me from playing cer-
> tain roles, maybe luckily, because I was never cast as the
> hero. And this short nose! Full lips, yes, but I've always
> preferred thin lips, like Jean Gabin's, and an aquiline
> nose. I should also cite [Vittorio] Gassman. And also the
> Ethopians and Abyssinians: they have beautiful, aristo-
> cratic noses.[1]

Mastroianni's self-image departs from the traditional pose of the Latin
lover, the star persona that was ascribed to him by the international film
community and came to be the dominating icon of Italian masculinity
in post-war Italy. Rather than self-confident, Mastroianni appears self-
deprecating; rather than heroic, he sees himself as the anti-hero; rather
than a sex symbol, he looks to others as models of masculine beauty.

Italian masculinity, with its cultural associations with Ancient Rome,
Renaissance sculpture, and the Latin lover, has been widely seen as the
masculine ideal of Western civilization. Rather than the dashing and
debonair Don Giovanni, however, the *inetto*, the particularly Italian incarnation of the schlemiel or anti-hero, comes to dominate the representation of masculinity in Italian cinema, and in Mastroianni's films in
particular. This figure is a man in conflict with an unsettled and at
times unsettling political and sexual environment. Since the fall of Fascism and the end of World War II, Italy has been mired by radical
change in the social and economic fabric of daily life. Mastroianni's roles
provide a window into important shifts in gender roles in this turbulent
and unstable period as they came to be reflected on the silver screen.

This chapter serves as a general introduction to the fundamental issues that form the backbone of my approach to Marcello Mastroianni's
films. The first section begins with an examination of the psychological,
cultural, and anthropological tropes of Italian masculinity in its traditional and often stereotypical forms: the sexually potent and protective
male concerned with preserving his honor, and the ideal of the *bella
figura*, which reinforces the performative nature of Italian masculinity.

1

2

In the period following Fascism and World War II, and even to some extent before, these ideals began to unravel, revealing a conception of Italian manhood which was threatened by a constantly shifting political climate and changing gender roles. The result was the emergence of the *inetto* as the dominant cultural representation of masculinity in literature as well as the cinema, and especially in Mastroianni's films. The next section gives a brief overview of the history of the representation of masculinity in Italian cinema, with an emphasis on the post-Fascist rupture and how both neorealist and post-neorealist films of all genres speak to an Italian masculinity in crisis. The final section explores the construction of the Mastroianni star persona and his career within the field of star studies and the Italian film industry. While using the Hollywood model as the paradigm for my analysis of the Italian star system, I also underscore the fact that many unique aspects of Italian society and culture contributed to Mastroianni's success and the trajectory of his career. Finally, throughout the chapter, the reader will encounter "previews of coming attractions," so to speak: brief references to subjects and themes that will be explored in greater detail in subsequent chapters.

Italian Masculinity Defined and Unmasked

David Gilmore's work on Mediterranean manhood has important consequences for an analysis of contemporary Italian masculinity, for it combines anthropological study with psychological insight into the present-day Italian male character. Subscribing to the theory that masculinity is not predetermined but, rather, "culturally and publicly sustained," he notes how Mediterranean masculinity is defined publicly rather than privately. Gilmore unifies the Mediterranean countries of Spain, Italy, Morocco, and Greece in their ecology, settlement patterns, economic adaptations, and—most significantly—a "sense of cultural homogeneity" in a shared image of manhood. A good Spanish/Italian/Greek man is "good at being a man": public space is the proving ground of his masculinity through sexual potency (the spreading of the seed), and then providing for and protecting the family.[2]

This notion of publicly performed masculinity relates specifically to the Italian concept of the *bella figura*, the manifestation of the private self in the public arena. Gloria Nardini observes how the *bella figura* is, in many ways, a primary metaphor in the Italian way of life, constituting "the notion of self as a social presentation for the consumption of others."[3] The *bella figura*, according to Nardini, is circumscribed, on the one hand, by the ideal of honor, the source of his good name and reputation. On the other hand, the negative pole is shame (*vergogna*), the fear of making a *brutta figura*—showing a bad face in public. She traces the *bella figura*'s origins back to the Renaissance, specifically to Baldassare Castiglione's concept of *sprezzatura* as elucidated in *The Book of the Courtier*. The opposite of affectation, *sprezzatura* denotes a naturalness in appearance without revealing the effort that went into its preparation. The result is the projection of grace:

> So you see how art, or any intent effort, if it is disclosed, deprives everything of grace. Who among you fails to laugh when our messer Pierpaolo dances after his own fashion, with those capers of his, his legs stiff on tiptoe, never moving his head, as if he were a stick of wood, and all this so studied that he really seems to be counting his steps? What eye is so blind as not to see in this the ungainliness of affectation; and not to see the grace of that cool *disinvoltura* [ease] (for when it is a matter of bodily movements many call it that) in many of the men and women here present, who seem in words, in laughter, in posture not to care; or seem to be thinking more of everything than of that, so as to cause all who are watching them to believe that they are almost incapable of making a mistake?[4]

Performance is thus integral to the self-fashioning of the courtier: he must exhibit a lack of affectation and exude a graceful ease in the construction of his public persona.[5] Also primary is the use of the body as a means of projecting the spirit of *sprezzatura:* grace is both ethereal and material in the display of *disinvoltura*.

Similarly, although in the completely different realm of political theory, Niccolò Machiavelli integrates the role of performance into *The Prince*. In citing the qualities necessary for a prince to be successful (compassion, faithfulness, integrity, kindness, and religion), Machiavelli, in a key passage, notes that if one does not possess them, one must "appear" to embody them:

> Furthermore, I shall be so bold as to assert this: that having them and practising them at all times is harmful; and appearing to have them is useful. . . . Let a prince therefore act to conquer and to maintain the state; his methods will always be judged honourable and will be praised by all; for ordinary people are always deceived by appearances and by the outcome of a thing.[6]

For Machiavelli, the public is essentially separate from the private: "Everyone sees what you appear to be, few touch upon what you are" (60). Thus, performativity is vital to the successful prince: he must appear kind and merciful in order to be a thriving leader, with the final result justifying the pretense. Later, Machiavelli even notes that just as important as savvy and intelligence is precisely the "impression" of having those very qualities.

The body, performance, and public space come to play an essential role in the courtier's modern descendent, the *bella figura,* as well as in its Northern European counterparts, the English dandy and the French *flâneur.* The dandy, although not necessarily a member of the aristocracy, nevertheless came to epitomize, like the courtier, many of the values traditionally associated with the ruling class: superiority, arrogance, restraint, and refinement. The dandy's attitude and way of life was above all conveyed through clothes. He redefined men's clothing with his form-fitting precursor to the modern-day suit, made predominantly of wool and linen in the restrained colors of blue, white, and black, and highlighting the lone touch of individualism: the cravat, the forerunner to the modern necktie.[7] Whereas the dandy attempted to distinguish himself from the masses, the *flâneur* was a man of the crowd. Giuliana Bruno notes how the French concept of *flanerie* relates to the Italian terrain of "leisure pleasure," or *dolce far niente,* where the focus is the erotics of spectatorship rather than active participation in urban life.[8] He is a "sovereign spectator" who watches and witnesses modern daily life as it develops in bourgeois urban settings, particularly Paris, and is seduced by the capitalist consumerism epitomized in the shopping arcades.[9] Yet the modern *flâneur* is capable only of watching, not of action, mired by crises of insecurity and ineptitude.

Whereas the *flâneur* is the subject of the gaze and the dandy the object, the *bella figura* is at once both spectacle and spectator. His aim is both to be seen and recognized as important and full of honor, as well as to see that others recognize this trait in him. This dual function is possible because an essential component of the dandy, the *flâneur,* and the *bella figura* is public space, the site of display and performance of masculine style.[10] In Italy, this spectacle occurs in the main piazza or the main street of a town or city when the Italian male literally puts on a show for an admiring public.[11] The time of display is more often than not the evening *passeggiata,* when Italian citizens traditionally congregate after work to discuss politics, sports, local gossip, and other events of the day, as well as, once again, to see and be seen. The architectonics of the *bella figura* thus breaks the typical spectator/spectacle dichotomy. The structure of public space, as opposed to the private stage, allows for the simultaneous situation of looking and being looked at.

Furthermore, that public space in Italy has traditionally been coded as masculine in an attempt to differentiate itself from the private, domestic, feminine sphere. These masculine/feminine and public/private dichotomies lie at the foundation of Mediterranean masculinity, particularly in the construction of Sicilian masculinity. The examination in chapter 3 of the Sicilian male in the 1950s and 1960s reveals how both gender and space are rigidly coded and bound by social expectations: that a man's virility depends not only on his sexual prowess but also on his ability to preserve his own honor by protecting the virginity of the family's female members. The Sicilian emphasis on virility and sexual performance (*gallismo*), as well as how female chastity codes are fundamental to the maintenance of his masculinity, are the subject of two Mastroianni films of the early 1960s which examine the issue within the larger context of Sicilian culture: one through melodrama, Mauro Bolognini's *Il bell'Antonio* (1960), and the other through comedy, Pietro Germi's *Divorce—Italian Style*.

This separation between masculine/public and feminine/private is necessary, according to Gilmore, because the greatest threat to masculinity is precisely feminization. Although Gilmore's work is based on extensive field research, psychoanalytic models of male subject formation reach much the same conclusion regarding the masculine/feminine dichotomy. Traditional psychoanalytic theory has attributed the formation of masculine identity to the castration complex, when the male child must renounce the pre-Oedipal world of the mother and identify with the authority of the father. Pre-Oedipal desire is either repressed into the unconscious or channeled into socially acceptable heterosexual desire in the post-Oedipal economy. In order for the masculine ideal to be sustained, the penis must be equated with the phallus: the male subject must align himself with what Kaja Silverman terms "the dominant fiction," or, rather, the psychic and ideological modes of assimilation into proper male subjectivity.[12]

Gilmore observes that this glorification of the phallus is an essential factor in the construction of Mediterranean masculinity:

> Faced with these challenges to masculine autonomy and sensing peril in a world run secretly by women, Mediterranean men seem to fall back on the one unambiguous distinction between the sexes: anatomy. Thus they honor the penis as the repository of manhood and the mirror of the masculine ego. The proof of this precarious manliness is the demonstration of phallic potency through erotic triumph.[13]

This need to prove one's masculinity sexually has manifested itself culturally and cinematically in the perhaps most well-known trope of Italian masculinity: the Latin lover, discussed in detail in chapter 2. The

Latin lover is a symbol of exotic sexuality, the epitome of Mediterranean (as well as Latin American) masculinity, which Mastroianni came to symbolize.

Gilmore notes, however, that in Mediterranean countries, primary pre-Oedipal identification is difficult to overcome because of the primacy of mother/son intimacy and father distance. Because the man's domain is the public sphere, precisely the proving ground of his masculinity, he spends as little time as possible at home, and even less in the child-rearing situation. The primary responsibility of raising the child falls on the women—mother, grandmother, and/or female siblings —resulting in a greater symbiosis with the maternal figure. Although puberty marks the time when the young male leaves the domestic arena for the homosocial public sphere, there is no rite of passage to initiate this transformation, and thus no clear-cut rupture with femininity. As a result, the feminine is a constant menace to the masculine, for the boundaries between them in the construction of masculinity are tenuous at best.[14]

Another threat equal to pre-Oedipal regression is that of homosexuality. Just as the feminine is othered in the Mediterranean world, the homosexual is equally if not more vilified as a threat to traditional masculinity, for he fails to prove his manliness through the most visible means: sexual reproduction. For Lee Edelman, the homosexual in heterosexual culture is the incarnation of the death drive which endangers the sanctity of the family and effaces heterosexual reproduction.[15] The Mediterranean man who does not publicly manifest the honor of masculinity through "virile performance" is shamed, cuckolded, and feminized. As a result, Mediterranean cults of masculinity are "at the same time powerful and inherently fragile," requiring "constant vigilance and defense" against the threat of feminization, regression to the pre-Oedipal state, and homosexuality.[16]

On screen, Marcello Mastroianni's characters epitomize the instability of Italian masculinity through the cultural configuration of the Italian *schlemiel* or anti-hero. Sanford Pinsker, in his study on the *schlemiel* as metaphor in Jewish literature and culture, defines the *schlemiel* as someone "who handles a situation in the worst possible manner or is dogged by an ill luck that is more or less due to his own ineptness."[17] As opposed to the *schlimazl*, who is more the victim of pure bad luck, the *schlemiel* is usually an agent in his own destruction. In Yiddish and Jewish culture, the *schlemiel* assumes many different forms: the cuckold, the inept businessman, and the brow-beaten husband.

Gian Paolo Biasin has isolated the Italian version of the *schlemiel*— the *inetto*—in twentieth-century Italian poetry and prose. Biasin notes how the modern and contemporary protagonists of Western literature have departed from the models of Greek and Roman epic heroes. They are defined not by action but, rather, by passivity, intellectualism, and artistic sensibility; they are failures rather than successes, mired in bourgeois mediocrity rather than stellar achievement.[18] For Biasin, the classic *schlemiel* in twentieth-century Italian literature is Zeno Cosini, the protagonist of Italo Svevo's novel, *La coscienza di Zeno* (1923; *The Confessions of Zeno,* English trans. 1930), whose total egocentrism and self-consciousness reveals a weak, passive anti-hero. *The Confessions of Zeno* is a modern parody of the *Bildungsroman,* the novel of formation and assimilation: the protagonist never changes and never assimilates into proper bourgeois citizenship, despite undergoing the necessary rites of passage as well as psychoanalysis, which leave him "worse than before." A hypochondriac, Zeno's "disease" is a pure exterior manifestation of his internal crisis. Zeno remains outside and alienated, projecting his own "illness" onto society as a whole: "Life is a little like disease, with its crises and periods of quiescence, its daily improvements and setbacks. But unlike other diseases, life is always mortal. It admits of no cure. It would be like trying to stop up the holes in our body, thinking them to be wounds. We should die of suffocation almost before we were cured."[19]

The literary *inetto*'s origins, however, predate Svevo's creation. It can be traced, among other places, to the mid-to-late-sixteenth-century theater, in particular the *commedia dell'arte,* whose characters and scenarios formed the foundation for much of Italian humor. The *commedia dell'arte*'s stock characters and improvised scenarios draw on the use of grotesque masks, dialects, various plot devices (such as mistaken identities and lovers' games), and *lazzi* (comic interruptions in the plot) for their comedic effect. Of particular relevance to the figure of the *inetto* are several characters: the Venetian merchant Pantalone and the Dottore, pompous elderly gentlemen often foiled by their ineptitude; and the *Zanni,* the buffoons and the clowns such as Brighella, Arlecchino, and Pulcinella, whose exploits revolve either around their cunning or, depending on the servant and situation, their ignorance. One notable scenario, transcribed by Flaminio Scala in 1620, "The Jealous Old Man," recounts the story of Pantalone and his much younger wife, Isabella, who is in love with a handsome young man named Oratio. Although Pantalone is extremely jealous and maintains strict watch over Isabella, Oratio manages to enjoy her after Pedrolino, Pantalone's servant, helps arrange a tryst between them. When Burattino, a grocer in whose house the liaison takes place, declares the truth to Pantalone, Oratio jumps in to reveal that Isabella was in fact a virgin, and Pantalone impotent. After confessing, Pantalone gives permission for Isabella to marry Oratio. Pantalone, despite his constant vigilance over Isabella, ultimately fails to maintain his honor. In the end he is revealed to be the consummate *inetto:* an impotent cuckold.[20]

The Italian *inetto,* while rooted in the comic tradition of the *commedia dell'arte,* does not, in its twentieth-century incarnation in film as well as literature, necessarily fall into the categorization of comedy as traditionally defined. Luigi Pirandello's concept of *umorismo* (humor) provides a more appropriate and more modern definition of humor for this literary and cinematic figure. Pirandello traces the notion of *umorismo* back to the Renaissance epic and Cervantes's *Don Quixote,* whose exploits evoke both humor and tragedy, laughter and pity, or what Pirandello terms an anti-rhetorical *sentimento del contrario* (feeling of the opposite)—the essence of *umorismo.* This contradiction is the result of a clash between the real and the ideal, with the latter ultimately revealing itself to be illusory.[21]

Pirandello's own quintessential *inetto* is the protagonist of his novel *Il fu Mattia Pascal* (The Late Mattia Pascal, 1904). Mattia is a good-for-nothing spendthrift who is forced to marry Romilda, a woman of a similar economic class, despite having impregnated another girl. His married life is far from blissful: his nasty mother-in-law evicts Mattia's mother from her home, and he is constantly at odds with her and his wife. After a particularly severe encounter, he escapes to Montecarlo without informing anyone and wins a small fortune. While he is away, a corpse, believed to be Mattia, washes up on the beach in his hometown. Free to fashion himself any way he chooses, Mattia moves to Rome and creates a new identity as Adriano Meis. Yet Adriano Meis, like Mattia Pascal, still remains on the social margins: never able to completely assimilate his new persona for fear of getting caught by the authorities, he, like the *flâneur,* is a witness to, rather than a participant in, modern bourgeois existence, describing himself as an "estranged spectator" lost in the crowd.[22] Freedom, which Mattia once described as an intense feeling of "lightness" soon weighs down on him as "masked tyranny" because he ultimately realizes that he is forever subject to social expectations and constraints—the humoristic clash between the real and the ideal. In the end, Mattia Pascal kills off his alter ego via another water suicide and returns to his previous existence, only to find his wife remarried to his friend. He moves in with his aunt, returns to his job at the library, and resumes his life as "the Late Mattia Pascal."

A modern incarnation of the *inetto,* Mattia Pascal actively chooses passivity and ineptitude as a way of life when he opts to return to his former life. For Biasin, this is precisely the strategy of the *inetto:* "When applied to the hero, 'strategy' has an active, aggressive connotation; when applied to the anti-hero, it has a passive, self-defensive, self-ironic quality. . . . In any case strategy points to the environment, not to the subject, and this environment is definitely hostile, if not cruel and violent."[23] The anti-hero's circumstance, in contemporary Italian literature, is one of alienation, as well as the self-conscious ironization of that condition. For Mattia Pascal, the notion of individual identity, and the freedom to choose that identity, is an illusion. The *inetto* is the cardinal character caught between the real and the ideal, and from this situation derives his humor. At the same time, however, his struggle reveals the tendentious relationship between the individual and the reality in which he lives.

On a psychological plane, the *inetto* shares some characteristics with the classic narcissist as articulated in clinical psychoanalysis. Concentrating specifically on secondary as opposed to primary narcissism— that is, the subject's relation to other objects as opposed to the subject's relation to the mother—the psychiatrist Otto Kernberg and the cultural theorist Christopher Lasch note how the narcissist, like the figure of the *inetto*, aims to quell his own feelings of inadequacies and mediocrity through external validation: his self-esteem is dependent on the approval of others. Like the *bella figura*, the narcissist attempts to mask these perceived inadequacies through the outward manifestation of grandiosity and excessive self-worth. What separates the narcissist from the *inetto* is the subject's relation to the external environment, and how each reacts differently to what Lasch terms "the tensions and anxieties of modern life." Although the narcissist often becomes aggressive toward those who do not immediately satisfy his needs, the *inetto* is passive. Aggression does not fall into his modus operandi—his response is internal as opposed to external self-absorption.[24]

Finally, what is it about the *inetto* or the *schlemiel* that necessitates his being gendered masculine? The *inetto* articulates the traditional binary opposite of the masculine, as it is constructed in Italian culture and society, and as it relates to sexuality: the cuckold, the impotent and feminized man.[25] Rather than active, the *inetto* is passive; rather than brave, he is cowardly; rather than sexually potent, he is either physically or emotionally impotent. His shortcomings and failings are in direct opposition to the prescribed masculine norms deeply rooted in Italian culture.

Thus, in twentieth-century Italy, the *inetto* emerges beneath the façade of the *bella figura*. The Italian male is "good at being a man" precisely because he masks the *inetto* through the performance of hypermasculinity: protection of honor, procreation, and sexual segregation. Post-war Italian cinema examines and dismantles this notion of traditional masculinity by highlighting its performative nature. For the male protagonists as brought to the screen by Mastroianni and others, alienation, social constraint, and ineptitude come to be a way of life. The crucial turning point in the emergence of the *inetto* as the dominant presence on the Italian screen is 1945, as radical changes in Italian society, culture, and politics led to new cinematic representations.[26]

The *Inetto* and Italian Cinema

After the Risorgimento and Italian unification in the nineteenth century, the newly formed Italian nation was faced with the question of national identity: specifically, what did it mean to be an Italian, when the nation itself consisted of stark regional differences and economic as well as social discontinuities? These historical developments, as George Mosse observes, had much to do with the formation of modern masculinity. At the beginning of the nineteenth century, the stereotype of modern masculinity in Western Europe had begun to take shape, mirroring the imperatives of modern society. Bourgeois ideals of moderation, self-control, and order supplanted aristocratic and feudal notions of excessive chivalry. Greater attention was placed on the athletic male body, which, after the French Revolution, came to symbolize both physical and moral virtue. Italian schools and the Italian army institutionalized gymnastics as a means of creating "manly men: disciplined, industrious, modest, and persevering." Significant as well, particularly into the early twentieth century, was the rise of nationalism as a political movement, which relied on the male stereotype as symbol of a new national consciousness. The sculpted body and the brave soldier contrasted with the degenerate enemies of the status quo: the effeminate man or manly woman, the androgyne, homosexuals, and Jews.[27]

In silent cinema, one popular and particularly masculine genre, the Strong Man films, projected the need for strength in the formation of the still-young Italian nation on the male body proper. These films revolve around a specific character placed in various situations and feature a sculpted male performing feats of bravery to show off his strength and virility. The character of Maciste, for instance, is initially featured in Giuseppe Pastrone's *Cabiria* (1914), in which he is a Roman slave whose astounding strength enables him first to protect and later rescue the beautiful and innocent Cabiria.[28] Although a supporting character in this film, Maciste proved so popular that he spurred a cycle of approximately twenty films before the advent of sound. Echoing the glories of Ancient Rome, the Maciste films re-incorporate and re-write the virile feats of the valiant Roman soldier for the twentieth century. Moreover, they re-inscribe masculine virility on the body. In the case of Maciste, race also played a significant role. In *Cabiria*, Maciste is a dark-skinned African. In his later films such as *Maciste* (Guido Brignone, 1915), *Maciste innamorato* (Maciste in Love, Luigi Romano Borgnetto, 1919), and *Maciste nella gabbia dei leoni* (Maciste in the Lion's Cage, Brignone, 1924), he is white. This racial shift is significant for several reasons. Richard Dyer notes how the muscleman's hard, muscular body signifies both white mental and physical superiority: the white man is not born with the hard, muscular body—it takes both brains (mental discipline) and brawn to achieve it. As a super-hero and symbol of a newly integrated Italian nation, Maciste had to be white.[29]

Maciste did not appear during the cinematic productions of the Fascist period after government intervention in the industry in the 1930s, as he was replaced by new models of masculinity. As Italian Fascism consolidated its power in the 1920s and 1930s, the government set about to fabricate, with varying degrees of success, what it saw as proper male and female appearance, codes and modes of behavior, and sexuality. Individual citizens were the present and future building blocks of the Fascist nation, and the regime saw that educational reforms, organized leisure, and mass media all contributed to the shaping of the proper Fascist subject. Drawing on works in late-nineteenth- and early-twentieth-century research in anthropology, sexology, and psychology, Fascist ideology incorporated new theories on the radical irreconcilability between the sexes, men's spiritual and intellectual superiority over women, and a woman's role as housewife and mother.[30] On a more immediate and tangible level, however, Fascism found its greatest ally in the Catholic Church, which had always emphasized the woman's total subjugation to male authority, doctrinally reaffirmed first by Pope Pius X in 1909 and again during the Fascist period by Pope Pius XI in 1930.[31]

What were these male and female Fascist ideals? The Fascist woman was deemed to be small yet corpulent and robust, not too pretty, and of modest intellect and cultural level. She was Woman, Wife, Mother, Widow, a symbol on whose shoulders rested the respectability of the nation. One article in *Critica fascista*, the cultural mouthpiece of Fascist ideology, listed her tasks as "producer of children, ruler and director of new lives, requiring sacrifice, a lack of concern for oneself, and an individualistic anti-hedonism."[32] Fascism also fostered a cult of virility as an essential part of its ideology, requiring duty, sacrifice, heroism, strength, obedience, and authority in its male citizens, brought to life by Benito Mussolini himself. Even more than the fasces (the bundle of sticks with a protruding ax blade), Mussolini was the unifying icon of the Fascist regime:[33] he was the ideal man and male-ideal rolled into one. An integral component of "manliness" was sexual potency, prowess, and promiscuity, while still reinforcing the man's duty as husband and father.[34] The number of children one had came to be considered proof of one's masculinity. Also essential was the image of the athletic male body, embodied by il Duce himself and appropriated by the arts.[35] As with the regime's politics regarding reproduction, the sensual was stripped from the sexual, reducing the male (and female) body to a nationalistic procreative machine.[36]

The cinema of the Fascist period, like many aspects of the Fascist government, was not a monolithically controlled state apparatus. Both the more commercially oriented products and the propagandistic films presented conflicting views of masculinity, often in opposition to the dominant ideology. What emerged was a representation of masculinity that, in the so-called "white telephone" films, the escapist parlor comedies featuring the well-to-do, veers from the masculine model personified in Mussolini's ubiquitous public persona and takes the form of a more liberated American-influenced representation. The propagandistic films, by contrast, reveal complex negotiations among ideological constructions, cinematic codes and conventions, and extra-cinematic conditions of existence.[37]

While the cinema of the Fascist period has been copiously examined elsewhere,[38] I would like to use as brief examples two different films by the same director to illustrate the contradictory images of masculinity which arise in many films of the Fascist period: *Il grande appello* (The Great Call, 1936), falling under the rubric of the military film, and *Il Signor Max* (Mister Max, 1937), a more Hollywood-style comedy, both directed by Mario Camerini. Military films such as *The Great Call* often follow what Marcia Landy has called the conversion narrative, whereby a male character, beginning as a cowardly, self-serving individualist, is psychologically and socially transformed into a heroic, virile, and productive leader who places collective interest over egotism. In these films, however, belief in the Fascist cause is not a necessary pre-condition.[39] *The Great Call,* for instance, revolves around a father-son relationship: an Italian man (Bertani) resides in Africa as the owner of a bar, making money on the side in nefarious dealings, including selling arms to the enemy. His estranged son Enrico, by contrast, is a radio operator in Somalia at the front and does not understand his father's lack of patriotism. The Italian characters must learn to embrace Fascism, with reluctance met along the path to proper Fascist subjectivity. Despite the fact that the father realizes the error of his ways and also sacrifices his life for the cause—his last words are "Italia, Italia"—the film raised some eyebrows among the Fascist elite, who felt that it was not patriotic enough.[40]

Camerini's 1937 film, *Il Signor Max*, proposes a radically different model of masculinity than the military conversion narratives. Gianni, a Roman newspaper vendor played by Vittorio De Sica, assumes the identity of his wealthy friend Max while on a vacation in order to woo an upperclass woman, Paola. He lives the high life but must leave when he loses all his money gambling in San Remo. Paola's maid, Lauretta, sees him one day at the newspaper stand, but he pretends not to be Max and plays the part of Gianni. Eventually Gianni/Max must choose between his two identities and the two women. He learns the error of his ways when, disguised as Max, he sees Paola mistreat Lauretta. Lauretta and Gianni are reunited in Rome and become engaged, with Gianni deciding not to tell Lauretta the truth about his masquerade.

The film proposes two distinct archetypes of masculinity: one tied to Anglo-American leisure culture and the other to petit bourgeois Fascist ideals. The Americanized Max reads *Time* and *Esquire*, dresses like an Englishman (the model of men's fashion) and plays tennis, golf, and bridge. The bourgeois Max dresses in a drab uniform and sings in a choir for the *Opera nazionale del dopolovaro*, a national after-work leisure program. *Il Signor Max* thus serves as a paradigmatic lens into the contradictory picture of masculinity under Fascism. The protagonist clearly aspires to escape the trappings of his work and leisure. He, like the protagonists of the propagandistic military films, must learn to embrace the status quo. The prescribed life of the ideal Fascist petit bourgeois male, however, contrasts with the vacuous yet still fascinating appeal of the Hollywoodized fantasy of aristocratic freedom. Although Gianni in the end rejects his Americanized alter ego, that lifestyle clearly holds the greatest fascination for the male protagonist, and presumably for the audience as well.

World War II, the end of Fascism, and the civil war that followed brought out a re-alignment in terms of gender and ideology. Women's emergence from the domestic sphere and into the workplace (a phenomenon which slowly began during the Fascist and war periods) garnered them greater public visibility as well as, finally, the right to vote. The brave Resistance fighter replaced the icon of the Fascist soldier in the post-war masculine imagination, and the new leaders became Gramscian-inspired intellectuals rather than uniformed party ideologues. Despite the failure of the Left to emerge as the dominant political force in post-Fascist Italy, the "organic man" and brave fighter found expression in popular cultural forms: in the neorealist literature of Italo Calvino, Cesare Pavese, and Elio Vittorini, and the neorealist films of Vittorio De Sica, Giuseppe de Santis, and Roberto Rossellini.

The year 1945 signified an important rupture in Italy's history: a break from the Fascist past, a second attempt to re-create and re-define the Italian nation, and the beginning of an era of constant political conflicts both between and within the dominant parties, economic swings, and radical social transformation. The historical and cultural legacy of Fascism and World War II had a profound impact on the Italian economy, Italian society, and the individual Italian citizen. The ensuing years of physical and political reconstruction, high levels of unemployment and inflation, and governmental instability shook the foundations of the Italian nation in ways that destabilized rather than solidified the Italian Republic, even after the Christian Democrats became the dominant political force in 1948.[41]

The representation of new post-Fascist masculine ideals in Roberto Rossellini's *Roma, città aperta* (Open City, 1945) mirrors the reconstruction of post-war and post-Fascist Italian society. The film recounts the story of the German occupation of Rome and the resistance against it. The male standard which looms large in this film is embodied in the characters of the martyred priest Don Pietro and his sacrificial lamb Manfredi, as well as the young band of Partisans who walk off together at the film's conclusion, with the panorama of Rome and St. Peter's in the background. These model men are emblems of the post-war masculine principles of courage and solidarity. The film intends to teach by example, basing its ideology on the principles of Christian humanism, Communist solidarity, and heterosexuality (with the Fascist depicted as the "perverse other").[42] Good and evil are unproblematically and neatly divided between the Partisans inspired with lofty quasi-religious goals and the barbaric and sexually deviant Nazis and collaborators.

De Sica's *Ladri di biciclette* (The Bicycle Thief, 1948) by contrast, reveals a profound sense of melancholy, loss, and ambiguity, reflecting the many conflicting emotions about Italy's past, present, and future in the crucial period between 1945 and 1948. This neorealist classic tells the story of Antonio Ricci, as he finally gains employment after two years without work, only to have his recently un-pawned (and necessary) bicycle stolen on his first day on the job. Gone is the solidarity of *Open City:* here the individual is alienated from the social institutions and the bureaucrats who run them. Nor is the division between good and evil as neatly delineated as in Rossellini's film: the presumed bicycle thief is himself a victim (of epilepsy), and Ricci eventually attempts to steal another bicycle as the only way out of his situation. Even the family, which in the end serves as the one safe haven in a cruel society, is emasculating for Antonio. His young son Bruno has been supporting the family with his job at the gas station, and often assumes the paternal role in their relationship in various stages during their journey through Rome.[43] Antonio Ricci in many ways stands in for the Italian everyman at a financial and emotional loss in the period of reconstruction: he is just one of the unemployed 25 percent of the Italian workforce whose life has been thrown into turmoil by the political events of the past decades.

As neorealism began to decline as a dominant cultural mode of cinematic expression, filmmakers explored other genres in order to reach a wider audience and achieve greater commercial success. In one such genre, later termed the *commedia all'italiana* (comedy, Italian style), the *inetto* emerged in full force. As opposed to the *film comico*, which featured renowned comic actors such as Totò in various situations,[44] the *commedia all'italiana* usually showcased the collective protagonist, a group of inept, bumbling, self-absorbed males who fail to assume the roles of responsible adults. Unlike the earlier "white telephone" comedies, these films, borrowing from neorealism's legacy, were often shot on location: in the countryside (Luigi Comencini's *Pane, amore e fantasia* [Bread, Love, and Fantasy, 1954]) or in the city (Rome in Dino Risi's *Poveri ma belli* [Poor but Beautiful, 1956]). Many female stars also emerged in the 1950s comedies: Gina Lollobrigida in *Pane, amore e fantasia*, Sophia Loren in Alessandro Blasetti's *Peccato che sia una canaglia* (Too Bad She's Bad, 1954) and *La fortuna di essere donna* (What a Woman! 1955), and Claudia Cardinale in *Big Deal on Madonna Street*. Gian Piero Brunetta notes that, although female emancipation was a distant goal for these characters, they nonetheless challenged traditional notions of femininity by working outside of the domestic sphere and used their sexual guile to obtain their goals.[45] This gradual female emancipation and its impact on Italian masculinity will be the focus of the analysis of the Mastroianni/Loren collaborations in chapter 5. Loren's incarnations of what Kathleen Rowe has appropriately called the "unruly woman" constantly challenge phallic authority and female subservience.[46]

As the genre matured in the late 1950s and early 1960s, films such as Monicelli's *La grande guerra* (The Great War, 1959) and Risi's *Una vita difficile* (A Difficult Life, 1961) took on a more politically committed tone. Through humor, they were able to be critical of the social system by focusing on the very individuals who were defeated by it: the poor, the marginalized, and the criminal. They probed the effects of historical events such as World War I, Fascism, and the Reconstruction, which had brought about changes in Italian economic, political, and social institutions. Often bordering on grotesque black comedy, many of these films presented a "darker, more ironic, and cynical vision" of contemporary Italian society.[47] The bond between male characters was based on the mutual experience of economic hardship and social disenfranchisement, reflecting an Italy caught in the middle of an economic boom but little equipped to deal with the social ramifications. The Italian character—particularly the male—did not escape ridicule and criticism. As Dino Risi observed: "We did not create myths and heroes, as opposed to American films. . . . On the contrary, we destroyed the myth of the great scoundrel, of the lower middle class coward, the profiteer, the lady-killer. The Italian cinema in general has never had either the great, good hero or the evil monster: the protagonists of Italian films are neither good nor bad, or may be both at one and the same time, with everyone's weakness and defects."[48]

Federico Fellini's *I vitelloni* (1953), one of the earliest *commedia all'italiana*, sets the prototype for this character type and challenges the traditional norms of masculinity as set forth by Gilmore and others.[49] The term *vitellone* refers to a young bovine but also intends a frivolous and idle young man. The film, set in Fellini's hometown of Rimini, tells the story of a band of five young men who define the *inetto* of the postwar period: they are unemployed, supported financially by their female relatives (mothers, aunts, sisters), and evade marriage at all costs— Fausto (Franco Fabrizi), the so-called spiritual leader of the clan, even tries to flee to Milan when he finds out he must marry Moraldo's sister after getting her pregnant. As opposed to the hypermasculinized heroes of the Resistance in films such as Rossellini's *Open City* and *Paisà*, these characters are decidedly feminized throughout the film: Alberto, played by Alberto Sordi, cross-dresses for *Carnevale;* Leopoldo, an aspiring playwright, is pursued by a homosexual actor; and Moraldo refuses to physically defend the honor of his sister (and his name), preferring instead to wander the streets until dawn. Fausto, the consummate Casanova, eventually surrenders to the law of the Father as he receives a beating from his own father for cheating on his wife, and is reduced to a sobbing wreck. In the end, it is only Moraldo who acts; but his sole act is flight, not confrontation, and it is uncertain where his journey will lead.

As Fellini told us several years later, Moraldo went off to Rome; his escapades were to be recounted in the film *Moraldo in città*, Fellini's "sequel" to *I vitelloni*, after his highly successful *Le notti di Cabiria* (Nights of Cabiria, 1956). Based on the director's own experiences in leaving the provinces, the character Moraldo was to arrive in Rome in the late 1930s. As he was preparing to make the film in 1958, Fellini realized, however, that the Rome of that era no longer existed—it was now dominated by photojournalists, cars, Vespas, and the café society of the Via Veneto. Working with Ennio Flaiano and Tullio Pinelli, he threw out the old script and began work on *Moraldo '58*. Moraldo soon became Marcello, with an eye toward casting Marcello Mastroianni, whom Fellini believed had "an everyday face," one which could best capture the emotions he wished to project onto it. *Moraldo '58* subsequently became *La dolce vita*, the film that launched Mastroianni's career and made him an international star.[50]

Mastroianni and Stardom

Research on what exactly constitutes a star has concentrated mostly on Hollywood studios, with works charting the development of the star system from the silent era, the studio system, through the interrogation of popular stars of the past several years. Even more theoretically oriented treatises use American actors and actresses as examples to support their ideas.[51] Nonetheless, research on Hollywood stardom provides important paradigms that can be applied outside the American studio model. For example, Richard Dyer, the pioneer of star studies, was the first to underscore the importance of stars as bodies, signs, and commodities. The star, according to Dyer, is a representation, embodied with certain meanings which change over time: "Stars represent typical ways of behaving, feeling and thinking in contemporary society, ways that have been socially, culturally and historically constructed."[52] For Dyer, stars are about the production and fabrication of the public self. He/she is a product, deliberately marketed, distributed, and sold in the greater economy, promoting both the film and his or her career. In many cases, the star even uses his or her name to sell a particular product, be it the film itself, a promotional commodity tie-in, or an unrelated item for consumption to which he or she has attached his or her name.

Each of these categories can be easily applied to Mastroianni, despite the fact that he did not make a film in Hollywood until the very end of his long career. His multiple appearances on both the screen and the international stage made him the most recognized international actor of his time. Like many other actors, Mastroianni was a bankable name that was used to promote, advertise, and sell the films in which he starred. He became a commodity unto himself, epitomizing a particular construction of Italian masculinity for a national and international audience. What Mastroianni eschewed was the role of public spokesman.

Unlike Sophia Loren, he never pitched commercial products, nor did he create a brand name line, as Loren did with her eyeglasses, perfume, and, most recently, cookbooks.

Mastroianni, moreover, represented a physical body with a specific relation to political, social, and cultural institutions, including the film industry. Because Mastroianni's career spanned fifty years, various historical events—what Gaylyn Studlar has called "cultural intertexts"—are important keys to his films, and they impact not only the interpretation of his star persona but also its construction.[53] For *La dolce vita* (Federico Fellini, 1959), the subject of the next chapter, the primary cultural intertext is the post-war economic boom of the 1950s, and in particular the emergence of an Italian style in the international marketplace. The effects of Italy's industrial rise to power after the devastation of World War II and its increasing presence as cultural commodity directly influence the character Marcello's ultimate failure in his search for meaning and spiritual redemption in an increasingly materialistic world. In chapter 4, I discuss how the feminist movement of the 1970s ridicules Mastroianni's middle-aged Don Giovanni in Fellini's *City of Women*. Each film effects a representation of masculinity thrown into crisis by social, political, and economic changes.

The reception of stars by the film-going public plays a crucial role in both their circulation and interpretation in Italy, where star-worshipping (*divismo*) is an important phenomenon. Italy has often been cited as the birthplace of *divismo*, with the emergence of the silent stars Lyda Borelli and Francesca Bertini, and as the birthplace of America's first major male film idol, Rudolph Valentino. In the heyday of the studio system, American actors such as Clark Gable, Jean Harlow, and Rita Hayworth were the subject of numerous pieces in Italian fan magazines and drew large box-office numbers. Many Italian stars who achieved fame, particularly in the 1930s and 1940s, were billed as Italian versions of popular American stars: Chiaretta Gelli was known as the Italian Deanna Durbin and Isa Miranda was marketed as the Italian Marlene Dietrich, even in her unsuccessful Hollywood sojourn. After the fall of Fascism, however, the aesthetics of neorealism, with its penchant for non-professional actors as icons of the everyday, failed to produce the new faces to replace many of the now-disgraced stars tainted by their associations with the Fascist regime. It was not until Silvana Mangano's magnificent emergence from the rice fields in Giuseppe de Santis's *Riso amaro* (Bitter Rice, 1948) that a new post-war Italian stardom was born. Mangano's breakthrough role, which successfully sold both the film and her image, opened the door for other former beauty queens, such as Sophia Loren, Lucia Bosè, and Gina Lollobrigida, to make their fortunes in Italian cinema. On the male front, the 1950s saw the continued presence of such popular stars as Totò and Amedeo Nazzari, as well as the appearance on the national and international film scene of Sordi, Gassman, and Mastroianni.[54]

There are several factors, however, which differentiate the Italian star system from its American counterpart. The primary factor is the lack of a coordinated public relations institution to help promote and circulate the star persona. Stephen Gundle has noted that, during World War II, Cinecittà—the major site of Italian film production created in 1937— functioned somewhat in the same capacity as the Hollywood studios in terms of star fabrication and publicity. After the fall of Fascism, however, stars emerged through other means: via alliances and marriages with important producers, as was the case with Mangano and Dino de Laurentiis as well as Loren and Carlo Ponti, or through their own personal determination. In addition, the permeation of Catholic morality in Italy's everyday life initially inhibited the open circulation and publication of various star exploits. Rigid social gender expectations also figured into the production and consumption of stars. Although the Italian public often overlooked Mastroianni's many love affairs (with the exception of his out-of-wedlock child with Catherine Deneuve), both Ingrid Bergman and Sophia Loren lost support in Italy for their respective extramarital and premarital liaisons, in part because of the often vitriolic attacks against them by the Catholic Church.[55]

The trajectory of Mastroianni's early career demonstrates how individual initiative and talent, rather than outside influence, was the basis for his success. Mastroianni began acting as an extra during the late 1930s, not only, as he often said, as a "game" or a "dream" but also to help support his lower middle-class family.[56] He appeared on stage at first with his church group and then at the university theater in Rome. In February 1948, Giulietta Masina, the actress and wife of Federico Fellini, had agreed to participate in the staging of Leo Ferrero's *Angelica*, an anti-Fascist satire, in which Mastroianni was performing. The play attracted the administrator of the director Luchino Visconti's theater company, who was impressed by Mastroianni's performance. After a stint with Nino Besozzi's theatrical troupe during the spring of 1948, Mastroianni met later that year with Visconti, who offered him, on a trial basis, the role of Mitch in *A Streetcar Named Desire*. Successful in the role, Mastroianni continued to work in the theater for the following ten years in plays such as Arthur Miller's *Death of a Salesman* and Chekhov's *Three Sisters* and *Uncle Vanya*. Throughout his theatrical work during the 1950s, Mastroianni never abandoned the more financially lucrative film industry. During the period between his theatrical debut and his first Fellini film, Mastroianni appeared in more than forty films, including Blasetti's *Peccato che sia una canaglia* and *La fortuna di essere donna,* which also were his first two collaborations with Loren, Luchino Visconti's *Le notti bianche* (White Nights, 1957), and *Big Deal on Madonna Street.* He played, with the exception of Visconti's film, which he also helped produce, mostly *bravi ragazzi,* young urban innocents or the "happy boy next door"[57]; in short, the young Italian everyman looking for love and happiness in post-war Italy.

There are other important characteristics of Italian stardom that are significant to Mastroianni's rise to fame in both Italy and abroad. Gundle points to the fact that Italy's recent status as a unified nation-state as well as its continued fragmentation on both a political and economic level contributed to the celebration of sports and actors as "shared national cultural symbols."[58] Both Mastroianni and Fellini, on their respective deaths, were placed in state as thousands came from all over Italy to pay their respects: Fellini at Cinecittà in front of the backdrop of blue sky from his 1987 film *Intervista,* and Mastroianni at the Campidoglio in Rome.[59] In memory of Mastroianni, the waters of the Trevi Fountain, the scene of Mastroianni's famous romp with Anita Ekberg in *La dolce vita,* were shut off, attesting not only to Mastroianni's association with one of Italy's great monuments but also the enduring image of Mastroianni as Marcello, the elegantly attired journalist with his omnipresent dark sunglasses and cigarette. Another factor Gundle cites is the importance of regionalism in determining a star's popularity. A prominent figure's ties to his or her native city or town underscore the bond of regional allegiance which still exists in Italy today. Mastroianni was born on September 28, 1924, in Fontana-Liri, halfway between Rome and Naples. Although he moved around quite a bit as a child, eventually settling in Rome, his ties to his native region remained strong and reveal themselves in his successful collaborations with two other "Southerners," Vittorio De Sica and Sophia Loren: *Ieri, oggi e domani* (Yesterday, Today, and Tomorrow, 1962) and *Matrimonio all'italiana* (Marriage—Italian Style, 1964), both examined in chapter 5.

The fact that most Italian actors who achieved fame on an international level were from the South speaks, in many ways, to the extranational image that international audiences desire. For Dyer, interpretations of any particular star change with respect to cultural context, be that regional, national, or international.[60] In the consumption of Italian stars, the dark, voluptuous, sensuous earth mother (à la Anna Magnani), the "mamma mia" (à la Gina Lollobrigida and Loren), or the dark,

1. Mastroianni in Luchino Visconti's *White Nights* (1957). Courtesy of Photofest.

brooding, sensuous Latin lover (Rossano Brazzi and Mastroianni) echoed American notions of Mediterranean ideals of exotic and erotic femininity and masculinity, as well as class—this dark eroticism has its origins not so much in the industrialized and Europeanized Northern Italy but, rather, in the more agrarian and impoverished South.[61] The ubiquitous image of Italy as a primitive, earthy, and uncomplicated nation continued to proliferate precisely because of the South's persisting economic, social, and political troubles.

Mastroianni came to embody the dark, Mediterranean eroticism of the Latin lover. At the same time, he took roles which deliberately played off that image, for instance, the impotent protagonist of *Il bell'Antonio* and the self-fashioned but inept Barone Cefalù of *Divorce—Italian Style*, both addressed in chapter 3. Despite Mastroianni's star persona, ineptitude rather than sexuality is what I will show to be the more common trope of modern Italian masculinity in post-war cinema in general and in Mastroianni's films in particular. It is against the cultural, political, and cinematic backdrop of the Italy of the 1950s—a country recovering from the physical destruction of war and attempting to build a new republic and restore the economy—that Mastroianni emerges as the international male star *par excellence*, and the incarnation

2. Mastroianni's play on the Latin lover image in Pietro Germi's
Divorce—Italian Style (1961). Courtesy of Photofest.

of Italian masculinity on the screen. That image, however, is far from
the hypermasculine ideal often associated with Italian masculinity. Brunetta notes that, in the 1960s, male stars such as Mastroianni (including
Sordi and Gassman) began to eclipse their female counterparts in terms
of recognition and star power. He explains their appeal in two ways:
(1) unlike the female stars, who seemed larger than life, they appeared
as regular guys, in both their good and bad qualities; and (2) rather than
epitomizing a gender icon, they ridiculed "national mythologies of virility and power."[62]

In Italy, the various tropes of masculinity (the *bella figura,* the Latin
lover, and the Sicilian *gallo*) all have roots in Italian culture and society.
Post-war films, particularly in the post-neorealist phase, destroy these
masculine ideals and reveal the *inetto* underneath their façades. This deconstruction of gender mythologies arises from the political and social
uncertainty of the post-war era as traditional gender roles became destabilized during Italy's transformation from the devastation of war to
one of the world's major industrial forces. Italian cinema's constant
interchange with the historical condition produced films which overtly
and covertly addressed changing roles for men in the second half of the

twentieth century. Mastroianni, as Italy's most renowned star on a national and international level, sold a certain image of life, Italian style, epitomized in *La dolce vita*. At the same time, however, Fellini's film and others probe the very nature of Italian masculinity as international commodity through a contrast between surface and substance, between Mastroianni as Latin lover and Mastroianni as *inetto*.

Undressing the Latin Lover

La dolce vita,

Fashion, and Italian Masculinity

> The six months of *La dolce vita:* perhaps the most beauti-
> ful period not only of my life as an actor, but of my life as
> a man. It was like being on a great raft on the open seas
> blown around by the wind in all directions, in a constantly
> festive climate: because with Fellini there were no mo-
> ments of drama—except for a few problems with the lack
> of money, or with something that didn't arrive on the set
> on time. For him making movies was always a game, a
> party, an endless party.[1]

Italy of the late 1950s and early 1960s was, in fact, in quite a celebratory
mood. Rebounding from the devastation of World War II and the political turmoil of post-war reconstruction, the unemployment rate was
dropping and the economy was booming. The country, in particular the
city of Rome, was the destination of choice for the international jet set.
Federico Fellini's *La dolce vita* arose out of this post-war cultural climate as Rome evolved from "open city" to the hot party spot of the rich,
famous, and beautiful. As Tullio Kezich notes in his diary chronicling
the making of this film, "*La dolce vita* was born on transatlantic jets, at
celebratory dinners, galas and above all on the margins of the Via Veneto,
where the beautiful people played during the carnival of these years."[2]

As represented in Fellini's *La dolce vita*, however, the carnivalesque
atmosphere that was Italy during what came to be known as the economic miracle proved to be an exhilarating but ultimately an empty
and alienating experience. The film centers on seven days in the life of
Marcello Rubini, a tabloid journalist on a futile quest for salvation in
the spiritual wasteland of late-1950s Rome, a city in which ethereality
has been subsumed by materialism. Marcello's character epitomizes
post-war masculine subjectivity in crisis, this time in response to the
economic transformation and resulting spiritual degradation of late-
1950s Italy. Even his many encounters with women, for which the actor
would become notorious off screen, only reinforce his impotence in the
hollow crusade for spiritual meaning.

Yet ironically the film came to epitomize and even celebrate the "sweet life," and Mastroianni became the dark, mysterious, and sexy Italian male, the latest incarnation of the Latin lover icon, with which the actor would be forever associated. This attribution of the Latin lover label to Mastroianni begs to be interpreted in light of the Italian post-war economic boom and the commodification of Italy at an international level. The Latin lover is above all a product, a cultural commodity offered up to an international public. What was being consumed in *La dolce vita* in 1959 was not only the European Don Giovanni but also an Italian style, based on the emergence of Italian design, Italian sensuality, and, most significantly, Italian fashion on the international scene.

This chapter examines the interrelated phenomenon of the Latin lover, fashion, and 1950s consumer culture in light of Italian cinema and Fellini's *La dolce vita*. In the end, Fellini's film unmasks the superficiality and the materialism of this growing consumer culture precisely through a baring of the fashion system. Clothes do not make the man—they only offer a temporary mask of a growing malaise in the alienating atmosphere of post-war consumer culture. Moreover, through its critical presentation of fashion and clothing, the film subtly critiques the Italian notion of the *bella figura*, the public manifestation of the private self through behavior and appearance, revealing the façade behind this performative aspect of Italian masculinity. In *La dolce vita*, Fellini dresses up the journalist Marcello Rubini, as played by Mastroianni, in the latest Italian fashion, but ultimately strips him bare to reveal a man at odds with rather than triumphant over a rapidly changing economic, social, and sexual environment.

The Latin Lover

When discussing why the media, particularly the American press, had dubbed him a Latin lover, Mastroianni expounded:

> The Latin lover! A crazy thing, really, a stupidity. And it makes me vulgar. And I said [in response], "Have you seen my films?" After *La dolce vita* . . . I made a film where I played an impotent man: *Il bell'Antonio*. And right after that *Divorce—Italian Style:* a foul cuckold. I also played a pregnant man; I was a homosexual in *A Special Day*. I've played wretches, where sex didn't even enter the picture. . . . And there's nothing to do about it, nothing to do. It's been 72 years now and journalists continue to describe me as a Latin Lover. But what am I? A side show? . . . This is one of the more unpleasant aspects of my profession. The press grabs hold of

an image that doesn't fit you at all and continues to use it, in a very, very irritating manner. I made a successful career by working in my profession, not by being a dandy.[3]

How did the Latin lover label come to be applied to Mastroianni, if, as this project reveals, most of the roles he played on screen did not conform to this image? The reasons have little to do with Mastroianni himself—although his offscreen and very public affairs with beautiful women such as Faye Dunaway and Catherine Deneuve helped to magnify this image—and more to do with what exactly a Latin lover is, and how it relates to the international image of Italy and Italian masculinity. The Latin lover is both a product marketed and distributed by the Hollywood and tourist industries and a symbol of national and cultural difference.

A cultural symbol of the Italian as other, the Latin lover has become the "imagined" embodiment of the primitive whose unrestrained and exotic passion contrasts sharply with the more civilized and restrained Northern European or American society.[4] Much of this differentiation is because Italy has consistently been seen—and has seen itself—as a backward as opposed to a modern nation. The origins of this concept of backwardness lie, according to John Agnew, in Italy's many historical failings and inadequacies in achieving a modern state: its inability to fulfill the promises of Renaissance glory; its failure to develop into a concrete and stable political identity, particularly after the Risorgimento; and the growth of positivistic science that typified Southern Italians in particular as "primitive." Furthermore, Italy's late industrialization and consequential slow development of a bourgeois ruling class, its ties to a more traditional, family-based way of life, and distrust of government have created spaces of difference between it and other more Westernized countries.[5]

The Latin lover also can be seen as a product of popular culture, a consumer icon turned real, which played off these cultural clashes. Both the tourist and film industries exploited his status as a marker of the exotic and the erotic. As Giannino Malossi observes:

> In media terms, the Latin lover leaps from the screen and bursts onto the stage of Italian holiday culture: as female tourists holidaying in Italy well know, Italian males become the stars of the show based on the interaction of the spectacular image of seduction and its execution, which takes shape in a set of rituals, codifying identity, gestures and language, which in turn rejuvenate and consolidate the stereotype and its media appeal.[6]

Thus an essential component to the Latin lover, and of Italian masculinity in general, is the notion of performance. The concept of performative masculinity has been extremely influential in recent studies of masculinity and the cinema.[7] Along these lines, the Latin lover literally puts on a carefully staged show for his admiring public, be it at the beach, which Latin lovers were known to frequent, or in the mass-produced fantasies for and by Anglo-Saxon women. These female "spectators" came to expect displays of passion of the Latin lover's "Mediterranean heat," his creative means of seduction, active sex drive, lack of inhibitions, and exceedingly polite, sophisticated, and cultured manner.[8]

The cultural archetype of the Latin lover, despite coming to fruition in the 1950s, dates back to the literary, musical, and theatrical incarnations of the Don Juan/Don Giovanni myth, which engaged European culture from the Renaissance onward in the works of Tirso de Molina, Molière, and Mozart.[9] It also involved the mythology of actual figures such as the infamous Giacomo Casanova (1725–1798). The hysterical fan culture surrounding Rudolph Valentino created the first cinematic Latin lover: the Italian immigrant who achieves the American dream first through dance, then through onscreen exoticism. The cult of the sensuous, even feminine "woman-made" man skilled in the tango and seduction contrasted with the "sincere, stalwart, American male" and defied American normative masculinity.[10] The case of Valentino and his successors shows the essential role Hollywood played in both creating and fueling the Latin lover image. After Valentino's death, despite noble efforts, successors such as Alberto Rabagliati, the Italian winner of the studio-sponsored "Next Rudolph Valentino Contest" in 1928, and John Gilbert, the American attempt to fill the void, failed to achieve the same status as Valentino in the eyes of the female public.[11]

Latin American actors also benefited from Valentino-mania, reflecting, according to Luis Reyes and Peter Rubie, a "cultural clash between an extrovert Latin culture and a predominantly introverted Anglo-Saxon, puritan society."[12] Figures such as Ramon Novarro, Antonio Moreno, and Gilbert Roland of the silent era and later Ricardo Montalbán and Fernando Lamas with sound film came to fill the Latin lover void created by Valentino's demise. Novarro more than Roland and Moreno became an extremely popular silent screen star, beginning with the starring role in MGM's legendary *Ben-Hur* (1926) up through the development of sound in *Mata Hari* (1932). Montalbán's and Lamas's Hollywood careers resulted from the U.S. and the film industry's Good Neighbor Policy of the late 1930s and 1940s. Between 1939 and 1947, as World War II closed off many of the European markets for American business, Hollywood turned to Latin America as a potentially lucrative audience. Films made during this period focused on presenting an image of Latin Americans that, according to Ana López, would appeal both to the Latin American and U.S. public. Latin American stars and characters became "a special kind of other," "nonthreatening, potentially but not practically assimilable (that is, nonpolluting to the purity of the race), friendly, fun-loving, and not deemed insulting to Latin American eyes and ears."[13] To cast its films, Hollywood exploited its already established Latin American and Spanish talent (Novarro and Dolores Del Rio are two good examples) and looked to the Latin American cultural industries for star imports, Carmen Miranda being the most famous example. Both the Mexican Montalbán and the Argentinian Lamas had successful careers in their respective countries, and each was brought over by MGM for specific Hispanic Latin lover roles and subsequently placed under contract. As Fernando Lamas noted in a 1979 interview in the *Los Angeles Times*, "I was the Technicolor Boy; get me the guitar, the horse, the girl, and get it over with. We were bottled and sold as products. Audiences then were buying trips, not truth."[14] Montalbán's first appearance was opposite Esther Williams in *Fiesta* (1947), in which he plays a Mexican classical composer who dances Spanish flamenco. This fusion of Continental and Latin American cultures is indicative of much of the representation of Hispanics in the cinema. National and cultural identity is lost, blending into the Spanish-speaking hybrid for an indiscriminate and often ignorant American public.

Rhythm, music, and dance are essential elements of the 1950s Latin American incarnation of the Latin lover, one of several factors that differentiates it from Italian Latin lovers. The most popular genre of the Good Neighbor films was the musical, featuring performers such as Miranda and Del Rio. López notes that Hollywood's attention to Latin American developed simultaneously with the rise in popularity of Latin American music, immortalized in both film and nightclub culture by figures such as Xavier Cugat and Desi Arnaz. The Latino/a character appeared as spectacle, an "exotic performer" rather than a "regular citizen." Songs performed in the original language became a "marker of generalized Latin otherness, empty of specificity and indexing only the romanticized sexuality of the exotic."[15] A perfect example of this tie to music and performance is in Mervyn LeRoy's *Latin Lovers* (1953), starring Lana Turner as Nora Taylor, a wealthy heiress with commitment issues, and Montalbán as Ricardo Santos, the uncompromising Brazilian who cures her neurosis. Santos accomplishes much of his seduction of the willing Nora through music and dance. He serenades her with the catchy Basanova tune "[I need] A little more of your *amor*," and teaches her the correct, more Brazilian (read passionate) way to samba. Throughout the film, Montalbán, rather than Turner, is the designated object of the gaze, and these scenes of performance, as well as the obligatory bare-chested beefcake shot, underscore Montalbán's and the Latin lover's pretty-boy status.

Another striking difference is that of class. The Spanish-speaking Latin lovers are often relegated to the working class, or, in the case of Montalbán, cast as athletes, giving the actor an opportunity to flaunt his toned physique. Their Italian counterparts, although poor, are striving to be members of the professional set: Vittorio Gassman is an aspiring musician in *Rhapsody* (Charles Vidor, 1954) and Rossano Brazzi is a future lawyer in *Three Coins in the Fountain* (Jean Negulesco, 1954). For a point of comparison, Montalbán starred in two "social problem" films in the 1950s: *Right Cross* (John Sturges, 1950) and *My Man and I* (William A. Welman, 1952). An outgrowth of the Good Neighbor policies and recent waves of Mexican immigration, these films ostensibly were concerned with presenting the "reality" of the Mexican-American experience, but mostly in terms of appealing to the growing Mexican(-American) film-going public. Chon A. Noriega notes that, in these films, although Montalbán's "light skin color" allowed him to "pass" and marry the blond American, played by June Allyson and Shelley Winters respectively, his characters nonetheless remained marginalized: Allyson's character is a working-class Irish-American Catholic, and Winters plays one of her many blond floozies. Thus the Mexican American "can leave the *barrio* behind but still be placed within class and ethnic boundaries."[16]

In contrast to Latin Americans, after Valentino, just being an Italian male was often enough to secure a future as a "Latin lover" for Italian stars in Hollywood. A perfect example is the case of Rossano Brazzi, the Italian Latin lover of the 1950s. Brazzi was first brought over to the United States by the producer David Selznick in 1947. His heavy accent initially impeded him from obtaining choice roles, but he eventually landed the part of Professor Baer in Mervyn LeRoy's *Little Women* (1949), for which he unhappily donned a fake beard and stomach padding. The film was an enormous disaster and hastened his return to Italy. After a series of failed theatrical and film ventures at home, Brazzi was offered the part of Giorgio, an Italian translator who falls in love with an American secretary, in *Three Coins in the Fountain*, followed by Joseph Mankiewicz's *The Barefoot Contessa* (1954) and David Lean's

Summertime (1955). His characters in these three films played off the myth of the exotic, erotic Italian seducing the prim, responsible American woman with his ardent behavior and diatribes on love.[17]

These roles were specifically designed to position Brazzi as Valentino's successor as the Latin lover of the sound era, and both the actor and publicity machinery heavily reinforced this label. Just as female fans adored Valentino for his intense gaze and hot-blooded hand movements, Brazzi's admirers relished the way his nostrils quivered before he would passionately kiss his American conquests.[18] Contemporary interviews with Brazzi had titles such as "Don't Talk Love—Take Love" and "Continental Charmer," featuring quotes such as this one in the *New York Daily News:* "You must understand that I'm an Italian who can't say no"—reinforcing his national connections to Valentino as well as positioning him as the potential lover of any woman, including the average female spectator to whom his films were actively marketed. Gossip columnists followed his alleged exploits with such famous women as Liz Taylor, Ava Gardner, and Grace Kelly, among many others. When the studio brought him over to the United States to promote *Summertime,* they refused to let him bring his rather corpulent wife Lidia, fearing it would destroy Brazzi's image. Eventually, Brazzi became bitter about his incapacity to escape the very image that catapulted him to fame.[19]

Thus the rubric of the Latin lover was well established in the United States and just waiting for Mastroianni, in spite of the fact that the actor did not make a movie in Hollywood until 1992. His films came to the United States at a time when the boundaries between mainstream and art-house cinema were beginning to break down. Although the roles he played did not subscribe to the Latin lover formula, the fact that he was an Italian male who dressed the part was enough for him to garner that label. As the latest incarnation of the Latin lover, Mastroianni was to become one of Italy's greatest and most successful exports.[20]

The notion of costume and fashion plays an important role in the commodified figure of the Latin lover. The Latin lover depended on projecting a casual but "elegant and refined manner," epitomized in the cravat and open-necked shirt.[21] Even in the 1920s, Ramon Novarro was known as one of the best-dressed men in Hollywood. Dubbed "Ravishing Ramon" by the press, he always insisted on wearing a black suit and tie to the studio, despite the more casual style of his colleagues.[22] In the 1950s, the Latin lover was a product enhanced by the growing vogue of Italian fashion. Rossano Brazzi had a whole new wardrobe made for his 1957 trip to the United States to film *South Pacific,* saying, "I must carry the bold flag of Italian elegance."[23] Mastroianni astutely relates the attribution of the Latin lover label to the stylized clothes he wore in *La dolce vita*. He notes bitterly how after he made that film, producers and distributors only wanted to cast him as the Latin lover because they "only wanted to see me in the V-shaped jacket with gold buttons."[24] Perhaps Vittorio Gassman's failure to succeed in American films and adapt to the Latin lover image had to do with the fact that he was never fashion-conscious. In his autobiography, he wrote: "For me, going to the tailor was worse than going to the dentist."[25]

Fashion and Performative Masculinity

The Italian economy at the end of World War II was, like much of the country, in need of reconstruction. Hurt by the protectionist policies of Fascist autarchy, it profited enormously after the war from free trade and the modernization of systems of production. By the late 1950s, Italy experienced a "miracle" as the economy rebounded to become one of the major players on the international economic scene. The country benefited from several key factors and initiatives during the 1950s: the infusion of American capital in the 1940s, the comparatively low cost of labor, and strategic public investment in the economy. The integrated European Economic Community in the 1950s, formally established in 1957, secured the abolition of protective tariffs, allowing Italy's export-driven economy to reach a wider consumer public. By 1958, the Italian gross domestic product was growing at an annual rate of 6.3 percent.[26]

Initially, exports were the driving force behind this expansion: they grew 14.5 percent during the years of the economic miracle (1958–63). Italy soon emerged as an international style maker and trend setter with the success of such products as the Vespa (1946), the Fiat 500 (1956), and the portable Olivetti typewriter (1950).[27] Eventually, the Italian public joined the consumption mania for cars, televisions, and domestic electric appliances, which, at the time, often cost less proportionally than certain food products. With the introduction of RAI (Radiotele-visiva italiana) broadcasts in 1954, television and consequently advertising were tuned to the national consumer, now with more disposable income to spend in this growing consumer culture.[28]

The Italian fashion industry was integral in popularizing the "made in Italy" style and rejuvenating the Italian economy. As Italian borders opened up to international markets after the fall of the Fascist regime, one of the main areas of interest for consumers and investors was Italian fashion and design. During the Fascist period, Italy had attempted to create a self-sufficient fashion industry, the prototype of its autarchic policies. Italy's alliance with the Nazis and its entrance into the European conflict complicated this effort, as the already over-extended economy was now forced to prepare for and then endure the hardships of war.[29] After World War II, Italian textile and garment companies, located predominantly in northern and central Italy, actively promoted international trade, particular with the United States, as it shifted from a home-oriented to an export-oriented industry. Italy had long enjoyed the reputation of being the site of superb craftsmanship, particularly in the accessories market of shoes and leather goods as well as with fabric, especially silk. Gucci handbags and Ferragamo shoes had been popular abroad for years. The industry was aided by Italian financial groups that saw fashion as the best product to circulate in the global marketplace. These groups actively recruited the participation of Italian tailors and designers who had emigrated to the United States and enjoyed success there. Oleg Cassini and Salvatore Ferragamo had planted the seeds of "Italian chic" on American soil, with their work in dressing prominent female figures, including Mrs. Douglas MacArthur and the daughter of President Truman.[30] These designers set the stage for the wave of Italian fashion that would sweep the United States in the 1950s.

Another important factor that contributed to Italian fashion's rise to prominence was a series of financial and image problems afflicting the French fashion industry, long the dominant trend-setter for women's fashion.[31] Many famous French couturiers such as Coco Chanel were no longer participants in the fashion scene, and newcomers struggled to take their place. An exception was Christian Dior, whose "New Look," which liberated women's fashion from the rigid constructions of shoulder pads and lower skirt lengths, became an important stylistic model for Italian fashion.[32] Ultimately, the protectionism of many fashion houses, which had refused widespread access to their collections for fear of imitation, and their high prices kept many private clients and public buyers away.

Taking their cue from the French, the first Italian designers, many of whom had worked behind the scenes in the Paris ateliers, preserved the lines of French style. However, they made their clothes with the high-quality fabrics for which Italy was known, with cheap labor as a result of the high post-war unemployment rate, and with superb attention to line and detail. The various figures involved included important custom dressmakers, who wanted to follow the paths set by Italians living in America, and the aristocracy, such as Emilio Pucci, who invested what remained of their family fortunes after the war in the fashion industry.[33] Beverly Allen has shown that Italian fashion often draws on historically contextualized images in its construction of national identity through clothing.[34] Pucci's early collections, for instance, looked back to Italy's regional and historical past, in particular the Palio of Siena, for inspiration. This trend indicates the unique path Italy would take in incorporating its customs and traditions into its designs, a fact that insured its popularity with the American consumer public.

The official birthdate of Italian fashion is given as February 12, 1951, when Giovanni Battista Giorgini, a wealthy aristocrat, organized the first Italian fashion show for American and Canadian buyers at the Pitti Palace in Florence. Designs by Pucci, the Sorelle Fontana, and Emilio Schuberth reflected a simplicity in style, an attention to detail, and a sophisticated use of color which would come to characterize Italian fashion for the next decade.[35] Their clothes were also half the cost of the French designs, an added attraction. The show established Florence as the center for Italian fashion in the 1950s. Rome became the capital of official fashion, with Papal audiences, state ceremonies, and aristocratic weddings as the showcase for new Italian designs. Milan, in addition to housing such influential new designers as Mila Schön and Enzo, functioned as an important showcase of Italian designs for high society at La Scala and other venues.[36]

After World War II, the money invested in the Italian fashion industry did not exclude the male sector. While the French served as the point of reference for Italian women's fashion, it was Great Britain that operated in the same capacity for men. France originally dominated as trendsetter in the Middle Ages and the Renaissance, but, from the seventeenth century, English fashion became the global model for much of European men's wear, because of its status as the dominating colonial and economic force. The well-dressed Englishman was a walking symbol of that nation's wealth and power—clothing became an indicator of his class difference and social status.

Focusing again on detail, fabric, and craftsmanship, Italian designers, led by the Roman fashion house of Brioni, departed from the often restrictive and crusty British designs. Their clothes reflected greater awareness of the body, infused with a sensuality lacking in classic English style. They advocated a more individualistic approach, through new combinations of different pieces, and, in Brioni's case, vivid and vibrant colors. Finally, rather than tying clothing to class and power, men's fashion on the Italian front came to be associated with a more relaxed way of life, liberating it from the rigidity of an aristocratic legacy and anchoring it firmly in the growing middle class. The idea was to project the new ideology of informality, leisure, and pleasure, essential qualities of the new *dolce vita* which post-war prosperity allowed, and from which Fellini would draw inspiration.[37] For the American male consumer, Italian fashion symbolized an "alternative masculine style."

The soft boxy jackets, tapered trousers, and brighter colors reflected a sensuality in style that was lacking in the ubiquitous male uniform of the 1950s: the gray flannel suit, the double-breasted jacket, and wide legged trousers.[38]

Tourism played an important role in the popularity of Italian style and the Italian way of life. American money from the Marshall Plan and other sources poured into the country in order to help it rebuild its economy and industry after the war. As a result, more and more foreigners visited Italy, particularly after the Holy Year of Jubilee in 1950, in which Italy experienced a tourist boom as many Roman Catholics made their faith-affirming pilgrimages to Rome. While there, the lower prices and superior craftsmanship attracted many consumers to return to their homes with new purchases of leather goods, accessories, and clothing in order to imitate the Italian way of life.

For female tourists, shopping was not the only activity of interest. Greater consumer spending power because of the healthy American economy opened holiday culture to the middle class. In the 1950s and 1960s, crowds of female foreigners flocked to the beach resorts of Rimini and Riccione in search of summer holiday fun, which included the obligatory tryst with one of the many Latin lovers who were happy to offer their services. The gradual liberation and relaxation of sexual attitudes allowed for greater numbers of women to travel unchaperoned.[39] Numerous popular Italian and American songs, such as "Arrivederci, Roma" (composed by Rascel, Garinei, and Giovannini, 1957) and Louis Prima's "Buona sera, Signorina" (1957), popularized this fantasy as they recounted the love story between the Italian male and his foreign conquest.[40]

Visitors were struck by the elegance that pervaded Italian everyday life: men in particular took both pride and pleasure in their appearance, whether hanging out at the cafés or taking an evening walk.[41] One key factor in the appeal of the Italian style was its broad appeal to all classes, not just the rich and famous. From what J. C. Flugel has termed the Great Masculine Renunciation of the late eighteenth century, when men's clothing lost its decorativeness and exchanged the beautiful for the useful, men's fashion has aimed to be inclusive rather than exclusive, extolling simplicity, uniformity in adherence to the new social codes but still, as Jennifer Craik has pointed out, highly stylized.[42] According to Ted Polhemus, Italian men of differing social status considered dressing well both a privilege and a responsibility. This emphasis on appearance and show is connected to the male ideal of *pavoneggiarsi:* the peacock male who "struts and preens to his heart's content, oblivious of a more northern view that only women should concern themselves with cutting a 'fare figura' [*sic*]."[43]

This emphasis on projecting an Italian male style is linked to the Italian cultural heritage of the *bella figura* (examined in detail in chapter 1), reflecting a taste for public display of self-worth through appearance. If the public arena is the *bella figura*'s stage, then fashion, in particular the suit, becomes his costume. The *bella figura*'s suit is his sign of honor and self-worth—both individual and national identity are written on the body through clothing and grooming and paraded for the community, be it urban or rural.[44] According to Anne Hollander, suits, from their birth in the later seventeenth century, have been seen as "naturally masculine." She traces their modern evolution, as does Flugel, back to the Enlightenment, when, influenced as well by a rediscovery of classical antiquity, the suit began to adhere to the contours of the Ancient Greek and Roman male ideal. Broad shoulders, small waist, and long legs became the "new anatomical foundation" for the modern man, "expressed not in bronze or marble but in natural wool, linen and leather." Hollander believes that the modern suit has survived because it has retained its ability to suggest that classical nudity and exude a "confident male sexuality."[45]

Hollander's use of Mediterranean models of masculinity in her analysis of the relationship between men's clothing and male sexuality is particularly appropriate for the Italian scene. Her discussion, however, presupposes a unified and unconflicting definition of masculinity, as well as a definite correspondence between clothing and male subjectivity; that is, what a man wears reveals who he is socially and sexually. This theory is questioned if that correspondence is negated: What if a man's attire becomes instead his costume, a mask which not only conceals the fragmentary nature of male subjectivity but also projects a radically different social identity? Stella Bruzzi, in her work on fashion and cinema, notes that men's clothing in film often works against character. In her analysis of the Franco-American gangster films, the emphasis placed on dressing well often masks unstable masculinity. In films such as *Le Samourai* (Jean-Pierre Melville, 1967), *Reservoir Dogs* (Quentin Tarantino, 1992), and *Goodfellas* (Martin Scorsese, 1990), when the characters don these suits, modeled on *la linea italiana* (the Italian line) of the late 1950s, they are allowed to assume the traditional position of power and control. Without the costume, however, they may as well be naked. Vulnerable and frail, they reveal, as does Mastroianni's character in *La dolce vita,* the tendentious state of "conventionalized masculinity."[46] Fellini takes this notion one step further: even though Marcello's wardrobe would soon become trend-setting in Italy and abroad, this costuming fails to mask his moral, spiritual, and sexual failings.[47]

Fashion and Italian Cinema

Fashion was in fact an inspiration for Fellini for *La dolce vita,* in particular the women's sack dress. The sack dress, a popular style in the late 1950s, was an unconstructed sheath-like dress which, according to Brunello Rondi, one of Fellini's collaborators on the film, "possessed that sense of luxurious butterflying out around a body that might be [physically] beautiful but not morally so; these sack dresses struck Fellini because they rendered a woman very gorgeous who could, instead, be a skeleton of squalor and solitude inside."[48] The growing divide between surface and substance is a theme which runs throughout Fellini's film, and one which hinges, in many aspects, on the fashion system, as well as fashion's relationship to Italian cinema.

Fashion and cinema were intertwined in Italy from the film industry's inception. Stars such as Lyda Borelli and Francesca Bertini influenced modes of dress and behavior, appealing predominantly to the middle-class spectator with the mythologies of upper-middle-class aristocracy and nobility.[49] During the Fascist period, films such as Mario Camerini's *Grandi magazzini* (Department Store, 1939) showcased Italian autarchic designs in the department store setting. Many films after the war were more concerned with either highlighting social and political injustices or entertaining the masses than with promoting Italian designs. Others, such as Giuseppe de Santis's *Bitter Rice,* put the focus on the female body and her clothing, be it the sexy uniform of the rice workers or the American-inspired fashions which covered the protagonist Silvana's dormitory wall. Michelangelo Antonioni's *Cronaca di un amore* (Chronicle of a Love Story, 1950), as well as his subsequent films *La signora senza camelie* (The Woman without Camelias, 1953) and *Le amiche* (The Girlfriends, 1955), shifted the focus to an upper-class milieu. These films featured women's fashion from Italian designers such as the Sorelle Fontana (*Le amiche*) and incorporated fashion itself into the narrative, with characters working in or frequenting the fashion houses. In these films, notes Roberto Campari, fashion functions not only in terms of mise-en-scène but also becomes a means through which the female characters express "integral parts of their personality."[50]

At the same time that Italian fashion found a place in its national cinema, it also made inroads abroad. Italian actresses such as Alida Valli and Valentina Cortese, who crossed the Atlantic in the late 1940s to make films in Hollywood, brought with them the designs of Schuberth. In the 1950s they were followed by Sophia Loren and Gina Lollabrigida. American actresses such as Joan Bennett and Myrna Loy were photographed on visits to Italy in Sorelle Fontana dresses, and actors such as Clark Gable, Henry Fonda, and John Wayne went to Brioni for their custom-tailored suits.[51]

Men's fashion played a smaller role, for, during the 1940s and 1950s, actresses such as Loren and Lollabrigida gained national and international attention. This is not to say that actors did not serve as inspiration for everyday fashion. The understated elegance of Totò speaks to and often satirizes the *bella figura,* highlighting the contrast between the morning coat, which became his signature garment, and the ironic ineptitude of the characters he played. Similarly, Alberto Sordi represented not only middle-class sensibility in behavior and dress, but also parodied Italy's fascination with American culture in films such as Steno's *Un americano a Roma* (An American in Rome, 1954).

In addition to individual stars, Rome attracted the American film industry as a whole. In the 1950s, as production costs increased and the power of the studio system declined, American film moguls looked to Italy as a place where films could be made for much less money. The Italian landscape offered the perfect settings for the large-scale biblical epics that attempted to combat the influence of television with new special filming techniques such as Cinemascope. Some of the most popular films made during this period set in contemporary Italy showcased Italian design and fashion, such as *The Barefoot Contessa*. The Sorelle Fontana designs for Ava Gardner in the film deliberately evoked the Italian line and tradition: the flowing fabrics and tight bodices of her dresses suggested the Ancient Roman costumes of Classical sculpture. Many Hollywood films employed Italian actors in supporting and eventually starring roles.[52] Rossano Brazzi revived his sagging career and solidified his Latin lover image playing Italian men who seduce American female tourists in *Three Coins in the Fountain* and *Summertime,* both major Hollywood productions filmed in Italy.

This phenomenon, known as Hollywood on the Tiber, also provided food for the gossip columnists and photojournalists, who saw the lucrative potential of selling the exploits of American and other stars to the public.[53] In doing research for *La dolce vita,* Fellini spent many an evening on the Via Veneto engaging the photojournalists Sergio Spinelli and Tazio Secchiaroli, the models for the film's character Paparazzo.[54] In fact, the film's narrative draws on several real-life episodes that were captured in the tabloids. Among them was the episode of the sighting of the Madonna, based on a July 1958 article in *Settimo Giorno* with photographs by Secchiaroli. In that same year, the photographer Pierluigi Praturlon immortalized the image of Anita Ekberg wading in the Trevi Fountain after cutting her foot on the Roman pavement. In the following year, both Anthony Franciosa, in the company of Ava Gardner, and Farouk, the former king of Egypt, had notorious run-ins with the *paparazzi* on Via Veneto. Another infamous episode involved the Turkish dancer Aichè Nanà's striptease at the Roman restaurant Il Rugantino, also captured on film by Secchiaroli: it was the indirect inspiration for Nadia Gray's striptease during the orgy scene in Fregene at the end of the film. Fellini also drew inspiration from the photographs and articles the *paparazzi* published in magazines such as *Europeo* and *Oggi*, which featured stories and fashion spreads that glamorized and spectacularized aristocratic decadence.[55]

La dolce vita, Fashion, and the *Inetto*

La dolce vita recounts a week in the life of Marcello Rubini, a writer making his living stalking the rich and famous for the *cronaca nera*, or the gossip columns in Rome. The film's narrative trajectory is that of a journey or a quest: a quest for meaning in the morally and spiritually vacuous milieu of late 1950s Rome. Rather than a mimetic representation, Fellini's image of the eternal city is highly personal and allegorical. Frustrated by on-location shooting restrictions and unsatisfactory results, he re-created the Via Veneto at Cinecittà.[56] The image that emerges is a city which has lost its connection to its ancient roots, preoccupied instead with immediate gratification, be it sexual, personified in the character of Maddalena; exploitive, as with the *paparazzi;* or spiritual, as in the sightings of the Madonna. This loss is also expressed in terms of the city's architecture. There is a stark contrast in the films between the old (the Trevi Fountain, the Termi di Caracalla, San Pietro) and the new (the housing developments, the highways, the desolate industrial countryside). For Penny Sparke, this contrast epitomizes a loss of tradition in late 1950s Italy, in which urban modernization had corrupted the innocence of "an earlier Italy less dominated by the mass media and other appendages of modern life."[57]

Critics have traditionally broken the film down into a series of seven episodes taking place over seven days and nights, with a prologue (the arrival of the statue of Christ in St. Peter's square), an interlude (Marcello meets the young girl Paola at the beach), and an epilogue (Marcello's final encounter with Paola). Peter Bondanella has rightly pointed out that, while such a structuralist reading of the plot strengthens the narrative's Catholic and Dantesque allusions to numerology, divinity, and a descent toward Hell, it ultimately lessens the necessarily unstructured character of the fragmented and non-linear narrative.[58]

Rather than a sequence of event-based episodes, a reading of *La dolce vita* lends itself to a series of encounters Marcello has with important people in his life: his fiancée Emma; his father; his mistress, Maddalena; and his respected friend Steiner, as well as with those who provide the potential for salvation as he begins his downward moral spiral: Sylvia; the religious sightings; and Paola, a Beatrice-like figure who could be Marcello's guiding light toward deliverance.[59] Such a character-based interpretation preserves the narrative's break with tradition, by centering it not on the events, as the traditional three-act screenplay structure does, but, rather, on Marcello and the various visitors and inhabitants of Rome. Furthermore, it still allows for a Dantean reading of the text. The film is rich with allusions to *The Divine Comedy:* its episodic structure, the *Inferno*'s strong reliance on characterization, and the explicit reference to the *Inferno*'s Canto XXXIII and Ugolino by Marcello's father in the Kit Kat Club—he refers to his age as the *Disperato dolor che il cor mi preme*—"the desperate pain which burdens the heart." Much like the *Inferno,* it is also about Italy's spiritual, moral, and political decay. In the film, the Italy of the late 1950s has prostituted itself to consumer culture. Like Dante's poem, the film's critical reach, for Gian Piero Brunetta, includes all classes: the bourgeoisie as well as the *emarginati.*[60] In addition, John Welle has convincingly argued that Dante's *Vita Nuova* and its emphasis on the greeting is essential to understanding *La dolce vita,* beginning with the outstretched arms of Christ flying over Rome through Sylvia's doubly staged greeting at the airport, to Paola's failed greeting at the beach. The greeting, for Welle, economizes the narrative, for it reveals cardinal character traits of both the protagonists and the supporting players. Moreover, it reverses the salvific potential of that greeting: "Dante portrays the spiritual growth of a man which develops out of his love for a woman, a new life which began in a greeting; Fellini reverses this process to depict the spiritual decay of a man whose inability to love leads to his demise and to a final state of despair which closes with his powerlessness to respond to a greeting."[61] It also sets up parallels between Marcello and Dante the protagonist of the *Vita Nuova,* reinforcing the former's centrality to the narrative.

There are, in fact, no scenes in *La dolce vita* in which Marcello does not appear. More than Rome itself, he is the narrative's unifying element. But what is Marcello's character? Who is he? Rather than the Latin lover, he is the *inetto,* the Italian incarnation of the *schlemiel* or anti-hero. Throughout the course of the film, Marcello fails to accom-

3. Marcello (Mastroianni)
with Maddalena (Anouk
Aimée) in Federico Fellini's
La dolce vita (1959).
Courtesy of Photofest.

plish anything. Incapable of making a choice between journalism and
literature, he semi-prostitutes himself instead to the tabloids. Mired in
mediocrity, he succumbs to the temptations of bourgeois and aristocratic decadence. He even chooses the wrong masculine-ideal role models to turn to for potential guidance: the false intellectual Steiner, as
well as his narcissistically absorbed, aging father.[62]

Similarly, the case can be made for Marcello as modern *flâneur*.
Marcello is inextricably linked to the city. Throughout the course of the
film, we see Marcello at many of urban Rome's most famous sites: San
Pietro, the Trevi Fountain, the Termi di Caracalla, and the Via Veneto.
Moreover, Marcello's occupation as journalist, and his link to the *paparazzi*, locates his position as spectator of the frenetic spectacle that
is modern Rome. Marcello, like the *flâneur*, is on a journey, a quest
for meaning and satisfaction. According to Keith Tester, the *flâneur*
searches for a sense of self in the spectacle of modern life. Hence
flânerie is "the activity of the sovereign spectator going about the city
in order to find the things which will occupy his gaze and thus complete
his otherwise incomplete identity; satisfy his otherwise dissatisfied existence, replace the sense of bereavement with a sense of life." But the
flâneur's search is one which is, like Marcello's, ultimately futile, based
on both the "hollowness of the commodity form" and the "hollowness

4. Marcello and Emma (Yvonne Furneaux) in *La dolce vita.*
Courtesy of Photofest.

of egotistical individuals" of capitalist consumer culture. Thus the
flâneur shares some of the characteristics not only of Marcello Rubini
but also of the *schlemiel* or *inetto:* he is the passive and ironic spectator
of the modern world, self-consciously aware that his search for self-
identity will ultimately fail.[63]

Like the *bella figura,* however, Marcello is at once spectator and spectacle. On the Via Veneto, his aim is to see and be seen. To this end, Piero
Gherardi, the film's costume designer, clothed Marcello in a variety of
stylish suits, intended to epitomize the suave, debonair urban bourgeois
male. He wears highly tailored single-breasted jackets with thin lapels
and a single flap; slim-fitting pleated but narrow trousers; clean-pressed
white, thinly striped, or dark shirts with cuff-links and thin dark ties;
and the requisite pointed Italian shoes and dark sunglasses. As Stephen
Neale has observed, masculinity itself becomes spectacle, and men can
be eroticized on film.[64] But, unlike most images of masculinity, his
spectacularization does not denote omnipotence. Moreover, Marcello's
passivity and metaphoric impotence reveal themselves primarily in his
relationships with women.

In his encounters with Emma, Maddalena, Sylvia, and Paola, Mar-

5. Marcello's classic Italian
style in *La dolce vita*.
Courtesy of Photofest.

cello searches for some meaning to his existence but ultimately remains
frustrated. He becomes prey, albeit at first willingly, to Maddalena's sexual games in the prostitute's house and the castle. He fails to either
commit himself to or extricate himself from his relationship with his
fiancée Emma. He ultimately fails to embrace the purity and goodness
the angelic figure of Paola represents. With Sylvia in the Trevi Fountain,
however, in what has become the iconic emblem of the film, the era, and
Mastroianni's Latin lover image, Marcello's constitution as the modern
inetto fully exhibits itself.

Although the presence of the American actress Sylvia references the
cultural climate of late 1950s Rome, her character symbolically signifies
much more. For Marcello, at the party at the Caracalla Baths, she is
everything in a material sense: "the first woman of the first day of creation . . . the mother, the sister, the lover, the friend, angel, the devil, the
earth, the house." She also personifies an animalesque physicality, not
just in the corporeality of her statuesque figure but also in her connections to the animal world: she rescues a stray cat, howls along with
the dogs, and dons a fur stole. With her mane-like hair and her proximity to the earth itself—she consistently appears and walks barefoot
throughout her screen time—she stands out from her Roman counter-

6. Marcello and Sylvia (Anita Ekberg) in the Trevi Fountain.
Courtesy of Photofest.

parts and surroundings in both her Nordic features and her embodiment of an earthly sensuality lacking in the material city. Her primitive
and uncontrolled, rather than civilized and proscribed, existence offers
a possible alternative to Marcello's bourgeois malaise. As he removes his
shoes to join Sylvia in the Trevi Fountain, he says, "Yes, she's right. I'm
all wrong. We're all wrong."

Marcello joins the modern incarnation of Nordic, earthly Venus as
she bathes in the waters of the Eternal city, symbolized in the Trevi
Fountain's connection to both Ancient Rome (the ancient aqueduct is its
source) and Papal Rome (it was commissioned by Pope Clement XII and
completed by the sculptor Nicolo Salvi in 1735). Yet he is unable to
physically touch and metaphorically connect with his potential salvation. As she symbolically baptizes him into this new world, the fountain
shuts off, symbolizing, for Bondanella, "a clear sign of his spiritual impotence,"[65] or, rather, his incapacity to reject the material in favor of the
sensual.

The abrupt cessation of the flowing waters, however, does have important implications for the representation of masculinity, and not just
in terms of Christian iconography. This harsh interruption implies cas-

tration not only in the strictly Freudian sense; the figure of the woman, here directly associated with the waters, symbolizes that threat. It also denotes castration in more general terms: faced with sexual and sensual pleasure, Marcello is rendered immobile, rigid, and is denied release. His anxious re-awakening from his sensual stupor once the flow of water is suspended intends a sexual and psychological frustration in the face of both unbridled female sexuality and the salvific potential of abandonment to that earthly sensuality.

Fellini's use of proxemic patterns and high-key lighting heightens Marcello's initial attraction to Sylvia's way of life as well as his ultimate impotence when directly in contact with it. Her seductive invitation is filmed as a medium-long shot of her bathing in the fountain waters, followed by two medium close-ups, intercut with Marcello's reaction shots which also set up point-of-view. The two tight shots of the couple in the fountain highlight both intimacy (in their proximity to each other as well as to the camera) and distance (they never actually kiss). The high-key lighting throws Marcello and Sylvia into bright focus. Once the fountain shuts off, however, and Marcello looks around helplessly, the camera cuts back to a high-angle extreme long shot, and, in an apparent shift from night to dawn, the scene now appears filmed in natural (or natural-like) light, minimizing the physical significance of the characters and symbolically reducing the power of their encounter to a frivolous frolic in the waters. This change is underscored by the presence of the bystander who has stopped to watch the spectacle. He stands for the bemused spectator who has awoken from the splendor of the moment only to realize the frivolity and futility of this transitory rather than life-altering escape.

Marcello's narrative trajectory is the opposite of the classic Hollywood character archetype: rather than passing from a state of moral, spiritual, and social darkness into an awareness and light, he ultimately descends further into that darkness. However, in keeping with the modern *inetto*, he actively chooses that strategy. Devastated by the Steiner murder-suicide, he plummets into a moral, spiritual, and sexual abyss, epitomized by the orgy sequence near the end of the film. The carnivalesque setting, complete with transvestites, stripteases, and insinuations of homosexuality, cinematically codifies the scene as one of lascivious degradation and ethereal emptiness. Marcello's final rejection of Paola at the beach, framed by the encounter with the monstrous fish, underscores not only his alienation but also alienation as a dynamic decision.

This "strategy" is marked throughout the film in terms of fashion. Gherardi's limited use of color in Marcello's costumes, apparent even in the black-and-white film, created a classic rather than a

7. Marcello's moral inversion is marked in terms of fashion.
Courtesy of Photofest.

high fashion look, one that wouldn't date the film at its release.[66] Signs of Marcello's moral emptiness and inevitable decay, however, appear throughout the film. Physically, Fellini wanted Marcello to appear at once intense and hollow. His eyes were masked by fake eyelashes and very little attention was focused on them. The lighting on his face is full of shadows.[67] Hints of Marcello's impending demise appear at Steiner's apartment after the murder-suicide: having just woken up, his tie is loose, his top shirt-button undone, his normally carefully groomed hair out of place. In the final scenes at the beach, Marcello, whose moral and spiritual search has resulted in failure, wears the inversion of his original and signature outfit: the rumpled and disheveled white suit with the dark shirt. The *bella figura* has become the grotesque *brutta figura*: the cravat with open-necked shirt, the fashion emblem of first the dandy and then the Latin lover, here serves as ironic commentary on the emptiness of that label and the culture it embraced.

The phenomenal success of *La dolce vita* in Italy and in the United States reveals how popular reception and cultural context can thwart a filmmaker's intended social criticism. The film constituted the first real cross-over success between art-house and mainstream cinema, becoming the highest grossing foreign film ever released.[68] Distributed by Astor Films, the film premiered on April 19, 1961, at the Henry Miller Theater, New York, the first time this theatrical venue had ever screened a film. It was shown in a subtitled version, although much of the rest of the country saw the film dubbed in English. Its popularity in the United States was largely because of the pre-screening publicity it received, as well as the religious debates surrounding its morality, or lack thereof. The Vatican newspaper *L'osservatore romano*'s vehement demand for Catholics to boycott the film in Italy ironically helped the box office both there and abroad. In the United States, the American Catholic Legion of Decency gave it a "Separate Classification," in general reserved for such films which, "while not morally offensive in themselves, require some analysis and explanation as a protection to the uninformed against wrong interpretations and false conclusions." It found the film to be "a bitter attack on the debauchery and degradations of a hedonistic society," a "denunciation of the creeping paralysis of decadence," and with a "shock value" that is "intended to generate a salutary recognition of evil as evil, of sin as sin."[69] The film was praised in many articles and columns in religious newspapers; one Unitarian minister in Chicago even delivered a sermon entitled "The Religious and Cultural Significance of *La dolce vita*," as a moral lesson against self-absorbed materialism and decadence.

Ironically, that attack on materialism and the scandalous reputation of the film only fostered interest in all products Made-in-Italy, including Mastroianni himself, in the United States. Why was this the case? Because the United States was already in the grip of Italy-mania, and Mastroianni became the latest addition to the long list of products eagerly consumed by the American public. Marcello's ubiquitous dark sunglasses, his Triumph sports car, and his cuff-links all entered the American fashion lexicon. Even the style of the white linen suit with dark shirt, the symbol of Marcello's total decay, became a fashion trend.[70]

In terms of tropes of masculinity, this reception of the Mastroianni persona and the commodities he modeled reinforces his position as object of the gaze, and fashion's role in that positioning. Jennifer Craik, in reference to men's fashion of the 1960s and 1970s, has observed that "changing conventions of men's fashion have re-worked attributes of masculinity that have transformed male bodies into objects of the gaze, of display and decoration."[71] In Italy, however, this has always been the case with the *bella figura*. Italian men have never avoided fashioning themselves as objects of the gaze, by embracing male sexuality and eroticism in both their attitude and the clothes they wear. Although an *inetto* in most of his film roles, Mastroianni still embodied a certain Italian style. Even in the most dire of situations, he still looked fabulous.

In the end, Mastroianni had this to say about the role of Marcello in *La dolce vita* and the Latin lover image ascribed to him as a result:

> Yes, from *La dolce vita* on, this label of the Latin Lover, which doesn't fit me, stuck to me. At first I played chauffeurs, ingenuous workers, modest but very nice young men. After this film new proposals for more intellectually committed roles started to arrive, but there was always some story in the middle involving the Latin lover, with which I had nothing to do because I have never been one. In fact, I was always busy saying: "Excuse me, but in *La dolce vita* this protagonist is not a lady-killer—he doesn't conquer anyone. If anything he is the one conquered. It's women who use him and he, being provincial, innocently falls for it every time! The foreign actress uses him; his mistress uses him, even though she may be the only one over whom he has the least bit of authority; the woman in the castle of aristocrats uses him—he is only the victim!" So, I'm not exactly sure what this idiotic term palmed off on me means. People have labeled me as such evidently because I wore a blue blazer in the film and moved in a circle with a lot of women.[72]

Mastroianni's comments address several important issues stressed in this chapter. First, the Latin lover image, more than a direct reflection of the characters the actor portrayed throughout his career, is a consumer icon, marketed to the international (particularly American) public who hungered for Italian commodities (fashion, design, travel), including sexualized images of Italian masculinity. Second, Mastroianni as commodity was tied to other Italian products, specifically, as even he notes, Italian fashion (the "blue jacket" as indicative of the relaxed Italian style of the "sweet life"). Soon the term *dolcevita* even entered the fashion vocabulary: it became the Italian word for the turtleneck sweater, epitomizing, when worn with a blazer, the relaxed yet elegant chic which came to be associated with Italian style. Mastroianni himself in *La dolce vita* became a symbol for life, Italian style, which resonated with a national public experiencing greater prosperity after years of struggle and an international consumer market hungry for all things Italian.

The film's emphasis on materialism, superficiality, and spiritual abandonment has important consequences for contemporary masculinity.

Marcello Rubini is far from the masculine ideal of the *bella figura*. Rather, he is the modern anti-hero and *inetto,* among the first in a long line that Mastroianni would immortalize on the screen. Passive rather than active, conquered rather than conqueror, he reflects the crisis of masculinity in an Italy dominated by materialism and spiritual decadence. At odds with rather than triumphant over his environment, his final strategy is physical masochism, ethereal annihilation, and a major fashion faux pas.

From *La dolce vita* on, the marketing of many of Mastroianni's films, particularly in the international arena, played off the Latin lover image, despite the fact that Mastroianni continued to play *inetti,* including a young man suffering from impotence and a cuckold, as discussed in the next chapter. The cultural intertexts which provide social and cultural relevance for these films are a departure from the world of high living and high fashion that *La dolce vita* epitomized. Instead, the focus shifts from the material to the anthropological and the political, from Rome to Sicily, and from the *bella figura* to the Sicilian *gallo* and man of honor.

3

Masculinity, Sicilian Style

Il bell'Antonio *and* Divorce—Italian Style

Following the national and international success of *La dolce vita,* Mastroianni made several films that continued to draw on his appeal as the ideal Latin lover of the 1960s. He was often paired with beautiful foreign women who would succumb to his charms. In *Vie privée* (A Very Private Affair, Louis Malle, 1961) Mastroianni co-stars with Brigitte Bardot, who plays a young starlet eventually hounded to death by the press and the *paparazzi. La decima vittima* (The Tenth Victim, Elio Petri, 1965) features a blond Mastroianni wearing Sorelle Fontana–designed costumes in a science fiction cat-and-mouse chase with Ursula Andress. Vittorio De Sica's *Amanti* (A Place for Lovers, 1968) brought Mastroianni together with Faye Dunaway for what proved to be better chemistry off screen than on.

Mastroianni's best and most significant film roles of the 1960s, however, stray far from and even lampoon the Latin lover image. As in *La dolce vita,* they have more in common with the figure of the *inetto* than Don Giovanni. In Antonioni's *La notte,* for instance, Mastroianni's character epitomizes masculine bourgeois malaise as a writer suffering from creative block. His search for sexual and emotional satisfaction remains thwarted in both his marriage to Lidia (Jeanne Moreau) and in his encounter with the daughter of a wealthy industrialist (Monica Vitti). In Mario Monicelli's comedy *Casanova '70* (1965), Mastroianni's turn as Andrea, a diplomat who can perform sexually only if he is in some kind of imminent danger, satirizes both the Casanova myth and Mastroianni's extra-cinematic image.

The two films dealt with in this chapter examine constructions of

49

masculinity by engaging a specific configuration drawn from Italy's rich social and cultural history: the rigid gender codes of Sicilian masculinity. Mauro Bolognini's *Il bell'Antonio* (1960) engages the myth of sexual potency and prowess as the prime indicator of Sicilian virility. By featuring Mastroianni as a strappingly beautiful yet impotent young man, the film dissects the ideal of the Sicilian Don Giovanni by revealing the fragility of Sicilian masculinity and the contradictory constructions on which it was based, and by actively challenging Mastroianni's star persona as established by the success of *La dolce vita*. Pietro Germi's *Divorzio all'italiana* (Divorce—Italian Style, 1961) further deconstructs an idealized and stereotyped Sicilian masculinity by focusing on the code of honor, which plays a fundamental role in its fabrication. In contrast to Bolognini's drama, Germi's film uses comedy to criticize the ridiculously rigid Sicilian gender codes against the backdrop of the politically and religiously charged national issue of divorce.

Much of the contextualization in this section is provided by anthropological fieldwork conducted in Sicily during the 1960s and 1970s. What is revealed in these studies by American, British, and Italian scholars is the extremely constructed nature of Sicilian gender roles during the time these films were made. Also cited throughout the chapter are works by Sicilian writers—Vitaliano Brancati and Leonardo Sciascia, among others—which add unique native insight into the way Sicily's tumultuous history has shaped its culture and the everyday lives of its citizens. These writers and scholars address what Antonio Gramsci isolated as the Southern question, or, as phrased by the Italian anthropologist Sebastiano Aglianò, "What is this Sicily?"[1] This question as to both the essence of Sicilian life and its relationship to the Northern Italian peninsula is the primary cultural intertext of this chapter: how the political problems, depressed economy, and rigid social boundaries of 1960s Italy came to be represented on film and personified by Mastroianni's characters. In *Il bell'Antonio*, inter- and intrafamily relations become a metaphor for the patrimony and corruption at the heart of the Sicilian political system. *Divorce—Italian Style*, by contrast, directly confronts the duality between the legal system and the Sicilian honor code as well as the socially divisive issue of divorce.

Certainly, Mastroianni made many other important films during what Peter Bondanella has called the decisive decade of Italian cinema.[2] The examination of *Il bell'Antonio* and *Divorce—Italian Style*, however, presents a unique opportunity to explore the relationship between Sicily and the North at a time when the government was trying, mostly unsuccessfully, to bridge that gap. It also allows for an exploration of the similarities and differences between Southern and Northern masculine codes, and the way in which Mastroianni's star persona as Latin lover helps to unmask and demystify them on the screen.

Sicilian Masculinity

In *Nero su nero* (Black on Black, 1979), Leonardo Sciascia, one of modern Sicily's foremost public personae, provides insight into many of the myths traditionally associated with Sicilian masculinity. He recounts a newspaper article which told the story of a middle-aged German woman (Mrs. Goetze) who, when traveling to Sicily with her husband, felt the uncontrollable urge to console a despondent Sicilian man whose wife had left him alone. Her husband gave his consent not only once but twice for this encounter, and was extremely pleased by the outcome: his wife's two nights with the Sicilian has rejuvenated her. Whereas press accounts tended to focus on the liberal sexual attitude of the German couple, Sciascia was fascinated instead by the marginal character of the Sicilian male:

> I am interested above all in that character who remained on the sidelines, the distinguished Sicilian gentleman, who for two nights had, in his melancholic solitude, the consolation of Mrs. Goetze. Sicily (of trashy literature) made Mrs. Goetze a goddess: but, in reality, only through a Sicilian gentleman whose wife was at the beach or in the mountains. Having grown bored and melancholy, he was disposed to an affair with any type of woman (but preferably a foreign one).[3]

Sciascia goes on to note that the Sicilian male's attraction to Mrs. Goetze was not in the immediate sexual encounter but, rather, in the opportunity to tell about it later to his friends: "the pleasure to be able to recount is absolutely superior to the pleasure of doing."

In this tale, Sciascia underscores several important mythologies attributed to Sicilian masculinity: the ideal of a Sicilian hypersexuality, with the potential to transform an ordinary woman into a resplendent goddess; the masculine predisposition to any type of love affair; and the greater gratification in being able to recount it, in embellished version of course, to one's friends.[4] What studies of Sicilian masculinity reveal, however, is that these beliefs are tendentious in nature: that Sicilian masculinity, like other gender constructions, is fraught with contradiction and conflict, and is constantly threatened by social, political, and cultural factors beyond its control.

More than just another region in the multi-cultural mosaic that constitutes Italy as a nation, Sicily has attracted a multitude of scholars from history, economics, political science, and anthropology who have examined its difficult past, its present struggles, and its future place in an increasingly globalized and less regionalized world. Subject to intense foreign domination and colonial exploitation,[5] its culture, history, and language have been shaped by many determining national forces. As an island with a more rugged and brutal climate than much of the Italian peninsula, it has always appeared as the mainland's poorer sister in terms of its predominantly agricultural economy, its feudal-based society, rampant crime from individual bandits to the organized Mafia, and its rigidly structured codes of expected behavior for both men and women.

Much of these gender constructions derive from what Jane and Peter Schneider see as the three dominant cultural codes fundamental to understanding the Sicilian way of life: *onore* (honor), that is, the primacy of the nuclear family over all other institutions, with women as symbols of family worth; *furberia* (cunning), allowing for any action in defense of personal or familial interests; and *amicizia* (friendship), whereby coalitions of men are established to preserve *onore* and at times thwart the *furberia* of others, turning them into *fessi* (fools). The authors stress the fact that these traits are not inherent to the Sicilian character per se. Rather, cultural codes were "instruments of adaptation" to external forces. Nevertheless, all contribute to the construction and formation of masculine identity in Sicilian culture.[6]

How is Sicilian manliness defined and how does it relate to these cultural codes? Anton Blok, in his anthropological study of this subject, stresses the physicality of Sicilian masculinity. A masculine Sicilian is one who is strong both inside and out. His courage, strength, and endurance are expressed in bodily terms, as an *omu di ficatu* and *omu di panza*—literally a man with a strong liver and a strong stomach.[7] This stress on the body emphasizes the notion of self-reliance that is so essential to Sicilian culture—self-dependence instead of dependence on the state. Of extreme importance to this concept of self-sufficiency and government distrust is the Sicilian principle of *omertà*. Traditionally used in reference to the Mafia, the term is derived from the Sicilian word for man itself—*omu*—as well as the Spanish *hombredad*, meaning virility. Thus, *omertà* signifies not only the tie that binds a group (either criminal or not) into a bond of silence against others, particularly state institutions, but also incorporates a masculine ethos into that covenant.

Similar to the more Northern model of the *bella figura*, the Sicilian male strives for respect (*rispetto*) in the public sphere.[8] In the South, however, the emphasis on the public as key to the private runs deeper than the superficiality of the *bella figura* as derived from the dandy and the *flâneur*. The ideal of honor is very much connected to both the physical person and the *rispetto* he is supposed to command.[9] Honor establishes status in the public sphere, and it is in the public domain that honor must be preserved. In Sicily, preservation and control of honor rests within the family, the predominant institution of Sicilian daily life. According to Peter and Jane Schneider, the emphasis placed on the family (familialism) and the code of honor insulated the family against the hostility of the usually foreign ruling forces. At the same time, because so much of the agrarian-based Sicilian economy depended on family-inherited property, the best of which was at a prime, rivalries developed between Sicilian families and domestic groups in the defense and protection of family property.[10]

The honor of the family depends on the strict maintenance of both the physical and metaphorical boundaries of the family unit: property, masculinity, and—most important—female virginity. Maureen Giovannini, in her work on female chastity codes in Sicily, notes that gender roles are shaped from early age: boys are socialized to be aggressive and domineering (*che maschio*—what a man!) and girls are discouraged from such behavior (*che vergogna*—what shame!). Girls are instructed to be gentle and obedient as they are segregated into the domestic sphere after puberty.[11] At the same time, boys are taught to preserve the virginity of their sisters, on whose bodies the honor of the family rests:

> In general, a man's responsibility is to provide for the material needs of his family and protect the family patrimony, including its women, from predatory outsiders. Correspondingly, a woman's duties involve performing domestic functions and exhibiting chaste and modest behaviour at all times. The latter is especially important since, according to town norms, the honour or social worth of a family and its members is largely determined by the sexual comportment of its women.[12]

If the men of the family fail to ensure the virginity of the female relative, she assumes the role of *la puttana* (the whore), defined as a girl or woman who has engaged in premarital or extramarital intercourse. She becomes, according to Giovannini, a metaphor for "the family that fails to keep its boundaries intact." Consequently, when a woman is labeled a *puttana*, her father, brothers and/or husband are in turn branded *cornuti* (cuckolds), for they have failed to protect the family and defend it from penetration from outsiders (420–21). And as a *cornuto*, a man is no longer a *vero omu*: he lacks the essential male attributes of strength, power, and cunning, as he has failed to safeguard the virginity of the female members of his clan. Thus, women are seen as inherently weak

and in need of constant surveillance, while men "lack the intrinsic characteristics of manliness deemed necessary to protect the family and its
women from outsiders" (426).

In order to combat these potential threats to his masculinity, the Sicilian male makes recourse to another essential aspect of his identity to
exert his manliness: sexual prowess. Yet, even this manifestation is more
a discourse than an actual trait. Vitaliano Brancati coined the uniquely
Sicilian term for the ideal of a man whose masculinity is determined by
his multiple experiences with women: *gallismo*, from the Italian word
gallo, or rooster or cock. In his 1946 essay "Piaceri del gallismo" (The
Pleasures of Gallismo), Brancati sets forth a definition of this notion on
which he expanded in his two novels, *Don Giovanni in Sicilia* (1941) and
Il bell'Antonio (1949). He explains:

> In Southern towns, the male face is characterized by a singular
> pride in which one seems to see something vermilion. The reason
> behind this pride is not his having been good, truthful, generous,
> honest, tame, just, charitable, etc. but rather feeling or imagining
> himself to be "talented in matters of love."[13]

The "pleasures of gallismo" consist of a man believing himself and
showing himself to be blessed with an extraordinary virile force (*una
straordinaria forza virile*), a particular sense of dignity and honor.[14] He
cites the hypothetical example of a family whose son does not like
women: the walls of their house and the tombs of their ancestors would
rumble and shake as a result of this affront to their reputation. Similarly, David Gilmore, in his work on Mediterranean masculinity, notes
how manhood is equated with sexual potency, with the proof lying in
procreation: a manly man is one who fathers many children.[15]

The key difference between Gilmore's and Brancati's definitions is
the latter's emphasis on self-fashioning in the celebration of sexual
prowess. In fact, the words that Brancati uses to describe *gallismo*—feeling or imagining oneself as talented in matters of love—bespeak the
façade of sexual potency that underlies this myth. Similar to the Sicilian man described by Sciascia, the most important part of being a *gallo*
is not the man's sexual exploits themselves but, rather, *il discorrere della
donna*—that is, talking about women, and relating the often exaggerated
and fabricated details of the conquest to his companions. Sebastiano
Aglianò, a Sicilian anthropologist writing in the 1940s, relates this notion of talk to the Sicilian cultural code of *rispetto:*

> I would almost say that the Sicilian constitutionally feels the need
> to construct an enlarged and embellished image of himself, and to

regulate his attitudes and even his actions around it. Even in his more common and less serious conversations he does not fail to introduce a tenacious (if involuntary) reference to what is the grandeur and dignity of his person. In discussions and in arguments this tendency is accentuated to the maximum, relative to the ardor with which one discusses or one argues.[16]

As opposed to the Don Giovanni, whose focus is on the practice of seduction, the Sicilian *gallo* lives to talk about his exploits, sexual and other, rather than for the exploits themselves. Often this is the case because these men are almost always unsuccessful with the women they encounter, because of the strict codes of behavior for Sicilian women. In Brancati's *Don Giovanni in Sicilia*, for example, the protagonist Giovanni Percolla and his friends spend their days in Catania chasing after women and then talking about their "encounters" ad infinitum. According to the ironic third person narrator, however, the story of Giovanni's actual amorous past "could be told in ten minutes."[17] For Sciascia, the Catanese dedication to women is "an offering, the ritual of an offering more than a practice of the conquest, a game of imagination more than of action."[18] Aglianò observes that, even though men talk about nothing except women, they are "not part of their daily existence," that "there exists a real sexual barrier between them, an attitude of constant defense" against one another.[19]

The fragility of Sicilian masculinity, based traditionally on the tendentious preservation of female chastity, the archaic code of honor, and sexual talk rather than sexual action, brings to light the unstable nature of that gender construction. Thus Sicilian masculinity is similar in many ways to the various manifestations of Italian masculinity described in this study. It is a trait which must be acquired, one that is governed by specific norms of conduct established by cultural codes and conventions more rigid and fixed in nature than their Northern counterparts, and one which is constantly at risk of being destabilized and subverted by forces beyond its control. This male insecurity is at the heart of the character of the *inetto* and the challenges he faces to live up to these often impossible masculine ideals. Brancati's *Don Giovanni in Sicilia* provides us with the first model of the inept lover hobbled by doubt and uncertainty. His subsequent novel, *Il bell'Antonio,* and Bolognini's film adaptation delve deeper into the subject by featuring as their protagonist the consummate opposite of the hypermasculine ideal: the impotent male. The literary and cinematic representations of this negative polar, however, differ in striking ways. For the film, Mastroianni's participation, and the Latin lover label his extra-cinematic

aura brought to the screen, was essential in highlighting the contrast
between the ideal and the real in contemporary male sexuality and its
impact on contemporary Sicilian and Italian culture.

Il bell'Antonio: Novel and Film

Millicent Marcus, in her work on Italian literary adaptations, notes that
the Italian film industry, from its earliest days, drew inspiration from
literary classics, theatrical melodramas, and pulp and romantic fiction.
The propensity to adapt the classics, particularly Italian classics, to the
screen proliferated during the Fascist period, when directors such as
Mario Soldati and Luigi Chiarini made sumptuous costume dramas in
which ideology both corresponded to and conflicted with Fascist imperatives.[20] Neorealism's problematic relationship with literature, articulated in Cesare Zavattini's postulate that cinema must "tell reality
as if it were a story," highlights what Marcus sees as the contradictory
relationship between neorealism and literature: that the utopic ideal of
neorealist "storylessness" is unrealizable precisely because reality demands a narrative in order to be told cinematically. In the 1960s, however, literary adaptations shifted focus away from the story per se toward
the psychological examination of character.[21] Bolognini's *Il bell'Antonio*
falls into this category, as it probes the repercussions of impotence in a
society which places the utmost value on male virility.

Il bell'Antonio the novel forms the second component in what is considered Brancati's "trilogy of *gallismo*," including the earlier *Don Giovanni in Sicilia* and the unfinished *Paolo il caldo*, published posthumously
in 1955. The action takes place in Catania over the course of thirteen
years, between 1930 and 1943. The protagonist is Antonio Magnano,
who from the novel's very outset is said to be extremely handsome, "di-
abolically handsome,"[22] capable of inducing turbulent, erotic responses
in the women he meets. The local priest early on warned Antonio's
mother of the young boy's effect. The first-person narrator who ironically comments on events describes how even the priest "knew well
that his feelings for Antonio were not perfectly Christian" (11–12). At
twenty-six years of age, Antonio is summoned by his family to return
to Catania from Rome, where his sexual conquests were believed to be
numerous, in order to marry Barbara Puglisi, the beautiful but bland
daughter of a rich landowning family. At first hesitant, Antonio changes
his mind on seeing Barbara for the first time. They marry on July 5,
1935, and three years pass before rumors of trouble begin to surface. It
is soon revealed that Barbara is still a virgin. Her father proposes that
the marriage be annulled, since it is not recognized in the eyes of the

Church, and that she be allowed to marry the Duke of Bronte, a man rich in both money and girth. Antonio, still in love with Barbara, desperately tries to convince her to stay married, but she sides with paternal and ecclesiastical authority in agreeing to marry the duke. Antonio, shamed, takes refuge in his parents' home, where he confesses his secret to his uncle Ermenegildo: that the rumors of his prolific sex life in Rome were all lies, and that in fact he is impotent. Antonio's father Alfio is so haunted by his son's failures as a man that during an air-raid at the end of the war he goes to a brothel so that when he dies the whole town will know that he died as a man. Unfortunately, the act has an ironic effect, invoking only pity in the public arena. The novel concludes with Antonio in hiding at his mother's home. When his cousin Edoardo telephones to recount through sobs how he raped his maid, Antonio begins to cry as well, not for Edoardo but for himself, out of both jealousy and shame.

The novel's chronological framework, from the growth in strength of the Fascist dictatorship to its waning days, grounds its gender critique in the discourses of Fascist dogma and practice. Brancati himself was an early adherent to the Fascist cause. He joined the party in 1924 at the age of seventeen and as a young intellectual collaborated on many of the regime's cultural mouthpieces, including *Critica fascista*. In *I fascisti invecchiano* (The Fascists Grow Older), published in 1946, almost ten years after his open break with the party, he describes the appeal that Fascism held for him as a young man:

> In my twenties, I was a Fascist up to the roots of my hair. I do not find any extenuating circumstances for this: I was attracted by the worst of what Fascism had to offer, and I can't invoke the excuses a conservative bourgeois subjugated by the words Nation, Race, Order, Tranquil Life, Family, etc. might have. . . . Perhaps because of my frailness (and a little because of what I was reading: Ibsen, Anatole France, Pirandello, Bergson, Gentile, Leopardi of course) I looked with astonished admiration, like I would upon statues of Phydia, upon those contemporaries of mine, who were more robust and more idiotic. I would have given two thirds of my brain for a well-developed bicep muscle.[23]

In this autobiographical passage, Brancati makes no excuses for his allegiance to the party in a period when many intellectuals were openly and avidly disavowing their pasts. Furthermore, Brancati expresses the appeal that Fascism had over him in terms of his physical failings as a man, particularly his failure to live up to both the regime's ideology of health and fitness (*Mens sana in corpore sano*) as well as the importance

of strength and physicality for the Sicilian male. In *Il bell'Antonio,*
Brancati deliberately connects the Sicilian man's obsession with his virility to Fascist rhetoric. A Fascist is an *omu veru,* while Antonio the
a-Fascist (if not anti-Fascist) is its antithesis, the *cornuto:* thus, Fascism
is equated with *gallismo* and anti-Fascism its antithesis. The unmasking
of masculinity coincides with an unmasking of the emptiness of Fascist
rhetoric.

Antonio's affliction, which the novel presents as psychological rather
than physical, constitutes an affront to the Sicilian notion of sexual potency as proof not only of one's masculinity but also of a family's honor.
The character who best articulates this belief is Antonio's father, Alfio,
who sees his son's sexual failures as a stain on his own masculinity. For
Alfio, the relationship between father and son constitutes a generational
continuity of sexual aptitude. He tells a fellow townsperson, when boast-
ing about his son's presumed talents with women, "He got it from me
and his grandfather! With the Magnano men, my dear friend, women
melt even when we touch them with one finger. . . . When a woman has
been with him [Antonio], she is left licking her lips for the rest of her
life" (79). Dubious at first about the truth when he learns of his son's
marital problems, Alfio believes that Antonio is too much of a man for
Barbara, that he is too "passionate" (109) for her. When he learns the
truth, Alfio is so incredulous that he becomes obsessed with restoring
his son's virility. To deny the rumors of his impotence, Alfio wants to
take Antonio and his father-in-law to a bordello to watch the young man
"perform." When forced to face the truth, Alfio declares: "It means that
I no longer have a son! He died, my son! I had him, and he died" (218).
His remaining days are spent attempting to rehabilitate his own image:
he tells his wife about all the illegitimate children he sired (269), and in
his last act of frequenting the brothel he gives Antonio "the strongest
slap in the face that a father could give a son." An anonymous hand
writes on Alfio's tombstone: "He died 6 March 1942 to wipe clean the
honor of his family mudded by his son" (298). Antonio's own reaction
to his predicament is the opposite of his father's: rather than combat the
rumors, he withdraws into the safety net of the maternal womb. Part of
his retreat is because of societal constraints: no longer an *omu veru* in
accordance with Sicilian norms, he cannot show his face lest he be publicly ridiculed and humiliated.

There is another undercurrent to the novel: Antonio's latent homosexuality.[24] Throughout the novel Antonio is placed in a classically feminized position when it comes to his sex life. More often than not, with
women, Antonio is the pursued rather than the pursuer, thus revers-
ing the traditional ritual of *gallistic* courtship. Furthermore, his status

as symbol of beauty destabilizes traditional notions of masculinity for it provokes female desire to an aggressive degree, thus putting the all-important status of female chastity at risk. Not only does Antonio elicit non-traditional reactions in Sicilian women—his beauty also has a powerful effect on Sicilian men: "Antonio's ugly friends respected him, and they would have even envied or even hated him, if, induced and infected by the women whose company they frequented, they had not been in love with him" (9). His encounter while in Rome with a foreign couple underscores his own homosexual urges, for it is the man's beauty, a Viennese official, rather than his German companion (Ing), which really attracts his attention. Although he gives more detail to the description of Ing's physique when he recounts his tale to his uncle, Antonio repeatedly dwells on the powerful handsomeness of her fiancé. His uncle reminds him of how beautiful he is as well, thus reinforcing the connection between the two young men. When about to make love to Ing, Antonio learns that the Viennese official is impotent, and he soon loses all sexual desire as well, as if Antonio's sexual identification with her fiancé overpowered his sexual desire for her.

The novel seeks to undermine many of the traditional notions of Sicilian masculinity studied by anthropologists (*gallismo* in particular) by underscoring the very fragility of those ideals through humor and irony, relying on dialogue, description, and dialect to create a choral effect. The film, by contrast, turns to melodrama and psychological introspection in its examination of masculinity. Almost immediately after the novel's publication, Brancati, who had been collaborating on film scripts for several years, wrote the first draft of a screenplay for *Il bell'Antonio*, which he completed in 1953. The script underwent three subsequent re-workings before it was brought to the screen in 1960: first by Gino Visentini, then by Pier Paolo Pasolini (whose script harked back to the Brancati version), and ultimately a final tweaking by Mauro Bolognini, the director who had signed on to the production. For Bolognini, *Il bell'Antonio* was his ninth film, capping a series of literary adaptations often co-written with Pasolini, including *La notte brava* (On Any Street, 1959) and *Marisa la civetta* (Marisa, 1957). In this and other films based on literary texts, Bolognini is not primarily preoccupied with fidelity to the original. Instead, according to Gian Piero Brunetta, he tends to engage larger ideological issues in their historical and social context.[25]

This broadening of setting and atmosphere into a universalization of specific historical problems was the justification for the film's most striking departure from the literary source on which it was based: the elimination of the Fascist context and the transposition to contemporary Italy. This change has two effects. First, it shows how many of the myths on which the Fascist regime depended, in particular the notion of virility, still play an important role in the contemporary Sicilian male's everyday life.[26] Second, by de-historicizing the setting, the emphasis shifts from the historical context to character psychology and individual existential crises, universalizing rather than specifying the film's social commentary.[27] Thus, the displacement allows for a greater focus on the expectations and hypocrisies of Sicilian masculinity devoid of the baggage of Fascist ideology.

Several other changes from novel to film had profound effects on the final product. The time span was shortened from thirteen years to two years, with the elimination of most of the back story, including the story of Ing and the Viennese official as well as the character of Antonio's uncle Ermenegildo. As a result, the accent falls on the effects as opposed to the causes of Antonio's impotence. The camera captures the tension between setting and character which dominates the film. Much of the town, from the opening credits to the very end, is deserted and desolate, with the ancient architecture of Catania imposing on the characters' daily existence, rather than fading into the background.[28] The film's ending, unlike the novel, reaffirms Antonio's virility: it is he, not Eduardo, who has a sexual encounter with Santuzza the maid and, as proof of his masculinity, impregnates her. But the text, and in particular Mastroianni's performance as Antonio, reinforces the bittersweet and melancholy tone of the supposed happy end.

Mastroianni's portrayal of the tortured Antonio reflects the many changes both Pasolini and Bolognini imposed on Brancati's original text, primarily the focus on the character's psychological and sexual torment. Mastroianni was not the first choice for the part: he was called in when Jacques Charière, the French actor married to Brigitte Bardot, pulled out at the last minute.[29] According to Pasolini, Antonio as incarnated by Mastroianni became "an introverted, anxious, sweet character, sometimes too closed in and sometimes too open. His pain is contained but also contagious and passionate."[30]

The film, unlike the novel, immediately brings to the surface Antonio's sexual incapacity in a decidedly Sicilian context. The first scene features Antonio in bed with a beautiful young woman, nameless in the film as well as in the script, in a darkened room. Both she and Antonio are fully clothed and lying separately in the bed. The dialogue which breaks the silence (even before the musical soundtrack is heard) immediately alludes to Antonio's sexual dilemma. The exact line his female companion says in Italian is "*Non ti piaccio*," literally translated as "I am not pleasing to you," but more colloquially assigned the phrase "You

8. Antonio (Mastroianni) contemplates his sexual failings in Mauro Bolognini's
Il bell'Antonio (1960). Courtesy of Photofest.

don't like me" with sexual connotations. As the dialogue continues, the
camera pans to reveal that the previous image was a mirror-shot. Mirrors and reflections are a constant presence in the film. This contempla-
tion of the image, and in this first scene the mistaking of reflection for
reality, underscores several reoccurring themes in the film: the importance of image in Catanese society, the ideal of beauty in that image,
and the contradiction between that image and the real situation. Another important mirror scene in the film occurs just after Antonio has
seen the picture of Barbara. He dreamily contemplates her photograph
until he spies his own reflection in the mirror: the change in his facial
expression from one of bliss to one of horror bespeaks the truth of his
sexual shortcomings. The camera zooms in on his half-shadowed face,
reinforcing the division between his idealized notion of love and the
reality of his impotence.

The film's first scene not only forefronts the issue of Antonio's impotence, a fact insinuated but not directly referenced until well into
Brancati's novel. It also highlights how Sicilian masculinity is integrally
related to female chastity. The film depicts Antonio's problem from the
start as one tied to Giovannini's theories of the dichotomy between the
pure and chaste girl, the *vergine,* and her opposite, the *puttana*. In this

first scene, Antonio's female companion is a virgin, a fact she highlights by telling him that none of the most "narrow-minded or ridiculous of your Sicilian compatriots" would be disappointed if they were to marry her right now. Pre-marital sex with a good girl (the *vergine*) will turn her into a *puttana*, thus spoiling her for future marriage and ruining her family's name and honor. But Antonio, when faced with virgin beauty and female chastity, is paralyzed, guilt-ridden, and rendered impotent. Despite the fact that this woman is not Sicilian and thus more liberated, Antonio cannot overcome his madonna/whore complex and make love to her. In fact, Antonio reveals in a subsequent conversation with Edoardo that the only women with whom he can perform sexually are prostitutes, maids, and servants: women of dubious reputation or of inferior class status. Thus, the essential ideal of female chastity to Sicilian culture as depicted in the film, rather than reaffirming Sicilian masculinity, has the detrimental effect of turning it into its feared opposite: the impotent man.

The madonna/whore dichotomy extends to Antonio's relationship with Barbara, played by Claudia Cardinale. When he first sees her photo, he describes her as an "angel," and throughout the film she is consistently referred to as a "divine creature" by Antonio and others. Iconographically, the camera captures her beauty in soft-focus, with emphasis on her beautiful and angelic face as opposed to her shapely body (a trait showcased in Cardinale's other films of the era), which is hidden mostly under proper and chaste clothing. Barbara's virtuous presence provokes an intense sexual crisis in Antonio. In the film, the ideal of female chastity, rather than proving masculinity, subverts it: Sicilian culture has revered the figure of the virgin to such an extent, and tied it so inextricably to masculinity, that the violation of that virginity is perceived as sin itself. Antonio so worships the figure of the virgin in an idealized *dolce stil novo* type of love that sexual intercourse threatens to violate that quasi-beatific notion. When he does find it in the figure of Barbara, satisfaction continues to elude him as the material threatens to impinge on the spiritual, despite the Church's predications that a marriage involves both the flesh and the spirit. For Antonio the two, just like the ideal and the real, are irreconcilable.

Further underscoring Antonio's sexual confusion is his own beauty, a status alluded to not only in the film's title but also explicitly referenced throughout the film. Although beauty is a concept often associated with Sicilian masculinity (as a reflection of God's grace),[31] here it is expressed, as in the novel, in decidedly feminine terms. With his long eyelashes (a dominant style in women's makeup at the time), Antonio is the constant object of the sexual gaze, from his lustful neighbor Elena

9. The angelic Barbara (Claudia Cardinale) with Antonio in *Il bell'Antonio*.
Courtesy of Photofest.

to the women who watch him from their balconies to the guests at the wedding. Moreover, whereas Antonio's father, Alfio, sees his sexual prowess as bestowing honor on the family name (he invokes his own father as well in that tradition), Antonio embodies the shame of not living up to that social and sexual expectation and being more associated with its dreaded opposite: the feminine. In Sicilian culture, the sins of the son become the sins of the father, and the unhappy ends that father and son meet comment on the restrictive codes of masculine behavior. Just as in the novel, Alfio's hypermasculinity is the ultimate cause of his death (here presumed to be a heart attack, rather than an air-raid, while in bed with a prostitute). Antonio's impregnation of Santuzza, while re-establishing his virility, much to the joy of his mother, nevertheless dooms him to an unhappy existence devoid of the idealized notion of love that he constantly sought.

The fact that Antonio is able to perform sexually with Santuzza, the maid, underscores the class system inherent in Sicilian culture. Throughout the film there are hints about society's increasing preoccupation with financial gain. Alfio arranges Antonio's marriage to Barbara to lift him out of his dire financial straits: he had invested all the money he had in an orange grove which was failing to produce. Furthermore, the film insinuates that the Puglisi's intention in annulling Antonio's and Barbara's marriage is not entirely religious. When Barbara's father learns of Antonio's impotence, he waits many months before seeking an annulment to the union, after finding another suitable husband for his daughter. The man he chooses, the Duke of Bronte, is a millionaire. Even the Church accuses the Puglisi family of hiding behind the façade of the sacraments—that the marriage did not exist in the eyes of God because it was not consummated—in order to benefit monetarily. As one priest puts it to Antonio's mother, "[Barbara's] nostrils are filled with the smell of money."

Although the notion of the woman as a commodity of exchange to bring about familial financial benefit is nothing new to Sicilian culture, the contextualization of this transaction in Italy in the years of the economic boom comments on the growing importance of monetary wealth and its connection to political power. A discourse on contemporary politics runs throughout the film, stressing the divide between North and South (here exemplified in the split between Rome and Catania) and progressives and conservatives (rather than the novel's Fascists and anti-Fascists). At issue is not only local politics, as both Edoardo and Barbara's father seek to use Antonio's supposed Roman connections to their own benefit, but also the tension between the two geographic regions. The years of the economic recovery, rather than ameliorating the chronic Southern problems of unemployment, poverty, and corruption, exacerbated the division between North and South, with the former never really reaping the benefits of the prosperous economic times.[32] Edoardo alludes to this situation in a conversation with Antonio in the latter's room. After working for a time in the Roman government, presumably fighting for Southern reforms, Edoardo returns to Catania disillusioned, having lost faith in the moral capacity of man and believing all to be corrupt. He says:

> Leaving Catania, dear Antonio, I lost everything. I don't have anything left: I mean moral capital. I still have the income from my mother's land, thank God, and for this reason, not caring about anything, I'll remain a conservative. I assure you that the least painful thing to conserve is Catania's misery. Here at least we know each other and we know what kind of old wolves we are. At least everything that's ancient is noble.

Here Edoardo echoes the philosophy of another important Sicilian novel and film, *Il gattopardo* (The Leopard), written by Giuseppe Tomasi di Lampedusa in 1958 and brought to the screen by Luchino Visconti in 1963. The famous line in that novel relates the situation of Sicily during the Risorgimento, the age of Italian unification, to the 1950s: "If we want everything to remain as is, everything has to change."[33] Dwarfed by a Catania that he was unable to better, Edoardo leaves it to rot in its corruption and poverty, one that extends to the everyday life of inter-family relations.

The film's concluding shot highlights the hypocrisy and the cynicism at the heart of Sicilian society and its rigid gender constructions.[34] In the scene, Antonio contemplates his reflection in the glass as Edoardo congratulates him on his impending fatherhood via telephone. The camera begins its slow zoom-in to Antonio's reflection as Edoardo berates him for his pining over lost love instead of celebrating the impending birth of a son, to be named Alfio. The darkened image slowly becomes illuminated, but half of his face remains shaded as Edoardo tells him, "And now you can finally be what you really are . . . a man!" The irony of the happy end is not lost. Although now he has earned the label of a "real man," it is at the cost of what he most cherished: his love for Barbara. Thus, the personal is sacrificed for the social, here the restoration of family honor and masculinity. The final close-up on Antonio's teary face is the culmination of a single shot which lasts over two minutes and accents the bittersweet resolution of Antonio's sexual conflict.

One reason behind Mastroianni's successful performance as Antonio rests in the fact that the audience automatically assumed his sexual prowess, given the on- and offscreen image associated with the actor: that of the Latin lover, whom women fall all over and who is more than willing to satisfy them. Richard Dyer defines the star image as "made up of screen roles and obviously stage-managed public appearances, and also of images of the manufacture of that 'image' and of the real person who is the site or occasion of it."[35] A star's image can be used to construct character in three different ways: (1) a perfect fit between character and star, whereby the character on the screen corresponds precisely to the star's image both on and off; (2) selective use, whereby a role brings out certain features of a star's image and not others; and (3) a problematic fit, whereby the correspondence between character and star image is fraught with conflict and contradiction.[36] By his good looks, which reference both his onscreen physical appearance as Antonio as well as his extra-cinematic presence as Marcello Mastroianni, Marcello/Antonio is assumed to conform to the cultural gender expectations: sexual prowess and potency. What his behavior and psychology reveal, however, is that looks are deceiving, and that the sexual god is in reality the sexual *inetto*, no longer a man but a *cornuto* and a *fesso*, playing against the star image which Mastroianni had recently garnered.

10. Mastroianni as the antithesis of the Latin lover and Sicilian *gallo*. Courtesy of Photofest.

The film is thus able to at once reference and demystify the image of the Latin lover within the dramatic framework of a narrative and geographic context in which this gender construction is an integral part of everyday life.

Divorce—Italian Style

The casting of Mastroianni against type, and the play on his Latin lover image, is used to comic as opposed to dramatic effect in Pietro Germi's *Divorce—Italian Style*, one of the quintessential examples of *commedia all'italiana*, and the film from which the genre derives its name. The performative aspects of Sicilian masculinity, in particular the *bella figura*, *the gallo*, and public manifestation of the honor code, are ridiculed through Mastroianni's skillful performance as the ludicrous Barone Cefalù. Moreover, the narrative unravels against the backdrop of three of Italy's major social and political issues of the early 1960s: the disparity between Northern and Southern Italy, the struggle for power between the Communists and the Christian Democrats as well as the latter's particular hold in the South, and the parties' positions on the divisive national issue of divorce.

Pietro Germi, although Genovese by birth, consistently dealt with the problems of the South in his films, from his first neorealist-western *In nome della legge* (In the Name of the Law, 1949) up through his follow-up to *Divorce—Italian Style, Sedotta e abbandonata* (Seduced and Abandoned, 1964), which examined the issue of Sicilian female chastity codes and marriage. Whereas critics such as Andrew Sarris have supposed that Germi's affinity for the plight of the disadvantaged Sicilians has much to do with his own lower-class background, others such as Mario Sesti have noted that much of this interest stems from the common theme of justice which runs throughout Germi's opus. This tension between the law, on the one hand, and the rights of the individual, on the other, manifests itself in his two Southern *commedia all'italiana* (*Divorce—Italian Style* and *Seduced and Abandoned*) as "the unbridgeable conflict between the State and the Individual, between the adventures of desire and the code of honor imposed by society."[37]

For a director like Germi, neorealism provided the aesthetic framework within which to explore these and other pressing social and political problems. At the same time, to much criticism by many ardent neorealists, Germi also turned to Hollywood genres—in particular the western, the melodrama, and the screwball comedy—as a means of broadening his message to a larger populace. Thus, there is often a tension in Germi's films between realism, on the one hand, and its long tradition in Sicily, and escapism, on the other, provided by the formal structure of the classic Hollywood narrative. The success of these two Sicilian comedies rests precisely on their ability to strike a balance between realism and escapism, between social commentary and recourse to grotesque black comedy, finding humor in such taboo subjects as murder, castration, virginity patrols, and the Sicilian honor code.

Divorce—Italian Style begins as Barone Ferdinando Cefalù, also known as Fefè, returns to his hometown of Agramonte after serving a jail sentence for a crime of passion. His sarcastic voice-over introduction/flashback to life in the Sicilian town serves to anchor the film geographically, politically, and socially, as well as to align the spectator's identification in the film with Ferdinando. The tone of the opening sequence, a take on the serious documentary-style introductions of many neorealist films, including Roberto Rosselini's *Paisà* (1946) and Giuseppe de Santis's *Bitter Rice*, is decidedly ironic, intent on highlighting many of the social and economic problems facing Sicily in the early 1960s. Three elements of Sicilian life immediately come to the forefront via the presentation of statistical data: the importance of religion (the town's twenty-four churches), the high unemployment rate (seventeen hundred out of eighteen thousand people), and a faulty education system (forty-three hundred of them illiterate). The camera then observes men in the public sphere at their club, first gossiping about Ferdinando's father, Barone Gaetano Cefalù, and then returning to their "favorite subject," women, most of whom remain hidden behind the grated shades of Agramonte's buildings. Here the film nods to the difficult position in which women find themselves in Sicily: as the constant subject of male fantasy (and the men's conversations) yet subject themselves to restrictive female chastity codes. Germi experienced this aspect of Sicilian life directly: when shooting the film, all local female extras whom he hired for various scenes came accompanied to the set by male relatives to ensure their safety in the decadent world of filmmaking.[38] The next shot, based on a scene actually witnessed by Germi, features the local Communist Party headquarters, as men dance with other men to American lindy music, with the sardonic voice-over "Meanwhile proletarian Agramonte was gloriously marching on the road to progress . . . a slow progress perhaps." The antipathy of the Church toward the Communist Party, as well as its staunch support for the ruling Christian Democrats, is the subject of the Church litany which immediately follows this scene. The priest urges his parishioners to vote for a party "which is both democratic and Christian." The film, right from the introduction, intends to ridicule Sicily's perceived backwardness, the pervasive influence of Catholicism on Italian everyday life, and, as the narrative unfolds, Italian law's failure to legalize divorce.[39]

The passage of a comprehensive divorce law took much longer in Italy than in other European countries because of the dominant conservative politics, the strong presence of the Catholic Church, and regional differences. Twelve different measures were introduced from the Italian nation's earliest days (1878) until final ratification in 1970. In the period following the Fascist era and immediately preceding *Divorce—Italian Style*'s release, there were two attempts to introduce legislation: in 1954 and 1958, both of which failed, blocked by an alliance between the Christian Democrats and the Church. Resistance to divorce was particularly strong in the South where, once the law was passed, the divorce rate remained extremely low, because of a greater propensity toward the private as opposed to the legalistic resolution of domestic problems. In the cases which were filed, however, the fault more often than not was attributed to the wife as opposed to the husband, reflecting even in the 1970s the strict codes of sexual conduct for Southern women.[40]

The fact that divorce did not become legal until 1970 did not prevent Italians from seeking other alternatives. A couple could receive an annulment in either a civil or ecclesiastical court, petition for a legal separation, or seek a divorce abroad. Under the 1902 Hague convention, Italy was obliged to recognize foreign divorces, and this became a means, albeit a legalistically complicated and expensive one, to extricate a party from a marriage. The most famous case was that of Sophia Loren and Carlo Ponti. In 1957, Ponti, having been repeatedly denied an annulment by the Italian civil and ecclesiastic courts, obtained a divorce in Mexico from his wife of eleven years in order to marry Sophia Loren. The two were married by proxy in a Mexican court. The Vatican condemned the union in various newspaper editorials. Spurred on by the Catholic Action group, individual citizens filed legal complaints against the couple, charging Ponti with bigamy and Loren of concubinage, both criminal offenses in Italy. The couple stayed away from Italy for the most part to avoid arrest. Eventually, to solve their legal problems, they moved to Paris, proved residency, and became citizens, which allowed Ponti to obtain a divorce from his first wife and marry Loren in Paris in 1966.[41]

In *Divorce—Italian Style*, Barone Ferdinando Cefalù finds himself in a similar situation. Ferdinando has fallen in love with his beautiful young cousin Angela. Unfortunately, he is still married to Rosalia, and, as there is no divorce in Italy, he must find a way to extricate himself from his unhappy marriage and marry Angela. The only way to do so would be to kill Rosalia, and in a series of fantasy sequences he imagines doing so: by stabbing her and then throwing her in a pot of boiling soap, by watching her drown in quicksand, and by sending her to the moon. Because murder carries a heavy legal sentence in the court of law, Ferdinando must find a way to defend his act. Enter the Sicilian honor code. Inspired by the case of Mariannina Terranova, a woman who killed her unfaithful lover after he betrayed her, Ferdinando discovers his way out. Since Sicilians hold the honor code in much higher esteem than they do constitutional law, Ferdinando learns that he will get a lighter sentence for a crime in defense of his male honor (only three to seven years) if he can catch Rosalia in an adulterous affair. He finds his bait in the art restorer Carmelo Patanè, whom he spies lurking outside his house one day in search of Rosalia. After discovering love letters that Carmelo had written to Rosalia before her marriage to Fefè (Carmelo was believed killed in Africa during the war), Ferdinando hires Carmelo to restore the frescoes in his house, secretly tape recording his conversations with Rosalia. Eventually the two lovers run away, and Ferdinando must assume the role that all Sicilian men struggle to evade: the *cornuto*. According to Jane and Peter Schneider, there are two types of cuckolds in Sicily: the *cornuto bastionato*, the weak man (the *fesso*) who

11. Ferdinando (Mastroianni) courts his beautiful cousin Angela (Stefania Sandrelli) in *Divorce—Italian Style* (1961). Courtesy of Photofest.

is powerless to respond to the charges, and the *cornuto contento,* one who willingly gives his wife or daughter away, usually to an economic superior.[42] In the film, Ferdinando is the *cornuto contento:* he is happy to be rid of his wife in order to pursue his passion for Angela. However, a *cornuto* is still a *cornuto.* In order to achieve his goal, he must publicly be shamed as the *cornuto bastionato* and then be challenged to do something about it, as he is by Carmelo's wife. His plans work out: he kills Rosalia, is given a light sentence by the courts, and returns to marry Angela.

An essential component to the success of Ferdinando's plans is the fact that this scheme must involve the entire town. This lack of division between the public and the private is a constant of Sicilian life, particularly with respect to the honor code. A man's honor, as defined by Pitt-Rivers above, requires public validation. Thus, for Ferdinando, all aspects of his plan must be performed on the public stage: the main street of the town or the piazza. In full *bella figura* regalia, he parades Rosalia in front of the men of the town to make sure that she still garners their attention. Then, after arranging meetings between the ex-lovers, Ferdinando begins his own campaign of "anonymous" letters, a Sicilian tradition in which those outside the family warn of improper goings on within that particular family: "Barone Cefalù, Open your eyes! Your wife betrays you under the roof of your honorable house." After Rosalia and Carmelo flee, Ferdinando feigns a fever in order to entice the worst gossip in town, Dr. Palamone, to his house to later spread the news of Rosalia's departure throughout the town. Pretending to be distraught and not to eat (he had in fact hoarded food and cigarettes in his room to sustain him), Ferdinando revels in this public humiliation as *cornuto bastionato*, seeing it as part of his plan. Even the Church and the communists get involved, the former attributing Rosalia's betrayal to the pernicious influence of scandalous films, and the latter using it as an excuse to discuss the issue of female emancipation. A Communist Party member asks those gathered at a meeting for their "objective" and "democratic" judgment of Rosalia's actions. In a sign of the lack of appeal of Communist ideology as well as the deep-seated traditions of Sicilian machismo, the overwhelming response is the established one: *puttana*. The real anonymous letters pour in, arriving in bag loads and relished by Ferdinando as future "meticulous documentation" of his act of revenge. Aiming to sink even deeper, Ferdinando, unlike Antonio, does the unthinkable: he leaves his house and walks through the town, consciously assuming the role of the *brutta figura*. His public humiliation culminates in the scene after his uncle Calogero's funeral, when Don Ciccio Matara, the local mafioso, promises to find out where the lovers are hiding. Carmelo's wife, with the appropriate name of Immacolata, spits in his face in the main piazza, challenging him to vindicate his honor. Thus Ferdinando, in fulfilling his desires, successfully manipulates many of the cultural codes attributed to Sicilian masculinity. He has had to knowingly perform the role of the *fesso* and the *cornuto* in order to be justified in seeking revenge. Because he consciously assumed this role, however, he is also a *furbo*, using the cunning and manipulation of *furberia* to obtain his goal: Angela.

Ultimately, however, in one of the film's many ironic touches, Ferdinando ends up as a real *cornuto:* at the film's conclusion, as Ferdinando and his young bride honeymoon on a sailboat, she seductively plays footsie with one of the handsome crew members while simultaneously kissing Ferdinando. This ending underscores another aspect of Ferdinando's character: that he, like many other protagonists of the *commedia all'italiana*, is an *inetto*. Ferdinando fashions himself a Latin lover, a charming, debonair aristocrat whom women cannot resist. In the film's first scene, he is wearing a dark suit, sunglasses (a Sicilian version of Marcello in *La dolce vita*), and smoking a cigarette through a holder as he lasciviously eyes the young women he passes in the corridor. In reality, however, he is an ineffective, destitute failure. An aristocrat in decline, he

12. Ferdinando as the *bella figura*, parading his wife Rosalia (Daniela Rocca) in front of the lustful *paesani*. Courtesy of Photofest.

has no discernable means of employment, preferring to spend his days lounging at home in his pajamas and trying to avoid his wife's meddling presence. So preoccupied is he with his own plight that he does not notice that the honor of his family name is being jeopardized by his sister Agnese, who consistently flaunts the female chastity codes with her fiancé Rosario—Ferdinando interrupts them several times in compromising positions, only to ignore them in his determination to fulfill his own desire. This is in contrast to his uncle Calogero, who immediately calls in the midwife to ensure that his daughter Angela is still "pure" when he discovers her diary and confessions of love. Assured that her chastity is intact, he then sends her off to school in Catania at the Convent of the Seven Sorrows to ensure her purity.[43] Germi often considered the honor code from the female perspective, apparent in three instances in *Divorce—Italian Style:* the cases of Mariannina Terranova and of Carmelo's wife, who saw fit to use the masculine honor code to vindicate their own honor, and of Agnese who, dishonored by Rosalia's actions as well, is abandoned by her fiancé as a result. In Germi's view of Sicilian life, no one is spared the repercussions of the restrictive honor code.

When Ferdinando embarks on his mission to catch Rosalia in the act of adultery, he is consistently undermined by his own ineptitude. As she and Carmelo finally confess their love for each other, the tape on his

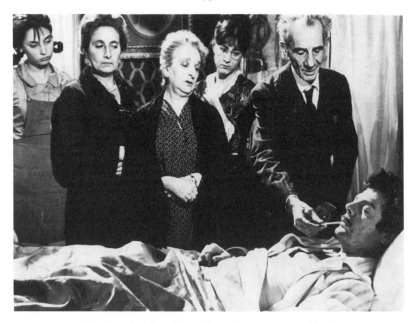

13. Ferdinando feigns illness in order to carry out his plans.
Courtesy of Photofest.

bugging device runs out, and he is unable to hear their plans. On the
day he intends to catch them, he misses them as they head for the train
station, thus thwarting his carefully laid plans of surprising them *in
flagrante delicto* and thus being justified in shooting them with the gun
he had conveniently planted nearby. Unfortunately, he arrives at the
train station late, missing the train, which has actually departed on
time. Finally, when he finds out where the couple is hiding, Carmelo's
wife arrives there first, fortunately leaving Rosalia alive to meet her appropriate demise.

Divorce—Italian Style, much like *Il bell'Antonio,* mocks the actor's
Latin lover image, this time through satire and irony.[44] Mastroianni's
successful caricature of the Barone, a role which garnered several awards,
including an Oscar nomination, depends on the physicality of his performance. His droopy eyelids and selectively unkempt or extremely
slicked-back hair reinforce his status as a self-involved, decadent aristocrat. Self-consciously aware of the importance of the male body's role
in the public display of honor, Ferdinando, after Rosalia's act of betrayal, slouches and shuffles, in contrast to his previous public prome-
nades exuding poise and power. His characteristic facial tic, which

14. Ferdinando attempts
to listen in on Rosalia's
conversations with her lover.
Courtesy of Photofest.

Germi at first thought to be Mastroianni's mocking impersonation of
him, seemingly provides insight into the character's mind, and specifically into his devious plots, but often reveals the ineptitude behind the
mask of strategic initiative.[45] The facial tic appears, for example, when
Ferdinando looks at himself in his mirror, once to admire his attractive-
ness and then to praise himself for his foresight in hiding the gun with
which he hopes to kill Rosalia. At the same time, the tic surfaces when
the tape runs out and he misses the lovers' plans, as well as when he
hears the shots fired by Immacolata Patanè as she beats him to the
crime. At first an apparent reference to his *furberia*, the tic also reveals
his status as *fesso* and *inetto*.

The text further parodies Mastroianni's image as the Latin lover
with a telling intertextual reference to *La dolce vita* itself, the film which
bestowed on Mastroianni that very star persona. Ferdinando uncovers
his wife's plan to meet her lover on an evening when the entire family
is out, allowing them the opportunity for their tryst. The event she
chooses is the screening of what is billed as "the most scandalous film
of all time": Fellini's *La dolce vita*, guaranteed to draw a crowd, because
the Church had warned spectators to stay away. Preceded by a montage
of Church litanies against the film, the scene presents a room packed to

the brim with mostly male spectators who remain transfixed by the screen, ignoring the Church's admonitions. The spectatorial scene features Sylvia, played by Anita Ekberg, dancing joyously around the Termi di Caracala to Adriano Celentano's version of Chuck Berry's "Ready to Rock-n-Roll." Although Mastroianni does not appear in the film within the film as Marcello the journalist, his association with both films would have been obvious to most spectators on a national and international level. Furthermore, the implicit comparison between the films exposes the sexual attitudes in each: Fellini's film, and this scene in particular, celebrates unbridled (female) sexual freedom, while Germi's film, by contrast, represents sexual repression at its utmost.

As opposed to *Il bell'Antonio*, *Divorce—Italian Style* relies on comedy for its ironic commentary on Sicilian life. Much of the humor in *Divorce—Italian Style* is derived from Germi's play with cinematic language. The film uses a variety of camera movements for comic effect, as when the camera rapidly zooms in on the men in town reading about Ferdinando's crime in the newspapers at various public sites: the club, the café, and the street. When Ferdinando returns from prison and seeks out Angela in the crowd that awaits him, the film speeds up to fast forward as he is forced to greet his friends and relatives but stops immediately when he spies Angela apart from them all. Likewise, the film goes into fast rewind of Carmelo's and Rosalia's first embrace as Ferdinando rewinds the tape. The last two examples provide further point-of-view identification with Ferdinando's state of mind—the frenetic joy of seeing Angela after several years in prison and the panicky and intense attempt to discover the lovers' plans.[46] Furthermore, Carlo Rustichelli's musical score firmly anchors the film in Sicilian culture and folklore, alternating three compositions: a funeral march, played not only at Don Calogero's funeral but also, in an implicit comparison, when the camera pans down Angela's body to reveal her game of footsie with the deckhand; the Ave Maria; and a Sicilian love ballad. As leitmotifs throughout the film, they comment on three important constants in Sicilian life: love, death, and religion. The fact that the sound is often commentative rather than actual, as well as counterpoint rather than parallel (as in the example of the last shot), highlights both the comic aspects of the film as well as the social commentary on Sicilian life and Sicilian masculinity that lies behind so much of the dark, grotesque humor.

If Germi's film is so heavily steeped in Sicilian culture and society, why the title *Divorce—Italian Style*? Much like Bolognini and Pasolini's decision to eliminate the Fascist temporal setting from their film, the lack of geographic specificity to Sicily extends the reach of the film's social and sexual commentary not just to Sicilians but to the entire Italian peninsula. Similarly, their engagement of gender constructions, while focusing on Sicilian masculinity and femininity, also has much to say about post-war Italian masculinity in general and its various incarnations on screen.

Each film attempts to undermine the mythology surrounding Sicilian masculinity. Much like in the rest of Italy, in Sicily a man's public appearance is a sign of self-worth and male virility (the *gallo*); however, in Sicily it carries the added baggage of family honor and female chastity. Like most gender constructions, masculinity is fragile, and Sicilian masculinity is no exception. What makes it unique is precisely what renders it tendentious. The irony of *gallismo* and the discourse which is at its base have much in common with Giovannini's and the Schneiders's observations that there are no innate characteristics of the Sicilian male which attribute to it a hypermasculinity. Rather, it is a construct, much like the cultural codes of *amicizia, furberia,* and *onore,* an "instrument of adaptation" to secular forces.[47] Furthermore, extra-national images of Italian male sexuality played a significant role. As the discussion of the Latin lover in chapter 2 elucidated, exotic sexuality goes hand in hand with Italy's status as a less civilized and restrained culture in comparison to other Western nations. That uncivilized and unrestrained characteristic is doubled in the case of Sicily, for its status within Italy itself as the backward appendage further enhances its status as primitive other.

Both *Il bell'Antonio* and *Divorce—Italian Style* zero in on the irony that belies Sicilian masculinity and its image of super-virility by revealing the *inetto* underneath the masquerade of sexual potency. Brancati's novel first explored the connection between Fascist ideology and Sicilian masculinity, specifically the preoccupation with virility and its basis in power and aggression. Its ironic and sarcastic tone gives way in the film to a serious if not melodramatic feel, suggesting the dire significance of Antonio's failures as a man in a culture still dominated by virile expectations. Sicilian masculinity's obsession with machismo and male sexual power is what drives Alfio to his death at the brothel and what leads Antonio into a loveless marriage. Germi's film satirizes the persistent divide between North and South, the honor code and the issue of divorce as it unmasks the *fesso* behind the façade of the self-fashioned *bella figura.* The citation of Fellini's *La dolce vita* self-consciously parodies Mastroianni's own Latin lover image by invoking the very film which garnered him that label and which this film seeks to consciously subvert and exploit for its own ironic and comic purposes—to expose the *gallo* as *cornuto* and *inetto*. Federico Fellini would have much fun playing off that Latin lover image in his next collaborations with Mastroianni. In *8½* and other films, he further scrutinizes traditional constructions of Italian masculinity by looking at them through a humorous lens, and laughs at both Mastroianni and himself in the process.

4

"Remember, It's a Comedy"

Mastroianni in the Films of Federico Fellini

Of his relationship with Mastroianni, Federico Fellini said: "I am frequently asked if Marcello is my alter ego. Marcello Mastroianni is many things to many people. For me, he is not my alter ego. He is Marcello, an actor who conforms perfectly to what I want from him, like a contortionist who can do anything."[1] The films Fellini made with Mastroianni include four feature films—*La dolce vita, 8½* (1963), *La città delle donne* (City of Women, 1980), and *Ginger and Fred* (1986)—and the two pseudo-documentaries *Block-notes di un regista* (A Director's Notebook, 1970) and *Intervista* (Interview, 1987). Mastroianni played an essential, self-acknowledged role in all of these celebrated, provocative collaborations. Their post-*dolce vita* artistic relationship, in which Fellini shifted away from a certain realism to a more dream-like world, turned an ironic lens onto Italian masculinity and through it exposed the fallacy of its myths and the shortcomings of its reality.

When Fellini began the actual filming of *8½*, he attached this phrase to the camera: "Remember, it's a comedy."[2] Although not everyone would call the film a comedy, Fellini's axiom gives impetus to a new reading of the film. The director was no stranger to the genre of comedy both on and off screen: as a young man he drew comic strips, wrote for humor magazines, and sketched caricatures of American soldiers stationed in post-war Italy. His first two films, *Luci di varietà* (Variety Lights, co-directed with Alberto Lattuada in 1950) and *Lo sciecco bianco* (The White Sheik, 1952), are set in what could be considered "humoristic" settings: the worlds of variety shows and *fotoromanzi* (comic books which featured photographs instead of drawings). Mastroianni has described working with Fellini as a "continuous game, a growing amusement, a total happiness."[3] According to Deena Boyer's chronicle of the filming of *8½*, Mastroianni and Fellini constantly played jokes on each other and the entire troupe. In one instance, after a false report appeared in the evening paper that Mastroianni had been in a car accident, the actor, whom the desperate filmmakers had been unable to contact, came in the next day with his head wound with bandages. In reality, the accident had happened to a man with the same name.[4]

Fellini's films give expression to many of these anxieties through the cathartic release of humor. I show how the use of irony, satire, jokes, and pranks in Fellini's films with Mastroianni reveals a deep-seated angst about masculinity and relationships among men, between men and women, and about the changing role of men in an Italian society in relation to profoundly unstable gender ideals. Humor provides an acceptable means for dealing with these anxieties. Jokes, irony, and slapstick allow Italian men to laugh at themselves and at what they fear most: their inability to live up to a culturally ingrained and idealized notion of masculinity.

The anthropological research of Stanley Brandes on the role of jokes in Mediterranean masculinity, along with the psychoanalytic theories of Freud and Jung, serves as guide to this analysis of the Fellini-Mastroianni collaborations, which concentrates primarily on *8½* and *City of Women*, with an interlude to *A Director's Notebook*.[5] Brandes argues that humor reflects shared assumptions about masculinity as well as "culturally acceptable outlet[s] for the frustrations, tensions, and other feelings that cannot be expressed directly."[6] However, as opposed to aggression, a concept which Freud sees as integral to his notion of the joke and the comic, Brandes identifies defensiveness as the dominant motivating agent: "In jokes, Andalusian men reveal and share their most deeply buried anxieties with one another, and thereby achieve a feeling of intimacy and camaraderie that they would find difficult to express through more overt means" (103). Pirandello's "umorismo" provides additional parameters of analysis in this discussion. Whereas Fellini denied ever having read Pirandello, Manuela Gieri, in her work on Fellini and Pirandello, individuates an "aesthetic and ideological 'affinity' or proximity" between the two. Fellini's cinema, like Pirandello's literature, "visually records the existential and psychological condition of modern man [*sic*]" through the transgressive social criticism of humor.[7] In light of psychoanalysis, anthropology, and cultural studies, Fellini's films are not, as many have claimed, misogynist and sexist. A nuanced view of his humor reveals that the films are in fact about male anxiety and anxious masculinity.

8½: The Director Laughs at Himself

8½ chronicles the story of Guido Anselmi, a filmmaker plagued by artistic self-doubt and personal conflict. On doctor's orders, he travels to a spa in the Tuscan town of Chianciano to rejuvenate his health as well as cure his writer's block. Unable to bring his most recent film project to fruition and incapable of reconciling with the many women in his life—his wife Luisa, his lover Carla, his mother, and Claudia, an ideal woman dressed in white who keeps appearing to him in various visions—the film's comic elements allow Guido to give expression to his artistic and sexual angst. *8½* was in fact born out of Fellini's own artistic crisis, as he did not know how he was going to proceed with his first feature-length follow-up to the phenomenally successful *La dolce vita*.[8] One day, as he was writing a letter to his producer Angelo Rizzoli withdrawing from the project, a grip working on pre-production on the yet-to-be-determined film came to invite him to a birthday party for another crew member. After they raised their glasses to toast the director and his next masterpiece, Fellini returned to his office and lost himself in deep thought:

> I listened to a fountain and the sound of the water, and tried to hear my own inner voice. Then, I heard a small voice of creativity within me. I knew. The story I would tell was of a writer who doesn't know what he wants to write.
>
> I tore up my letter to Rizzoli.
>
> Later, I changed the profession of Guido to that of film director. He became a film director who didn't know what he wanted to direct. It's difficult to portray a writer on the screen, doing what he does in an interesting way. There isn't much action to show in writing. The world of the film director opened up limitless possibilities.[9]

As the film has many echoes of Fellini's autobiography, it is not surprising that critics have found correlations between characters and their real-life counterparts: the relationship between Mezzabotta and his young girlfriend Gloria parallels Sophia Loren's relationship with Carlo Ponti; and Guido's problems with the foreign actress (Madeleine Lebeau) who relentlessly hounds him are reminiscent of Fellini's own troubles with Luise Rainer in the casting of *La dolce vita*.[10] Shooting of the film began on May 9, 1962, and proceeded through October 14 of that year; it premiered in Italy on February 15, 1963, and in France and in the United States the following May and June.[11]

15. Guido (Mastroianni)
contemplates his angst-
ridden mirror image in
Fellini's *8½* (1962).
Courtesy of Photofest.

The film revolves around Guido, from whose point of view the film takes its tone, a fact quickly established in the opening dream sequence: Guido dreams he is suffocating in a car during a traffic jam, unable to escape as others around him are oblivious to his pain. Fellini was fascinated by dreams on both a practical and theoretical level: he diligently kept a dream notebook with elaborate sketches of his visions. Eventually, in this opening scene, Guido escapes in a Christ-like drift over the sea, until he is pulled down by two men (one of whom we subsequently learn is Claudia's manager). For Carolyn Geduld, this dream constitutes pivotal clues to Guido's crisis, for it is the "unconscious material" released in the dream which encapsulates his various predicaments: the pressures of filmmaking, and the "binding quality of both his sexual needs and his masculine identity."[12] As Guido awakens before he plummets into the sea, the film abruptly cuts to Guido's darkened hotel room, where his doctors and a nurse examine him and prescribe his regimen at the spa. The first shot in this sequence is a pan from left to right and back again from Guido's point of view as he lies in bed (the back of his head is also visible). This shot serves to align the spectator's gaze with Guido, reinforcing the film's subjective perspective.

Guido represents, in many ways, a joint collaboration between Fellini and Mastroianni.[13] Fellini had originally thought of Laurence Olivier for the role of Guido, but, according to Mastroianni, Fellini felt he was too "great" for the part, that—like Marcello in *La dolce vita*—he wanted another average man (*un uomo qualsiasi*), but also one who could do a good imitation of the director himself. Fellini had Marcello's chest hair removed, made him lose eight kilograms, thinned out his temples, put gray streaks in his hair and heavy bags under his eyes to make him look older, less virile, and more fragile, as Fellini saw himself.[14] The director also had Mastroianni imitate his own behavior: his tics, facial expressions, and habits; he even had him raise his voice in order to resemble Fellini's higher pitch. At one point, Mezzabotta even calls Guido "Old Snàporaz," Fellini's nickname for Mastroianni (and the nickname of the protagonist in *City of Women*).

Although there exist many parallels between Fellini's life and the film, to reduce the film to an autobiography would miss the universality of the film's message. Not only is it a film about Fellini making a film, it is also a highly self-referential film about filmmaking and the many tensions involved: between film as a work of art and film as industry, between the artistic vision of the auteur and the collaborative nature of the filmmaking process, and between the filmmaker, who aims to communicate his vision to an audience, and an audience which may or may not appreciate that vision.[15] Guido is caught between these many contradictions, and his anxieties as an artist plagued by self-doubt often exhibit themselves through humor. Fellini's intention was to make Guido both a serious and comic character, and the film was to be a satire of a film which he would never make.[16] Even though Fellini admitted that the final product failed to be as funny as he had intended, the camera style—the rapid camera movements, the frenetic pace of certain scenes, the strategic use of the grotesque close-up—all contribute to the film's circus-like atmosphere in capturing both Guido's personal crisis and the filmmaking process.

As Guido awakens from his nightmare of falling into the sea, his first encounter is with the doctor, who greets him with the line: "Well, what exciting thing are you preparing for us now: another film without hope?" Soon the writer Daumier enters (played by Jean Rougeul, an existential writer in his own right). Of all the characters, Daumier, to whom Fellini himself refers as Guido's true adversary, is clearly the most castrating to Guido's ability to make the film.[17] Called in to comment on the integrity of the script, he spends most of the film chastising Guido on the banality and incomprehensibility of his ideas. A sarcastic caricature of the intellectual whose name evokes the French painter Honoré Daumier (and whose French-accented Italian underscores this parody), he functions as the mouthpiece of Guido's own self-doubt as well as the depository of the possible critiques that could be leveled at

8½. After Guido has asked him to read the script for the film he intends to make, Daumier disparages its disjointed narrative, its lack of a cohesive unifying argument or philosophy, and its self-gratifying excess.[18] The comic aspects of Daumier's character rest in the exaggerated harshness and intensity of his criticism as well as his physical appearance: his expressionless dour demeanor, his inability (or perhaps snobistic refusal) to integrate with the rest of the group, and his lack of social skills—rarely does he engage in conversation, with didactic preaching as his dominant mode of communication. Even in the hotel room sequence, Daumier remains on the margins of the action, sitting in a chair with his legs crossed, smoking, and responding to Guido's query about his impressions on the script with "We'll talk about it later." While in the bathroom after their conversation, Guido positions his body as if flatulating in Daumier's direction as Wagner's "Ride of the Valkyries" plays in the background. This obscene gesture, reminiscent of Dante and Chaucer, signals Guido's attitude toward Daumier and others in positions of power over him, yet it is a response that he can only perform in the secrecy of his bathroom, or in the privacy of his fantasy life, where he enacts the ultimate revenge on Daumier. During a viewing of the many screen tests made for Guido's soon-to-be film, Daumier cites their futility, and accuses Guido of self-absorption. Guido then imagines the writer's vivid death-by-hanging, accompanied by the light-hearted single piano version of the circus motif of Nino Rota's score. The humor in this scene rests in the correspondence between Guido's fantasy and that of the spectator, who rejoices in the demise of this smug, pestering intellectual boor. This brief fantasy perfectly illustrates Pirandello's feeling of the opposite (the humor in death), as well as the fantasy solution to Guido's artistic torment.[19] Guido, in watching the projections of his life as they appear in the screen tests, also projects his aesthetic angst onto the figure of Daumier.

Also subject to Fellini's angry satire are the journalists and members of the film industry who constantly hound him and feed his self-doubts. These players are involved in two of the most circus-like scenes: Guido's initial descent into the hotel lobby, and the press conference announcing the beginning of the film's shooting. In the first instance, producers, agents, managers, and even his assistants become part of the carnivalesque array of people from whom Guido attempts to escape, often through comic gestures: a low, squatting, duck-like walk reminiscent of Gelsomina's traveling circus act in Fellini's *La strada* (The Road, 1954), or the exaggerated obsequious bowing to his producer. The film benevolently enjoys this send-up of the film's producer (loosely based on Rizzoli, the producer of *8½*), who is more concerned with the

16. Daumier (Jean Rougeul) berates Guido at the spa for the banality
of his ideas. Courtesy of Photofest.

economic bottom line (and berating his young girlfriend) than making
a work of art. It reserves most of its wrath for the journalists who seem
to be more interested in Guido's love life and political views than in his
future film, and in exalting his failure rather than promoting his success. At the final press conference, with its fusion of reality and fantasy,
complete with visions of Luisa in her wedding dress and hallucinations
of suicide, Guido's anxiety finds its voice in the Pirandellian, humoristic
laugh of the American journalist who looks directly at the camera and
cackles: "He is lost. He has nothing to say."

The fact that the American journalist is a woman makes the criticism doubly caustic, for the women in the film are often the mouthpieces of the most severe criticism leveled against Guido's professional
and personal life. Much work on gender and Fellini has revolved around
Jungian psychoanalysis, because of Fellini's fascination with Jung as
well as his relationship with Ernst Bernhard, a prominent Jungian prac-
titioner. Fellini turned to Jung and Bernhard as a way of making sense
of the coincidences and omens which had always been a part of his
life, and as a way of finding a unifying theory to guide his artistic self-
therapy.[20] Most resonant for Fellini was Jung's notion of the collective

unconscious and its use of archetypes, which Jung defined as the expression of various forms of psychic content which are identical in all individuals and are inherited: "The archetype is essentially an unconscious content that is altered by becoming conscious and by being perceived, and it takes its colour from the individual consciousness in which it happens to appear."[21] Archetypes find expression in what Jung has called the "active imagination": dreams, myths, and fairytales, on which Fellini's films all draw.[22]

The most significant archetypes for a Jungian interpretation of Fellini's films are female: the *anima* and the earth mother. The *anima* represents the feminine element in man, which manifests itself in dreams, visions, and fantasies. Not a substitute for the figure of the mother, it corresponds instead to the maternal Eros, that is, the feelings and emotions associated with the mother. Jung writes that the *anima* "makes demands on the masculinity of a man, on his ardour, above all on his courage and resolution."[23] This struggle with the *anima* radiates in Guido's relationships with women. In *8½*, Luisa's disgust at Guido's lies, Claudia's sweet berating of his inability to love, and even his assistant Cesarino's nieces' observation that he doesn't know how to make a love story speak to the role of women in Guido's torment. According to Bondanella, women for Guido fall into two categories: either virgins/mothers or whores, because of the childhood trauma of the Saraghina episode, one of the film's funnier flashbacks. Saraghina was a local prostitute who sold herself to fishermen for the remains from their sardine nets. Her name was derived from the word for sardines in the dialect of Fellini's hometown of Rimini.[24] As schoolboys, Guido and his friends would pay money to watch her dance the rumba outside her beach shack. For the boys, Saraghina is simultaneously erotic and menacing: her unkempt hair and raggedy, revealing clothing contrast with the child-like glee she takes in entertaining the boys. When the priests from the school discover the boys, the scene takes on a slapstick feel: the film speeds up as Guido tries to escape their clutches, and they all end up in a pile on the sand.

Like Saraghina, the other women in his life are simultaneously nurturing and ominous, shrouded in a child-like fear and reverence or symbolic of guilty pleasure.[25] Guido's wife Luisa is completely desexualized in both demeanor and appearance: Fellini deliberately tried to diminish Anouk Aimee's natural beauty (he even had her famously long eyelashes cut) and makes direct associations between her and Guido's mother during a dream sequence. By contrast, Carla exudes sexuality from every pore: Fellini conducted an exhaustive search for the actress who would play Carla, and when Sandra Milo was found, he rejoiced in her

17. La Saraghina (Eddra Gale) dances the rumba for young Guido
and his friends. Courtesy of Photofest.

child-like laugh and her joyous gluttony.[26] She is Guido's adult version of Saraghina, at once sexual and motherly. This association is directly referenced in a scene at Carla's hotel, where Guido applies make-up to her face and directs her to snarl so that she resembles the prostitute.

The figure of Claudia exists, as do many of the characters, on several levels: as the subject of Guido's fantasy, as a character in Guido's film, as the actress Claudia who would play the character in Guido's film, and finally as Claudia Cardinale, recognizable by the film's spectators as such.[27] A fusion of the mother/whore, she reappears to him in visions throughout the film as both nurturing—as a nurse at the spa in a white uniform—and sexualized, appearing in one fantasy sequence in a sexy nightgown. Guido believes that only she can save him from both his artistic and sexual anxieties. Unfortunately, she is unable to calm them, for Guido realizes, in their first face-to-face encounter toward the end of the film, that Claudia only fuels his personal and career crises. She is, in Fellini's view, "the most disturbing sign of Guido's impotence,"[28] evidenced by the episode that follows their meeting: the press conference and suicide fantasy.

Perhaps no scene elucidates the contrast between the real and the ideal with women in Guido's life better than the harem sequence, also

known as *la fattoria delle donne* (the farm of women), in which Guido
fantasizes about a joyous reunion of all the women in his real and ideal
life. Lasting approximately twelve minutes, it is preceded by one of the
most comic of Guido's fantastic visions. As he, Luisa, and her sister
Rossella have coffee in Chiancano's main square, Carla appears and sits
down at one of the many empty tables (they are in fact the only custom-
ers there). After Luisa berates Guido for his dishonesty (he denied
knowledge of Carla's presence at the spa), Guido imagines a reconciliation between his wife and his lover: Luisa approaches Carla, kisses her,
and compliments her on her gaudy outfit. Their praise is mutual, and a
reaction shot shows Guido, legs up on a table, applauding approvingly.
Carla and Luisa then parade together toward him and dance with one
another, physically bringing together in his fantasy world what he is
unable to reconcile in real life: the desexualized mother and the over-
sexualized lover.

A dissolve shot transitions us to the farmhouse which is to be the
setting of *la fattoria delle donne*. The same location had figured prominently in a previous flashback to Guido's youth, where he and other
children, presumably his siblings and cousins, are lovingly cared for by
their nursemaids. During that earlier scene a young Guido is bathed
in a huge vat of wine, a ritual enacted on all the boys in order to
make them grow strong. After the young Guido is wrapped in a sheet,
cuddled by his nurses and maids, and lovingly tucked into bed, his play-
mate tells him to chant the phrase "ANANISIMASA" to ward off the
evil eye of the portrait hanging in the bedroom. The last image of the
scene, accompanied by the single notes of a harp, is of a burning hearth,
symbolizing the tender, emotional warmth evoked in the memory. The
hearth reappears as the first shot of the harem sequence, and is one of
many images which bind the two. The harem sequence thus melds the
past with the present, a child-like vision of sexuality with an adult fantasy world, but, unlike the memory, ends on a note of anxious melancholy rather than wistful nostalgia.

The harem sequence can be broken down roughly into three parts:
(1) an introduction to the characters and the establishment of the rules
of the universe; (2) the rebellion, led by the soubrette Jacqueline Bon-
bon, and her final dance; and (3) the sorrowful conclusion, in which
Guido has re-established order but experiences a profound sadness. It
is a fantasy of control over an out-of-control situation, as all of *8½*'s
women, with the notable exceptions of Guido's mother and Claudia,
are present to please and cater to him. Yet, in terms of a male fantasy
about women, it is decidedly uneroticized. For Guido, they are there
more for maternal comfort than sexual pleasure, evidenced by the dupli-

cation of both setting (the farm) and action (the bath, here water not wine) from the ANANISIMASA memory. Several of the women— Gloria, the "negretta" from Hawaii, and Jacqueline—are decidedly more sexualized, yet theirs is an exotic, animalesque, menacing sexuality rather than a docile eroticism.

Although appearing on the surface to tend to Guido's every whim, the women in actuality consistently subvert his authority. During their open rebellion, set once again to Wagner's "Ride of the Valkyries," the women criticize Guido's performance as a lover, saying he doesn't know how to make love, and that he falls asleep immediately afterward, to Guido's vociferous denials. In order to subdue the uprising, Guido brandishes the ultimate phallic symbol of power, the whip, and quells the insurrection, and in doing so references his own weakness (the need for an outside object to re-establish order) as well as the genre of the Hollywood western, in particular the short serial films. He even smoothes back the brim of his hat after controlling the masses, as if putting his gun back into his holster. In an important twist on the western, however, here he must establish dominance over women, something that would rarely happen in an American version, so as not to call the hero's masculinity into question. The scene's conclusion, rather than being triumphant, is infused with a profound sadness, for Guido realizes the impossibility of this fantasy. It also acknowledges an important subtext to the film, and one which will move to the forefront of Fellini's subsequent films: aging. Guido projects his own anxiety about aging onto the dancer Jacqueline, who, now that she has reached the age of thirty, must be banished to the second floor of the farmhouse, where all other former lovers are put out to pasture.[29] Thus in this scene, like in many others in the film, sexual anxiety encroaches upon artistic anxiety, displaying Guido's fear of failure to perform in more ways than one.[30]

Yet, although the ending of this scene rings with melancholy, the film's triumphant conclusion reconciles fantasy with reality as well as finds a solution to Guido's crises. All the disparate elements in Guido's life come together in a circus-like celebration of what was the original title of the film, *La bella confusione* (The beautiful confusion). After deciding to abandon his film project to the approval of Daumier, who praises the artist for ultimately discovering the artistic merits of silence when one has nothing to say, Maurice, the magician who had provoked the ANANISIMASA memory, appears to him and tells him that they are ready to begin. Guido soon envisions Claudia, his nurses, Saraghina, and his parents, all dressed in white as they walk toward his abandoned movie set. While Daumier continues his droning monologue about the

18. Guido attempts to suppress the women's rebellion. Courtesy of Photofest.

futility of Guido's sewing together of "the vague tattered pieces of your life, your vague memories, or the faces of the people that you were never able to love,"[31] Guido comes to the realization that the truth of his life lies in its confusion, and he is no longer afraid of accepting it.

After professing that "Life is a celebration: let's live it together," Guido, the characters in the film (except Claudia and Daumier), and much of the actual film crew begin to assemble as a band of clowns, featuring the young Guido, plays Nino Rota's famous refrain "La passarella di addio." The Fellini-Rota collaboration dates back to the director's first solo effort, *The White Sheik*, and continued up to Rota's death in 1979. Inspired by such diverse musical influences as nineteenth-century dance-opera, music-hall and variety theater tunes, melodic songs of the 1930s, and the scores of Chaplin shorts, these scores aimed, according to Pier Marco de Santi's study of Rota's music, for simple, melodic, and catchy refrains which "moved from a tenderly sentimental vein to a discrete and pleasing humorous one, which is best generically indicated by the term 'clownerie'," reflecting an "evocative symbiosis" between music and image.[32] From *La dolce vita* onward, Rota integrated well-known popular songs and classical compositions in the films' scores. For *8½*, Rota initially envisioned only one original composition, the "Equestrian Circus March," to be strategically inserted at various points throughout the film. In the film's final scene, therefore, it would be recognizable to the film spectator, and he or she would participate in the concluding "explosion" of the circus motif.[33] Eventually, other Rota compositions came to be integrated and reworked throughout the film score—Carla's theme, the music accompanying the press conference, and the cemetery scene—although, according to Rota, they did not take on the symbolic function of the leitmotif.

In this final sequence, Guido is now in his director persona complete with megaphone. It is, in fact, the first time we actually see him directing anything during the film. He guides the characters to their places, and soon the young Guido draws back a white curtain over the stairs of the abandoned space ship set to reveal the characters parading down, as the music swells into a full orchestral fanfare. They all form a circle, which Guido eventually joins, and dance together in a celebration of the confusion Guido has just embraced. The light then darkens to showcase the young Guido and the clown musicians surrounded by a circle of lights and highlighted by a single spotlight. Young Guido dismisses the other musicians, and as he exits the scene the screen soon fades to black. Fellini had originally envisioned this sequence as the film's trailer. The original ending instead featured Guido and Luisa returning to Rome on a train, and Guido imagines all the film's characters dressed in white and smiling at him in the train's dining car. Fellini remained unsure as to which ending he would select up to the last minute.[34]

The message of the chosen ending resolves many of the issues Guido has faced, but perhaps not so neatly: he has not yet settled his relationship with Carla, he still longs for the attention of his dead mother, and he remains isolated from his friend Mezzabotta, who is too preoccupied with his young girlfriend Gloria to notice him. The last image Fellini leaves us with, that of the young Guido, has important implications for both a psychoanalytic reading of the text, as well as the role of the comic in the film. For Jung, the child paves the way for future wholeness (often associated with roundness—here the circle) on both a conscious and unconscious level.[35] Guido embraces the non-logical and nonsensical elements of his life—the beautiful chaos—symbolized in the joyous celebration of dance, the figure of the child, and the comic image of the band of clowns. Guido rejoices in his sexual and artistic crises rather than being bogged down by them. At the film's end, Guido, and perhaps Fellini, has learned to accept and laugh at himself and all his shortcomings, be they related to artistic angst or male sexuality. As Fellini's career progressed, the world around him would change, resulting in the filmic representation of deeper and not-so-readily resolvable gender crises.

Transitions: *A Director's Notebook*

Fellini: A Director's Notebook (or, in Italian, *Block-notes di un regista*), the documentary Fellini made for the U.S. television network NBC, begins much like *8½* ends: on an abandoned set, this time for a project Fellini always envisioned but would never make, *Il viaggio di Mastorna* (Mastorna's journey), which was to have starred Mastroianni as well. Also a film about filmmaking, *A Director's Notebook* pushes the boundaries of the documentary genre through another disjointed narrative featuring his regular players (Masina, Mastroianni) as well as the expected unusual cast of characters as they parade through a series of personal visions: among them, the Mastorna set, an underground subway ride through Rome, and an encounter with possible non-professional cast members for Fellini's next project, *Satyricon*. The film, like *8½*, is highly self-referential, as it consistently calls attention to itself as film: Fellini and his crew are simultaneously in front of and behind the camera, with little distinction between fact and fiction, and reality and re-creation. In one scene, for example, a group of prostitutes on the Appian Way metamorphose into their ancient Roman counterparts and are soon joined by a group of truck drivers who undergo the same transformation. This infusion of *romanità*—the conflation of Ancient and present-day Rome—permeates the film, which takes place in and around the city and signals two subsequent Fellini projects: his adaptation of *Satyricon,* and another pseudo-documentary, *Roma* (1972), Fellini's homage to his adopted city.

Mastroianni was to appear in *Roma* as well, but his scene was removed during the editing process. In *A Director's Notebook*, however, he figures prominently in two segments: when Fellini visits his home on the Appian Way, and in a screen test for the role of Mastorna. A little more than mid-way through the film, Fellini blissfully parodies Mastroianni's star status as Latin lover. He encounters the actor in the gardens of his sumptuously appointed villa, posing with beautiful models for a fashion shoot during an interview by an American journalist. Here the object of Fellini's ironic satire is not only the publicity machinery that creates the star system but also Mastroianni's own love-hate relationship with it. Rather than responding to the journalist with answers to the questions she poses, he readily agrees with the answers she feeds him. He states how he's a little tired of being labeled a Latin lover and how it is a big responsibility, because he will be thirty next year (in fact,

Mastrioanni was pushing fifty when this film was made). While his assistant Cesarino (played by Cesarino Miceli Picardi, the actor who
played Guido's assistant in *8½*) tells him (in Italian, with no subtitles
in the American version) that Sophia Loren, Gina Lollobrigida, and
Claudia Cardinale have each called three times, he recognizes the lack
of veracity in that statement. Wearing a tuxedo and drinking cham-
pagne, he then greets a busload of foreign, female tourists who have
come to his villa on their bus tour of Rome's many famous sites and
institutions.

The scene is by far the most comic in this pseudo-documentary—at
one point Fellini even tells de Santis his cameraman to stop laughing
and keep shooting. Unlike the other episodes in the film, where Fellini
is an active participant, here he remains a bemused spectator. Clearly
for Fellini the theme of the permeability between reality and fantasy
has invaded the extra-cinematic discourse surrounding Mastroianni,
and he revels in its irony: the fabrication of the Latin lover image and
Mastroianni's seemingly gleeful participation in it. The next scene,
however, in which Mastroianni tests for the role of Mastorna, completely reverses the mythology of filmmaking and stardom, as Mastroianni, incapable of capturing Mastorna as Fellini envisioned him, appears distraught, out of control, and unable to perform. As he directly
addresses the audience while ostensibly looking into the mirror as he
removes his stage makeup, Mastroianni tells Fellini that if the director
had faith in him and believed he was Mastorna, then he would become
Mastorna, much as Guido in *8½* wished for Luisa to have more faith in
him.[36] Stripped down to his bare essence, Mastroianni here exposes the
anxiety which underlies the humor of the Latin lover sequence: an inability to perform, here artistically, but, as becomes more evident in
City of Women, sexually as well, due to an undeniable fear of impotency
tied to the aging male psyche.

City of Women: The Joke Is on You

Similar to *A Director's Notebook* in its ironic play on Mastroianni's Latin
lover image, *City of Women*, one of Fellini's most controversial films,
centers around a male protagonist, alternately referred to as Marcello or
Snàporaz, who descends from a train in pursuit of a beautiful woman
and finds himself in a nightmare world controlled by women. In an interview with the journalist Lietta Tornabuoni in 1980, Fellini said that
all his films are about women: "They represent myth, mystery, diversity,
fascination, the thirst for knowledge, and the search for one's own identity." Further elaborating on the connection between women and cinema,

the director compares the film-going experience to returning to the womb, adding that "one should go to the cinema with the innocence of a fetus."[37]

Of all of Fellini's films, *City of Women* addresses head-on Fellini's own self-professed fear and bewilderment of women, which, this time, he foregrounds in light of Italy's recent feminist movement.[38] For Bondanella, the film is all about men's failure to understand women, and functions in many ways as a projection of male sexual fantasies about women (325).[39] Like other Fellini films, *City of Women* is a journey, a journey of an aging *inetto* into a world changed by the social and political redefinition of femininity.[40] Yet, unlike other Fellini films, in which the journey implies self-realization (*La strada; 8½*), self-destruction (*La dolce vita*), or self-reflection in the world of memories (*Amarcord,* 1973), *City of Women* chronicles a regressive journey into the world of dreams and, ultimately, the safety of the pre-Oedipal womb. Within the guise of humor, Fellini gives expression to his own sexual anxiety about the changing roles of femininity in Italian society.

Significant for understanding the complex dream-like structure of *City of Women* is the relationship between dreams and jokes in psychoanalytic thought. For Freud, jokes possess many similarities to dreams: he relates the brevity of jokes to condensation, its nonsensical attributes to regression to the child-like world of perceptual imagery, and the displacement of inhibitions through the joke to the unconscious centralization in dreams of consciously marginalized elements.[41] The main purpose of the joke-work is to liberate pleasure while ridding inhibitions and lifting suppressions and repressions (164–68). Significant to the liberation of this psychic energy is cathexis: the idea that a certain amount of instinctive and often socially unacceptable psychical energy exerts pressure on psychical forces for release.[42] For Freud, the laughter involves the re-channeling of previously repressed psychic energy (180). Thus, the joke becomes a liberating process of the inhibited in a socially and morally acceptable form, and—and here lies the connection to dreams—it is most powerful when it reaches down into the self's unconscious. Perhaps no Italian director was more in touch with his unconscious than Federico Fellini, whose post-*dolce vita* films reflect a greater self-reflexivity and preoccupation with various modes of consciousness. The dream-like narrative structure and framework of *City of Women*, combined with the humor with which it is infused, particularly in the Pirandellian "feeling of the opposite," constitutes one long joke on Snàporaz/Marcello as the prototypical *inetto* out of place in the feminist world of gender revision.[43]

When Fellini was making *City of Women*, Italy was already in the throes of what became known as the third wave of feminism. The first wave, according to Susan Basnett, dates back to the *Risorgimento* up through the turn of the twentieth century, with a focus on the role of women in the new Italian nation; the second involved the post-war reconstruction and the formation of the constitution, with the debate centered around female suffrage. As Basnett and others have pointed out, this connection between feminism and politics in Italy is essential for understanding the fundamental characteristics of Italian feminism: that more often than not, it is tied to a volatile political issue, whether unification and nation formation in the nineteenth and twentieth centuries, constitutional rights in the post-Fascist era, or the social and political struggles for legalized abortion and divorce rights in the 1970s. Based predominantly in the North, this last wave of Italian feminism grew out of and went beyond the student and worker protest movements of the late 1960s. In contrast to Anglo-Saxon feminists, who looked toward self-definition through sexual awareness, and French feminists, who turned to psychoanalysis and the unconscious as a means of understanding women's oppression, Italian feminist organizations addressed issues of power. Groups such as *Lotta femminile* (Female struggle) and the *Movimento della liberazione della donna* (Women's liberation movement) raised awareness in several areas. They excoriated women's economic exploitation in the home and advocated a wages-for-housework campaign; they encouraged women to take control of their bodies, promoting birth control, abortion rights, and "take back the night" protests; they attacked the traditional gender constructions of the *madonna/ puttana* dichotomy so prevalent in Italian culture (see chapter 3); and they promoted legal equality for the sexes. In 1977, the "historic compromise" between the Christian Democrats and the Communist Party, a move designed to unite the country against terrorism, ultimately resulted in the gradual deceleration of various cultural revolutionary movements. Nevertheless, smaller splinter groups kept the ideals and the goals of the feminist movement alive. On the whole, Italian feminism was more of a cultural than a political revolution—it brought women into the public sphere, allowing them to break from traditional feminine behavioral expectations. Although on the wane, feminist consciousness was still very much present and alive when Fellini both conceived of and executed *City of Women*.[44]

A highly ironic and self-referential film, *City of Women* begins with a female voice speaking over the credits saying, "Marcello again? We're begging you, Maestro." Once again, the connection between Fellini and Mastroianni is noteworthy in this film. Not only does he use the actor's first name (as he did in *La dolce vita*), but he also invokes, as in *8½*, the personal nickname Fellini had for Marcello: Snàporaz. According to Mastroianni,

> Snàporaz's roots are the same as my other Fellini characters. Snàporaz is a little bit like Fellini, but also a little bit like me, and we represent so many other men. . . . The [film's] theme can be synthesized thus: that the changes in the feminine world found us, meaning us old men, very but very unprepared. But probably it will end up that the film in the long run will be seen with much more interest by those much younger than us, both men and women, in order to understand how we men were (and are, because we are still alive, that's clear), and how we saw, or loved, or feared women.[45]

This quote underscores two essential aspects of the film: (1) that Snàporaz/Marcello, rather than being a pure Fellinian alter-ego, really represents everyman, and every Italian man at a certain point in his life (middle age) at a certain point in history (against the backdrop of the feminist movement); and (2) it integrates the fears of an aging man into the equation. In many ways, the protagonist is a Guido seventeen years later who has still not resolved his issues with women. Mastroianni's turn as an aging lothario cannot help but recall Fellini's interpretation of the famous Venetian four years earlier—*Fellini's Casanova* (1976). Although Mastroianni expressed interest in the role of Casanova, a part he would later play in Ettore Scola's *Il mondo nuovo* (*La Nuit de Varennes*, 1982), this time Fellini did not choose him. Because of production constraints (the film would be released in English), the part had to go to a native English-speaking actor. It eventually went to Donald Sutherland, a decision Fellini later regretted.[46]

City of Women features additional self-conscious elements: Snàporaz, tossed about from one episode to another, at one point asks himself (and the audience), "What kind of film is this?" Later, a flashback to his youth references the sexual fascination that cinema, especially American cinema, held for the male audience in the 1930s. As proof of Fellini's ideas on the regressive nature of film spectatorship, the seats in this theater have been replaced by one extremely large bed, in which the entirely male audience becomes sexually aroused by the various female images on the screen, dating back to the silent biblical epics à la *Cleopatra* (probably here the 1917 version starring Theda Bara); and Greta Garbo, Marlene Dietrich, and Mae West–like stars, with fetishized close-ups of female body parts and reaction shots to the boys and men masturbating together in the bed. The segment concludes with a shot directly into the film projector, attesting to both the sexual power of the cinema and a nostalgia for the films of an era long gone.[47]

The film's narrative begins with Snàporaz asleep in a train compartment as the train enters and then emerges from a dark tunnel. He awakens to see seated across from him a mysterious beautiful woman (played by Bernice Stegers) in a fur hat, the first of many women Snàporaz will encounter in the film in various episodes: the feminist convention, the joyride of the nymphs, Dr. Katzone's house, and the feminist prison, among others. Critics have been quick to note the dream-like structuring of the film, in particular the repetitive pattern of ascending and falling and much phallic and vaginal symbolism.[48] The train is also significant, for it picks up where *8½* was supposed to leave off: with Guido and Luisa on the train ride home, and Guido's subsequent vision of all of the people in his life smiling at him. Yet, as Fellini himself has observed, *City of Women* represents "the nightmare aspect of Guido's dream in *8½*."[49] Rather than integral harmony between the sexes, there is only alienating distance.

After suggestively staring at the woman in the fur hat and perceiving her responsive to his sexual overtures, Snàporaz subsequently follows her into the bathroom for what he hopes will be a sexual tryst. Their liaison is soon interrupted when the train abruptly stops. It is clear from their initial encounter that Snàporaz fashions himself to be a Don Giovanni, but he is completely out of touch with the women he intends to seduce and remains inept at sexual conquest. Bondanella observes that throughout the film, none of his sexual encounters leads to complete sexual satisfaction (321). His lack of sexual success is due, in part, to the decidedly adolescent nature of his sexuality, one that relies on verbal vulgarities and egotistical satisfaction rather than reciprocal passion. Throughout the film, Snàporaz is consistently associated with the child-like and even infantile, be it the made-up exclamations he spouts ("Smick! Smack!" "Sloff!"), or the infant-like nightgown he wears for much of the second half of the film. Moreover, Snàporaz's journey parallels in many ways that of another famous literary child: Lewis Carroll's Alice. Like Alice, Snàporaz is caught between dream and nightmare; and, like the women who populate *City of Women*, Alice comes to represent, as Nina Auerbach has observed, "the perversities of the fallen woman and the distortions of the monster," a dichotomy apparent in what is perhaps the film's most notorious, and funniest, episode: the feminist convention.[50]

The mysterious woman descends from the train, and Snàporaz follows her into a forest. She is a menacing rather than reassuring Virgillike guide, who leads him to a feminist convention at the Mira Mare Grand Hotel.[51] As Snàporaz enters the hotel in pursuit, he is thrown into the middle of the most comically opposite of situations—the lone male (except the hotel's employees) and journalist among hundreds of women from different nationalities literally singing the praises of female solidarity and emancipation. He passes from a slide-show acclaiming the beauty of the vagina and condemning phallic power, to a vociferous rebuke of fellatio and sexual penetration, to a documentary and presentation about a woman with six husbands, and finally to his public berating by the woman in the fur hat whom he encountered on the train. The feminist convention clearly evokes the realm of the carnival: the world is literally turned upside-down with the women now "on top" in positions of power through patriarchal subversion. Moreover, as Àine O'Healy has observed, Fellini's female/feminist grotesques "simultaneously subvert conventional notions of masculine subjectivity, thus echoing the contemporary preoccupation with the crisis of masculinity."[52] In Fellini's world, no one is spared, as both the feminists and Snàporaz become objects of ridicule.

Fellini relies precisely on the mechanisms Freud individuated in the production of the comic to make this spectacle funny: mimicry, caricature, and parody. The segment that best illustrates this use of humor is a musically pantomimed skit entitled "The average housewife." A woman, dressed in rags and rag curlers with a baby attached to her breast, frenetically attempts to accomplish all her tasks—ironing, sewing, cooking, washing the stacks of dishes and vats of clothing, bathing and feeding her children—even after her husband, a Frankenstein-like monster, returns home, expecting her to sexually satisfy him while she continues to work. Filmed at a feverish pace with a piano score and choreography designed to evoke silent film comedies, the scene elicits boisterous laughter from the crowd, who shout *matrimonio-manicomio* (marriage = insane asylum) at the performance's conclusion. Throughout this and other encounters at the feminist convention, Snàporaz remains the passive, mildly bemused spectator who is at a loss to comprehend what is going on around him, proxemically expressed through his marginal positioning with respect to the action: he is usually shaded, standing by a doorway or in a hallway, literally on the sidelines. Also typical of his attitude is his verbal response to seeing two women who are the only ones to offer smiles amid the angry glares. He inquires: "What have we done? I understand the problems of feminism, but is it necessary to be so angry?" The irony here is that the women do not understand Italian, and thus this exchange takes on the role of metaphor

19. The life of the average housewife, as portrayed at the feminist convention in Fellini's *City of Women* (1980). Courtesy of Photofest.

for both man's failure to comprehend women as well as Snàporaz's, and perhaps Fellini's, ultimate incomprehensibility of the feminist movement.

Snàporaz's passive marginality reaches its culmination in his encounter with Donatella, who ultimately saves him from a feminist lynching. Donatella is a smiling, squeaky-voiced, extremely large-breasted woman who symbolizes both a feminine sensuality and a maternal nurturing and who reappears throughout the film in key episodes.[53] She leads him to a basement gymnasium, complete with roller-skating rink and a male dummy being pummeled in the testicles by women learning self-defense. Alternately referring to Snàporaz as "Grandpa" and "Daddy," Donatella makes him don roller skates in order to join the others. On skates Snàporaz is a klutzy buffoon, unable even to take the smallest steps on his own as the women energetically and athletically skate circles around him. His ineptitude at skating also functions metaphorically, as symbolic of an old man out of step with a changing notion of femininity.

Eventually Snàporaz falls down a staircase, where he encounters *la donna della caldaia* (the boiler woman), a menacingly matronly figure

who speaks in a hybrid of German and Triestine dialect and who promises to take him to the train station on her motorcycle. She is the first
of several characters with Germanic echoes, introducing an element of
militaristic and overpowering female sexuality into the film. Instead
of leading him to the station as promised, she makes a brief stop at a
greenhouse tent in a farm field, where she attempts to seduce him.
Saved by the boiler woman's mother who scolds her sexual promiscuity,
Snàporaz is then told to follow a waif-like young woman. She leads him
to a car of drugged-out punk nymphets, who transport him on a wild
ride into a forest where they are later joined by two other jalopy-like cars
filled with dancing, wild teenagers. Completely out of touch with the
rowdy image of this generation that enjoys cruising and shooting at air-
planes, he takes off into the forest on his own, only to be later chased
by the three cars onto the estate of Katzone, a Teutonic Don Giovanni
who is about to celebrate his ten-thousandth sexual conquest. Literally
meaning "big cock" (*cazzone* in a non-Germanicized Italian), the character of Katzone reportedly was based on the author Georges Simenon,
who since the age of thirteen had claimed to seduce precisely that number of women.[54] His villa is replete with phallic furniture and sexually
suggestive *objets d'art*, including a light with a long tongue that licks
Snàporaz's ear and an automatic vibrator with a speed of three thousand
rotations per minute. It is the site of Snàporaz's reunion with Elena, his
estranged wife, who berates Snàporaz's boring, bourgeois existence and
the demise of their love. Donatella also appears at the party, where she
reveals herself to be the daughter and niece of a famous showgirl duo
that Snàporaz had admired in his youth. The party is broken up by the
militaristic feminist police, including Francesca, a long-lost friend of
Elena, and the *donna della caldaia*, who embarrassingly strip-searches
Snàporaz for documents, making fun out loud of his flaccid penis.

Images of impotence abound in Katzone's hypermasculine villa, as
commentary on Snàporaz's own sexual failings and his lack of understanding of and control over female sexuality.[55] After Katzone shows
him the amazing vibrator, Snàporaz turns it on in secret after his host
leaves the room, but it spins out of control and he is unable to either
turn it off or to hide it. The unruly dildo suggests Snàporaz's own un-
ease with phallic expectations as well as the castrating power of female
desire. Similarly, in Katzone's hall of conquests, which features audio-
visual reminders of all the women with whom Katzone has had sexual
relations, Snàporaz finds marvelous wonder in each amusing photograph
and accompanying recording of sexual satisfaction. He pushes each but-
ton with great physical and verbal fanfare, using the adolescent comic
book–like exclamations described above ("Squish!" "Smick, Smack!").[56]

20. Snàporaz (Mastroianni) in Katzone's Hall of Women. Courtesy of Photofest.

But when these individual images and sounds join together in a cacophony as they spin out of control, they become a collective, menacing, and monstrous force, reducing the man to impotent insignificance. This attitude is foreshadowed in the establishing shot which begins the sequence: Snàporaz enters the darkened hall, shot from a high angle so that he appears small and inconsequential, encased, once again, by a liminal doorframe. In the end, the one who "mans" the controls of the rambunctious dissonance is Elena, and she is ultimately the power that reins them in. After the police break up the party and kill Katzone's beloved dog Italo, Katzone turns for consolation to the statue of his one true love, that of his mother, on whom he bestows kiss after kiss as he cries like a little boy. Katzone, like Snàporaz, is in an arrested state of sexual development, Oedipally attached to his dead mother as female ideal.

The protagonist, in search of Elena, subsequently finds himself in a room with an old maid and two women wearing white burkas. The women, after shedding their over-garments, metamorphose into the showgirls Raina and Vassilas, one of whom is really Donatella, and proceed to dance the Charleston in their skimpy costumes, with Snàporaz joining them as Fred Astaire in a soft-shoe dance. They lead him upstairs, where, much like Guido's flashback to his youth in *8½*, he is pampered by the women as he gets into bed, complete with the recitation of nighttime nursery rhymes warding away the evil spirits.[57] Yet, unlike Guido's fantasy, Snàporaz is stuck in his worst nightmare, and instead of bedding down with the two showgirls, Elena enters the room, with heavy nightcream around her eyes and her hair in rollers, declaring that she wants to make love between animal-like grunts and operatic arias. Unsatisfied, Elena rolls off him and falls asleep, while Snàporaz, following the whispers of young women (possibly the showgirls), discovers a tunnel under his bed, which takes him on an amusement park–like toboggan ride through the sexual memories of his youth.[58] Once again, a pleasant sexual memory/fantasy turns nasty, as he now finds himself encaged and subsequently interrogated by a gender-bending group of feminists, who list all of his many crimes against women.[59] After being dismissed, he still wants to see what the other men "imprisoned" here have failed to obtain: the ideal woman, who turns out to be a large, inflatable balloon in the shape of a voluptuous female resembling Donatella. The real Donatella, however, has other plans, and the lulling nursery rhyme music is interrupted by her gunfire as she shoots down Snàporaz and the balloon. As Snàporaz clings to the net and the balloon floats away, he is confronted by a series of menacing female eyes. Then he awakens to find himself back on the train, sitting across from Elena and soon joined by the first woman from the train, Donatella, and her friend. The film concludes with Marcello, perplexed by the real world, choosing to fall back asleep and return to the world of the unconscious as the train heads into a dark tunnel.

This final scene begs further detailed analysis, for it draws together several of the film's key themes as well as the role of humor and jokes in elucidating them. In terms of its communality, the joke is, for Freud, a shared process, necessarily involving three people: the self or the first person (the narrator of the joke), the object of the joke, and the outside person or the listener (176). The intimacy of the Fellini/Mastroianni collaborations, many of which feature inside jokes between the two men, underscore the intricate relationship between the self and the listener, who should share many of the same inhibitions in order for the cathectic release to be successful (184). Thus, the joke, for Freud, takes on a triangular structure in its performance: it involves a narrator, a subject, and a listener. This schema is revealed through a map of the gaze in the film's conclusion, in which the menacing eyes of his dream fuse into the laughing eyes of the women in the train's compartment with the spectator's gaze aligned with the protagonist. In this final scene on the train, Snàporaz, and the spectator, come to realize that the film, in essence,

21. Snàporaz with the showgirls Raina and Vassilas before his nighttime paradise becomes nightmarish. Courtesy of Photofest.

has been one big joke, with Fellini as narrator; Snàporaz, and by extension the spectator, as the subject; and the women as the "audience" of the joke.

The scene—indeed, the entire film—evokes the deep roots of the *beffa* in Italian culture. The traditional definition of the *beffa*—a joke or trick made with skill, so that whoever is tricked does not realize it—harks back to Giovanni Boccaccio's *Decameron* and proliferates in the Italian Renaissance *novella*. Valerio Ferme individuates three different functions of the *beffa* in Boccaccio's work: (1) to both entertain and educate the audience; (2) to stress the importance of *ingegno*—intelligence and/or wit—in post-plague Florentine society; and (3) as a projection of Boccaccio's attitude toward the moral and social issues of that society.[60] The *beffa*, in all its various forms, also involves, like Freud's joke, a tripartite structure in its intention to trick: the agent (the *beffatore*), the victim (the *beffato*), and the narrator. The importance of narration to the *beffa*—the idea that the story must be told—reinforces the verbal component in the "creation of a fictitious reality" which is then unmasked as non-truth, resulting in the successful deception of the *beffato*.[61] Although some critics, both in Italy and abroad, failed to see the entertainment and/or educational value of *City of Women*,[62] the film demonstrates how one man's lack of *ingegno* allows him to become the *beffato* throughout the film: as victim of the woman on the train, the feminist convention, his wife, and ultimately, himself. As narrator, a role reinforced from the film's title voice-over directly addressing Fellini as "maestro," the filmmaker has led us into the world of his own fantasies, tricked us into believing them to be real, until he reveals that Snàporaz's journey through the city of women was in fact all a dream/nightmare. Snàporaz, like the spectator, awakens to find himself as the butt of the *beffa*—pun intended, given Fellini's obsession with the female posterior and its dominant presence in this film—as Elena, the initial woman on the train, and Donatella and her friend conspiringly and knowingly look at each other with bemused smiles.[63] Elena, wearing the fur hat that appeared in the dream on the woman from the train, equates screen time with real time as she tells her husband that he has been murmuring in his sleep for two hours, the length (more or less) of the film up to that point. For Snàporaz, however, returning to the conscious world is far from comforting. The joke presumes regression rather than confrontation or change. Like the *inetto*, he chooses the passive way out: sleep. Moreover, given the exchange of looks and their role in the joke, as well as Fellini's own role as narrator of that joke, Fellini embroils the spectator's gaze into the conclusion, by implying that we are all the subject of the women's conspiratorial prank.[64] Frank Burke notes that women in the film become the locus of social anxiety: about terrorism, feminism, youth and drug-culture, and non-traditional gender constructions (244). Through humor, *City of Women* gives expression to those anxieties and sees a return into the womb-like safety of the tunnel as the only possible response.

Fellini once said: "Through the ages, from the beginning of time, I'm certain man has covered woman's face with masks. They are, however, his masks, not hers. They are the masks of the viewer, not of the woman, and what they hide is not what they seem to cover. The masks come from the man's own subconscious and they represent that unknown part of himself."[65] In Fellini's films, humor functions as a tool that removes the mask, bringing the subconscious fears and anxieties of Italian masculinity to the surface. If, as Brandes argues, jokes provide a locus of "protective fantasy"—a way for men to reveal and work through their own issues of sexual and social inadequacy (107)—then Fellini uses humor in much the same way, with the self-reflexive addition of artistic inadequacy in *8½*, and the fusion with the world of dreams in *City of Women*. There are, however, important differences between the films. In *8½*, these anxieties are predominantly related to the protagonist's personal and professional predicaments, while in *City of Women*, they resonate strongly with the extra-cinematic context of the 1970s feminist movement. *8½* becomes a celebration of the fragmentation and disunity of the individual's relation to the world around him, in particular women, whereas *City of Women* cowers in the face of that confusion, ultimately choosing to return to the safety of the dream world. Nevertheless, in both films, humor is, like Pirandello's *umorismo*, both serious and comic, giving expression to Italian masculinity's deepest fears and anxieties while allowing us to laugh at the *inetto*, and the *inetto*, in the guise of Mastroianni's characters, to laugh at himself.

The next chapter turns its attention to another fruitful artistic collaboration in Mastroianni's career: his work with Sophia Loren. As opposed to Fellini's films, in which cultural constructs of Italian masculinity turn the lens on themselves, in Mastroianni's work with Loren, mostly comedies themselves, the figure of the unruly woman further destabilizes traditional notions of both masculinity and femininity. Here, however, we regress historically, to Italy of the 1950s and 1960s, a time of a growing female presence in the public sphere, and economic prosperity at the cost of a greater divide between North and South and rich and poor. The battle between the *inetto* and the unruly woman challenges patriarchal dominance, and it is no surprise that, more often than not, the woman comes out on top.

5

The *Inetto* versus the Unruly Woman

Mastroianni and Sophia Loren

Of all of Mastroianni's various pairings with prominent directors and actors, arguably his most famous counterpart is Sophia Loren. Their production together—they co-starred in twelve films—constitutes Mastroianni's most prolific partnership on screen. In their collaborations, many of which were commercial successes that crossed national and art-house borders, Loren and Mastroianni had each come to symbolize Italian eroticism for both a national and an international audience. In these films, mostly *commedie all'italiana* shot on location in Rome and Naples, the wild female character who rebels against patriarchal authority meets the Italian *inetto*, the man at a loss to respond to the changing role of women in contemporary society, revealing the effects of a gradual post-war female emancipation on Italian masculinity.

In her work *The Unruly Woman: Gender and the Genres of Laughter,* Kathleen Rowe defines the unruly woman as a woman who disrupts the norms of femininity and social hierarchy of male over female through outrageousness and excess.[1] Rowe's theories are also applicable to Sophia Loren, whose exaggerated femininity exhibits itself in the cinematic and extracinematic emphasis on her body: the Italian term most often used to refer to her and other female stars like her during her rise to stardom was *maggiorata fisica*, or exaggerated, voluptuous figure. In her films with Mastroianni, Loren's characters are not mere spectacles: rather, they use the primary tools of the unruly woman—the body, speech, and performance—to get what they want, be it the man, a career, or freedom. Like the *inetto*, the unruly woman has deep roots in Italian culture, from medieval and Renaissance literature up through

105

the nineteenth and twentieth century variety theater and the post-war *commedia all'italiana*. Moreover, unlike the American texts that feature the exploits of the unruly woman, rarely are Loren's wild characters fully tamed and subsumed into the patriarchal order. As a result, Mastroianni's characters are at a loss to deal with this increasingly independent and emancipated female character, just as he was at a loss to deal with an increasingly materialist culture in *La dolce vita*, the outdated ideals of Sicilian masculinity in *Divorce—Italian Style* and *Il bell'Antonio*, and the militant feminists of *City of Women*.

Although it is difficult to generalize about the many films Loren and Mastroianni made together, important patterns emerge in their most commercially and artistically successful collaborations: *Peccato che sia una canaglia* (Too Bad She's Bad, 1954) and *La fortuna di essere donna* (What a Woman! 1956), both directed by Alessandro Blasetti; *Ieri, oggi e domani* (Yesterday, Today, and Tomorrow, 1963), and *Matrimonio all'italiana* (Marriage—Italian Style, 1964), both directed by Vittorio De Sica; Ettore Scola's *Una giornata particolare* (A Special Day, 1977); and Robert Altman's *Prêt-à-Porter* (Ready to Wear, 1994). Their first screen appearances together, the two comedies directed by Blasetti, establish the paradigm of the unruly woman/*inetto* clash.[2] Both set in Rome, they self-consciously play on post-war Italian film culture as they represent a more popular alternative to neorealism, and as they feature a confidently sexual female character intent on manipulation. In the 1960s, this populism continues with two significant shifts: in director (now Vittorio De Sica) and setting (Naples). Whereas Blasetti's films constituted a neorealist/Hollywood hybrid narrative, De Sica's films relocate that Hollywood paradigm with the context of Neapolitan culture, the shared roots of all three participants. In both films, Naples as city and way of life figures prominently in the image of the unruly woman, for Naples itself is the quintessential unruly city, where the world is constantly turned upside-down and rules, be they legal or social or gender-related, are made to be broken. Gender constructs are also the focus of *Una giornata particolare*, but this interrogation departs from the norm, in that it is a serious dramatic piece set against the backdrop of the Fascist period. Nevertheless, issues of sexual normalcy and deviations are configured within the *inetto*/unruly woman paradigm, when Loren's character literally becomes the woman-on-top through her encounter with the perceived heterosexual *inetto*: the homosexual. *Prêt-à-Porter*, which features a stunning Loren and a haggard-looking Mastroianni, provides both a fitting conclusion to this analysis of their collaborations and a nice transition to the following chapter's examination of the representation of aging masculinity in the final stages of Mastroianni's film career.

The Unruly Woman

Natalie Zemon Davis, in her work on gender in early modern Europe, observes how the female sex was believed to be "disorderly" by nature, possessed by an unruliness that needed to be tamed in order for a woman to assume her proper subjugated station in the dominant patriarchal order. Nevertheless, numerous cultural forms—literature, theater, popular festivals and carnivals—often celebrated "sexual inversion," that is "the world-turned-upside-down, the topos of the woman-on-top."[3] For Zemon Davis, these inversions gave expression to many of the conflicts about gender and power in early modern societies, allowing for a cathartic release within the confines of an established cultural paradigm. She argues that, although proper order is restored in the end, the image of the disorderly woman did not always function to keep women in their place. On the contrary, it was a multivalent image that could operate, first, to widen behavioral options for women within and even outside marriage, and second, to sanction riot and political disobedience for both men and women in a society that allowed the lower orders few formal means of protest (131). At the same time, it also had the potential to spill over into daily life, providing an "alternative way of conceiving family structure" (143), promoting resistance to the very constructions the "topsy-turvy" world intended to reinforce in the end.

Kathleen Rowe has adapted Zemon Davis's theories on the disorderly woman into what she calls the unruly woman and has shifted her focus to American romantic comedies of the 1930s, 1940s, and 1950s. Relying as well on Mikhail Bakhtin's work on the carnival and Mary Russo's observations on the female grotesque, she locates the unruly woman's outrageousness and excess in several different spheres: body, speech, and behavior.[4] The unruly woman is often portrayed as loud, fat, androgynous, or masculinized, prone to loose sexual behavior, and associated with dirt. At the same time, however, her sexuality is a source of potential power, becoming transgressive "when she lays claims to her own desire" (30–31).

Just like Zemon Davis's disruptive early modern texts, classical Hollywood films allow for transgressions of feminine norms through the persona of the unruly woman.[5] Much like the cultural paradigms described by Davis, the typical Hollywood film preserves the status quo by righting all wrongs and securing social and sexual order at its conclusion.

The conflicts that rise to the surface before the inevitable happy end, however, reveal many contradictions with respect to gender. For the female protagonist, romantic comedy constitutes the resolution of her Oedipal conflict and the acceptance of heterosexuality, signified by marriage. But the rebellion that precedes assimilation into the patriarchal order is rife with challenges to that very order, and those challenges are literally embodied in the figure of the unruly woman. She consciously uses her body through masquerade and performance to get what she wants: independence from familial structures, a career, or freedom from the norms of femininity. The tools she employs are either speech, as a way of taking control of the narrative, or her body, through which she parades her desire in a controlled spectacle or feminine masquerade. Thus, throughout the classical narrative, the unruly woman is on top and in control, before being ultimately tamed and subsumed into the heterosexual patriarchal order.

In Italian culture, Jane Tylus traces the presence of the unruly woman all the way back to the Middle Ages and the Renaissance. In a story told on the seventh day of Giovanni Boccaccio's *Decameron*, for instance, Monna Ghita takes a lover in order to get revenge on her philandering husband, eventually locking him out of the house and berating him from the upstairs window in front of all the townspeople. Tylus also cites Caterina Sforza's public display of her genitals at the walls of the Forlì citadel in Machiavelli's *Discorsi*, when she tells her captors that she would not care if they were to kill her children, for "she was still capable of bearing more." Both these female figures, as well as the female characters who populate Flaminio Scala's *commedia dell'arte* scenarios (see chapter 1), disrupt action from a liminal space of a window or a wall. By halting the primary action, the unruly woman employs spectacle as the tool of her disruption through words (Monna Ghita) or her body (Caterina). "Traditional passivity," that of the spectacle, is transformed into the "manipulative action" of the unruly woman.[6]

After the Renaissance, more modern incarnations of the spirit of the carnival came in the form of Italian popular theater, specifically the *teatro del varietà* as it developed in the late nineteenth and early twentieth centuries. Its origins in Italy can be traced to the influence of the French *café-chantant* (translated into Italian as the *caffè-concerto*), which indicated a place, usually a café or restaurant, where the clientele would be entertained by a show composed of short skits of music, comedy, and exhibitions of agility and ability. More popular than bourgeois mainstream theater and featuring a wide variety of performers from singers and comics to story-tellers, magicians, and dancers, it had cross-class and cross-regional appeal, especially as its locus shifted from the café to the theater proper. In Italy, its roots are strongly anchored to operas, operettas, and Neapolitan culture.[7] Each troupe featured a *capocomico*, the headlining male performer who would often be the creative force behind the show; the *diva*, the female star; and the *soubrette*, at first referencing the second-lead singer in the troupe but later used synonymously with the *diva*. The first site exclusively devoted to variety theater —the Salone Margherita, which opened its doors in 1890—was in Naples. The city had always been known as an important center of music and theater, with its famous *canzonette* (storytelling songs) and *sceneggiate* (skits based on popular songs of the time). Some of the most famous variety performers were Neapolitan, including Raffaele Viviani and the de Filippo family: Peppino, Titina, and Eduardo, on whose work two of the Mastroianni/Loren films would be based. Vittorio De Sica, who directed those two films, was steeped in this very tradition with his work in Mario Mattòli's Za Bum variety company, a collaboration which helped launch his early career as an actor in the cinema.

Just as in the American counterpart of vaudeville and burlesque, women played an important part in the variety spectacles. As Robert Allen has argued in his work on American burlesque, female spectacle "was built partially or wholly around feminine sexual display, and each contained its own strategies for producing male scopic pleasure and containing the moral and social transgressiveness that pleasure necessarily entailed."[8] At the same time, particularly after the turn of the century, there was an "insubordinate, inversive spirit" to burlesque, personified in female performers such as Sophie Tucker and Mae West. Similarly, in Italy, the independent female images that performers such as Anna Magnani perfected on stage countered the scantily clad dancers and chorus girls, whose function was pure sexualized spectacle. As Wanda Osiris, one of the more prominent *soubrette* of the *varietà* noted for her famous descents from large flights of stairs, said: "I was always completely dressed, in fact, because if the prima donna stripped down she had no class. But the other girls showed off their bodies—they were for the lower-class audience."[9]

Italian variety theater, as it developed into the twentieth century, gradually incorporated film into its repertoire. Shows exclusively devoted to performance skits gave way to the *avanspettacolo*. Literally meaning "before the show," it consisted of a performance of various sketches that would precede the film screenings and last about an hour. This phenomenon became popular after the introduction of the sound film, replacing the human contact of musical accompaniment.[10] Films that followed the *avanspettacolo*, in particular those of the late 1930s and early 1940s, were no strangers to the figure of the unruly woman. As the film industry expanded with Fascist government financing, filmmakers often turned to Hollywood genres as a model for artistic and aesthetic inspiration. The romantic comedy was no exception. Marcia Landy notes that comedies of the 1930s and 1940s use theatricality, specifically impersonation and spectacle, to reveal "complex portraits of courtship, familialism, and the forms of sexual conflicts which animate the films."[11] One example of romantic comedy that stands out is the schoolgirl comedy, which first arrived in 1934 but flourished in the early 1940s. These films feature rebellious female protagonists who, like Rowe's unruly woman, use cunning speech and active performance to subvert the authorities, be they academic and/or familial, that oppress them. One film, Raffaello Matarazzo's Il birichino di papà (Daddy's Little Devil, 1943), has the female protagonist, a rambunctious tomboy, disrupt a Fascist-inspired rhythmic gymnastics display with her singing from a window above the piazza, much like the commedia dell'arte's women at the window. Although these films conclude with the inevitable marriage and/or the taming of the unruly pupil, they nevertheless provided a space for female rebellion and subversion of patriarchal authority as they questioned the norms of proper feminine conduct within the heavily prescribed parameters of Fascist Italy.[12]

Post-war comedies shifted their emphasis from escapism to realism, as the aesthetic discourse of neorealism assumed the primary place among critics and filmmakers, if not audiences. Gian Piero Brunetta isolates various stages in the development of Italian comedy from post-war liberation up through the economic boom. The first Italian comedies to appear at the war's end drew their inspiration precisely from the variety theater and avanspettacolo that were so popular during the war. Not only did cinema turn to this medium for many of its performers (Anna Magnani, Aldo Fabrizi, Totò, among others) but they also had as their focus the world of popular theater itself, the most famous being Federico Fellini and Alberto Lattuada's Luci del varietà (Variety Lights, 1950), which chronicled a variety theater troupe as it traveled around Italy. In the 1950s, comedies developed in two ways. First, scripts became more fully realized by a group of screenwriters who specialized in film comedy, particularly the trio of Agenore Incrocci (billed as Age), Furio Scarpelli, and Ettore Scola. Second, as the decade progressed, they began to reflect a greater commitment to the ideological complexities and realities of everyday life in a reconstructed Italy.[13]

One of the realities that 1950s comedies brought to the surface was shifting gender roles in the post-war social and sexual economy. The figure of the unruly woman becomes the personification on film of these conflicts. During the 1950s, Italy began to recover from the effects of

Fascism and the war, and to recover with great gusto. The gross national product doubled, and personal income increased by over 60 percent. As families began to earn more money, their children, both boys and girls, were able to continue their studies longer: by 1955, enrollment in middle schools and industrial training schools was almost double that of 1947, and by 1962 it had more than tripled that initial level. In addition, their leisure time increased, as young girls in particular left the protective shadows of their homes and ventured out into the public sphere to enjoy music, dance, and the cinema.[14] In films, Brunetta notes how female characters in the 1950s are caught between traditional moral expectations and their own desire for sexual and social mobility brought on by the liberalization of Fascist gender policies and women's recently acquired right to vote in 1946. While their career ambitions are never extremely high, mostly relegated to aspiring actresses or models, they nevertheless express a longing for independence from familial constraints that conflict not only with parental expectations but also with the dominant ideology. These young women reveal a gap between the generations, as daughters rebel against the law of the father.[15]

The primary tools with which these unruly women pursued their desires were their bodies. With Silvana Mangano's infamous boogie woogie in Giuseppe de Santis's *Riso amaro* (Bitter Rice, 1948), the female body came to occupy a prominent position in many post-war Italian films. Labeled by critics as "pink neorealism," these films, by showcasing scantily clad female beauties, attempted to achieve the box office success that often eluded most neorealist films by making the social problems of the day appear "nice and rosy." Actresses such as Mangano, Lucia Bosè, Gina Lollobrigida, and Sophia Loren soon became extremely popular stars both in Italy and abroad, prompting critics to note how Italian cinema of the 1950s came to be dominated by a "star system of exaggerated bodies" and "the war of the breasts."[16] This emphasis on their bodies also emanated from their origins in show business: all these actresses were discovered in beauty contests. Lollobrigida finished third in the 1947 Miss Italy contest, behind the winner Bosè (Mangano was also a contestant). Recent studies on the nature of beauty pageants have argued that these contests are more than theatrically staged events intended to objectify female beauty. On the contrary, "beauty contests are places where cultural meanings are produced, consumed, and rejected, where local and global, ethnic and national, national and international cultures and structures of power are engaged in their most trivial but vital aspects."[17] The female body serves, for Stephen Gundle, as the site of inscription for what constitutes the national. The post-war Italian female body, as it appeared in films, theatrical productions, and pag-

eants, came to represent a new national dynamic based on a highly
sexualized feminine corporeality, one that would signify national pride,
modernity, and fecundity, reflecting a naturalness at harmony with the
national landscape.[18]

At the same time, however, the power attributed to the increasingly
prominent female body presented moral, sexual, and social challenges to
the patriarchal order, as the female used her body to turn traditional
notions of proper feminine conduct upside-down. The influence of
American cinema and the classical romantic comedy is not coincidental
here. In attempting to increase the box-office revenues of the dominant
neorealist aesthetic, filmmakers looked to the female body, in particular
the pin-up popularized in the post-war era by Rita Hayworth and Ava
Gardner, and incarnated by Mangano in *Bitter Rice* and Lollobrigida as
La Bersagliera in Luigi Comencini's *Pane, amore e fantasia* (Bread, Love
and Dreams, 1953), the first major success of 1950s pink neorealism.
The shrew-like outbursts of La Bersagliera, the poorest but most beautiful of the town's residents, underscore her rage at her economic situation. For Millicent Marcus, however, her taming is a necessary preclusion to the film's happy end, in which "the image of La Bersagliera as a
furious, caged animal is replaced by the sultry and seductive one of the
beautiful wench lying on the prison floor singing her heart out for
love."[19] With the emphasis placed on the economic issues raised and
gender inversions played out within the film's narrative, *Pane, amore e
fantasia* questions the social and sexual status quo through the rose-
tinted glasses of pink neorealism.

When Lollobrigida's salary demands became too expensive for the
planned third film in the *Pane, amore* series in 1955, Sophia Loren was
called in to take her place.[20] By this time, Loren had begun to establish herself as an unruly woman in her own right, with her role as the
adulterous pizza-maker's wife in De Sica's *L'oro di Napoli* (The Gold
of Naples, 1954). Wearing her sexuality on her sleeve (or in her case
her skin-tight dress), Loren's character exuded a confident femininity
which reduced men to weakness and allowed her to obtain what she
wanted, in this case both a husband and a lover. It would be the first of
many rebellious women she would capture on the screen, which would
classify her, according to Gundle, as "a cultural icon and even a national
symbol." Not classically "Italian," she embodied a more popular spirit,
that of a "highly subversive idea of unabashed female sexuality."[21] This
subversion was linked not only to her popular roots, specifically to the
region of Naples (as will be discussed below), but also to the very evident and very emphasized exaggerated proportions of her body. This
physical excess, for Rowe, is one of the essential qualities of the unruly

woman. Suggestive of an uncontainable physical appetite, Loren's curvaceous figure intimates instead a sexual uncontrollability, not so much
in her own sexual desire but, rather, in the uncontrollable response that
her body provokes in the men who are unable to resist her.

Loren's effect on screen as unruly woman brings us back to the central question of this study: Mastroianni and Italian masculinity. For
Rowe, the function of the unruly woman in classical Hollywood romantic comedy is to chastise the male hero and then bring him in line with
the norms of masculinity from which he has strayed (146–47). Once
proper virility is restored, the unruly woman can then become the domesticated ideal woman, whose body assumes a de-sexualized maternal
function. The Italian case, however, is not so cut and dried. Clearly,
much like his American counterpart, the Italian male victim of the unruly woman is castrated by her unruliness, rendered weak, immobile
and, in comparison to her successful exploits, inept. The presence of the
over-sexualized female body, however, has radically different consequences in 1950s American and Italian films. Rowe notes that in Hollywood films such as *Gentlemen Prefer Blondes* and *Some Like It Hot,* the
unruly woman "was stripped of her intelligence" and "reduced to a
pure sexual creature," whose power was replaced with a vulnerability
whose sexuality served the sole purpose of male pleasure" (170–71). In
Loren's comedies with Mastroianni, by contrast, the exaggerated display of female sexuality is not purely fetishistic. Rather, it is a site of
empowerment, one that castrates the male at the same time that it refuses to completely domesticate the female. On the narrative level, it
underscores the more open nature of post-war feature films with respect to narrative closure. Moreover, Loren's incarnation of the unruly
woman as paired with Mastroianni's *inetto* becomes a topos which does
not shift over time, unlike the Hollywood unruly woman who gradually
loses her independence in both love and career in the 1950s, culminat-
ing for Rowe in her replacement by men in the aforementioned *Some
Like It Hot.* In Italy she survives historical shifts, from the economic
boom to the cultural revolutions in the 1970s and into the globalized
1990s, as well as the various different movements in Italian cinema—
the *maggiorate fisiche, commedia all'italiana,* and the re-examination in
the 1970s of Italy's Fascist legacy—by remaining the woman on top.

The 1950s: How Lucky to Be a Woman

In Loren and Mastroianni's first film together, the first of three films
they would make under the director Alessandro Blasetti, they did not
appear on screen simultaneously. *Tempi nostri* (Our Times, 1954) was a

French-Italian co-production featuring eight episodes (and a prologue) based on short stories by some of Italy's most prominent post-war writers, including Alberto Moravia and Vasco Pratolini. Mastroianni was featured in the second episode, entitled "Il pupo," in which he played an unemployed husband and father who, no longer able to care for all of his children, sets out with his wife (Lea Padovani) to find an appropriate place in which to abandon their youngest child to ensure that he be taken in by a proper family or the proper authorities. At the time the film was made, over two million Italians were officially listed as unemployed, a figure believed to greatly under-represent the actual number, and an additional four million were considered "marginally employed."[22] Shot on location in Rome, the episode follows the couple in their futile quest, underscoring the social plight of the *figli di nessuno* (no one's children), while at the same time infusing it with lighthearted humor at the couple's indecisiveness and leaving us with a rosy ending (they are ultimately unable to abandon the child). Mastroianni's turn as the husband was typical of many of the early roles he played on screen: the proletarian *bravo ragazzo* (good guy) trapped in the hostile economic circumstances of Reconstruction Italy. Loren's role as foil to the comedian Totò in the film's last episode, "La macchina fotografica" (The Camera), showcases her status as female pin-up by having Totò take her photograph in a variety of seductive poses, promising her a career in fashion. Throughout the film she retains the upper hand, by refusing to submit to his sexual advances.

Peccato che sia una canaglia, also set among the working-class in Rome and based on a short story by Alberto Moravia, recounts the story of Paolo (Mastroianni), a taxi driver who one day picks up Lina Stroppiani (Loren) and her two male companions, who then attempt to steal Paolo's taxi. Paolo is an earnest, hard-working man without family ties (his entire family perished during a wartime air raid), who longs for a stable, middle-class family life. The not-so-subtle contrast that comes to light in the very first scene is between Paolo's serious dedication to making a better life for himself and the typical leisure culture of his generation, who pass their time at the beach or as con artists. It is Lina's job to distract Paolo while her accomplices carry out their mission. Lina accomplishes this task using the instrument of the unruly woman: her body. She changes into her bathing suit behind the bushes, splashes seductively in the water as she invites Paolo to join her on the beach, and then lies down on Paolo's chest in the sand. Paolo nonetheless is able to thwart the robbery but holds onto Lina, planning to turn her in to the police. Lina escapes when Paolo is cited for a traffic violation; later he sees her again and chases her down, only to get into an accident. Deciding that paternal law would be more effective in disciplining Lina, he brings her home to confront her father (Vittorio De Sica), who, unknown to Paolo, is also a thief. The culture of theft is rampant in the neighborhood: the children in the street below steal Paolo's tire (Lina secretly makes them put it back), and even Lina's grandmother pickpockets Paolo's wallet. As the scene progresses, Signor Stroppiani gradually seduces Paolo, pretending to be an honest person who scolds his wayward daughter. To Paolo, both the beautiful Lina and this surrogate family begin to seem attractive, especially when, as he returns to his garage, he finds Lina paying for the damage to the car. He resolves to reform Lina and help her be honest. He goes to the cinema with her family, and she gives him an engraved cigarette case.

Unfortunately, Lina had just stolen that cigarette case from the owner of Paolo's garage, and Paolo, on learning the truth, vows to end their relationship. Confronting Lina and her father as they attempt to steal suitcases at the train station, Paolo intends to take them to the police but has another car accident, this time with a group of Indian tourists: Paolo is taken to a hospital, and Lina and her father escape. Once again, Lina succeeds in winning over Paolo as she tearfully apologizes to him. He proposes marriage and gives her his mother's wedding ring. Although she slips the ring back on Paolo's keychain when he is not looking, Lina vows to help raise the 100,000 lira needed to pay for the damage from Paolo's latest accident. With her father and the two male friends from the thwarted taxi robbery, she boards a bus with the intention of pick-pocketing the passengers. Paolo sees them, boards the bus and, catching them in the act, takes them to the police station. Through both verbal manipulation and feminine charms, Lina (along with her father) manages to not only weasel out of the charges against her, but to get the money for Paolo to pay off his taxi. The film concludes with Lina's supposed "taming" into marriage with three slaps, a ring, and a passionate kiss in front of a cheering crowd.

Peccato che sia una canaglia is a prototypical example of the unruly woman in Italian romantic comedy. With its light-hearted tone and satirical look at black-market culture in post-war Italy, the film pivots around the antagonistic chemistry of the two stars, with De Sica providing additional laughs. It also provided the blueprint for future Loren-Mastroianni collaborations, with Loren's character emerging to dominate Mastroianni's. *Peccato che sia una canaglia* was typical of 1950s post-neorealist Italian comedies favored by Blasetti, in that they featured young, carefree protagonists who were not preoccupied with major social and political issues.[23] A scene of spectatorship reinforces this tendency in filmmaking. Paolo, Lina, and her family all go to see a

22. Vittorio De Sica, Sophia Loren, and Marcello Mastroianni in a scene from *Peccato che sia una canaglia* (1954). Courtesy of Photofest.

fictitious film entitled *Mano pericolosa*—Dangerous Hand—about, ironically, a thief. Signor Stroppiani disparagingly notes how unrealistic it is.
The scene's self-conscious irony is not lost here: the eminently recognizable Vittorio De Sica, neorealist director *per eccellenza*, criticizing a
film for being too superficial, childish, and unbelievable.

Throughout the film, Loren's body is the center of attention. Loren
was the choice of the film's two scriptwriters, Ennio Flaiano and Suso
Cecchi d'Amico, the latter of whom described the young Loren as
"beautiful, excessive and decorative as a Christmas tree."[24] The camera
reinforces her physicality, particularly her curves: she is usually photographed in a full-frontal medium shot highlighting her bust, waist, and
hips. In addition, her body is never still: she plays with her hair, moves
her arms, swings her hips, and pouts her lips. As opposed to being the
static object of the gaze, hers is a dynamic presence, reinforcing the
notion of activity over passivity as the unruly woman employs her female charms to achieve her goals. Moreover, Lina self-consciously acknowledges the power of the female body in the many mirror shots that
appear in the film. As Lina looks at her own image, she recognizes not

only her own beauty but also the power that lies within that recognition as it reduces men such as Paolo to bumbling idiots.

Conscious of her feminine powers, Lina constructs various feminine personae to get herself both in and out of trouble. Here she employs another tool of the unruly woman: speech and performance, which, according to Rowe, is a way in which the unruly woman gains control of the narrative (37). Every time Paolo tries to leave her—shown through repeating scenes of him castigating himself as he drives his taxi—she is able to manipulate him by assuming a traditionally feminine role. As the fallen woman, she feigns melodrama, moaning to Paolo that she is destined for prostitution, unless he drops his case against her and "saves" her from her impending doom. When confronted about the stolen cigarette case, she is the desperate sacrificing girlfriend, crying that she only wanted to give him a gift. Later, at the police station, she proclaims herself ready to go to jail for him. She even knows how to play the perfect future wife. As she serves coffee to Paolo and her father, the latter refers to her as *una perfetta massaia* (a perfect housewife), referencing the term favored by the Fascist regime in its attempt to both ruralize (hence, de-urbanize) and domesticate women.

The allusion here, like much of the film, is ironic, for Lina is never fully "tamed," even at the film's conclusion. In the last scene, as Lina and Paolo leave the police station, they are constantly struggling to see who is in control: he keeps pulling her aside and she keeps moving along, stopping to inquire with a vendor as to the price of onions, or heading out onto the sidewalk. Throughout this final scene, her defiant body posturing reinforces her status as unruly woman. When Paolo slaps her three times, an action she actually invites, she rebounds and smiles after each slap. Her physical insolence and her verbal response (*Finalmente*—"finally") belie submission to his authority. Their final kiss in front of a growing, admiring crowd, although setting the prototype for the Loren/Mastroianni consummation, nevertheless rejects the complete capitulation of the unruly woman into patriarchal domination, for it is her active desire rather than docile acquiescence which dominates the scene.

In the next Blasetti-Loren-Mastroianni project, *La fortuna di essere donna*, it is the Mastroianni character who, initially at least, has the upper hand.[25] Blasetti originally wanted to recreate the successful formula of *Peccato* by reuniting Loren and Mastroianni with De Sica, but the producers felt that Charles Boyer would be a bigger box-office draw. Set against the backdrop of the burgeoning Roman fashion and film industry of the 1950s, Mastroianni, departing from his usual *bravi*

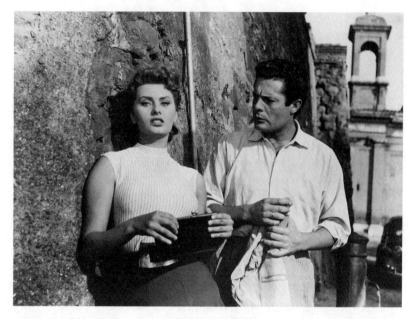

23. Lina (Loren) plays the role of the fallen woman to the gullible
Paolo (Mastroianni). Courtesy of Photofest.

ragazzi roles, plays Corrado Betti, a photographer, who captures the
stunning Antonietta Fallari (Loren) on film as she fixes her stocking.
After the photograph appears on a magazine cover without her permission, Antonietta's fiancé, Federico, confronts Corrado, but soon Antonietta finds herself seduced by Corrado's promise of making her a star
and by the photographer himself. After a passionate photography session
and the pledge of help in her career, Antonietta overhears Corrado dis-
missing their relationship to his friends. Now bent on revenge by arous-
ing Corrado's jealousy, she courts his neighbor Count Gregorio Sennetti
(Boyer), a shifty agent with a penchant for using his wife's money to
seduce young starlets. As she rises up the ladder of success with a contract from a movie producer, she suggests marriage to the count at a
party. A jealous Corrado calls the count's wife to the party, and rather
than embarrassing Antonietta, she and the count's wife bond over the
stupidity of men. Ultimately, she gets Corrado to confess his love for
her and the two once again seal their union with a kiss.

Even more than in *Peccato che sia una canaglia*, Loren's body dominates not only the screen but also the narrative of *La fortuna di essere donna*, as her physical attributes attract Corrado (and every other

male) to Antonietta. The film parodies the dominant presence of the *maggiorate fisiche* in Italian cinema and print culture of the day. Antonietta's world is populated with photographers, agents, and movie producers who fall all over her in an attempt to make money off her body. This parody, akin to the more serious examination of 1950s star culture in Michelangelo Antonioni's *La signora senza camelie* (The Woman without Camelias, 1952), is self-reflexive in nature. There are many insinuations to Loren's own rise to fame: her association with Carlo Ponti, a much older producer, is similar to her relationship with the count. Comments used to describe Antonietta—her fabulous body, her gorgeous "lines," her "advantages"—all play off the discourse used to describe Loren in the popular press, both in Italy and abroad.[26] As if to reinforce the Antonietta/Loren connection, the filmmakers use an interesting editing device to show Antonietta's initial surprise photograph. As she stands on the Appian Way in the film's opening sequence, we see a medium-long back shot of Antonietta as she fixes her stocking. The back shot is featured throughout much of the film, designed to show off Loren's narrow waist and curvaceous behind in her tight skirts. On screen right, a truck filled with photographers, including Corrado, approaches, yelling, "Signorina, over here." Classically, the next shot would be a reverse shot of Antonietta as she would soon be captured on film. Instead, the next shot is precisely the magazine cover, in a pin-up pose typical of Loren's publicity shots, as her horrified fiancé sees it at the magazine stand. The cover of *Le Ore* thus becomes both the inciting incident which sets the plot in motion as well as a self-conscious play on Loren's own image in Italian popular culture in the 1950s.

Yet, while those in the fashion and film industry attempt to create the proper performance of femininity, for Antonietta, as for Lina, it is a masquerade. Throughout the film, Antonietta is in constant motion: playing with her hair, seductively posing her body, and straightening her clothes. And, like Lina, she takes pleasure in the power of her appearance, as she is forever looking at herself approvingly in mirrors. In this film, her legs as opposed to her torso become the featured focus of the camera, but in the narrative they are used in such a way as is typical of the unruly woman: as a means of empowerment. Corrado's first accidental photograph becomes a means to an end: she tells Corrado that she will not sue him for failure to get her permission for its publication if he helps make her a star. And, although it was initially Corrado who urged her to pose provocatively in a towel, it is she who later rips off her skirt to pose with the count in just her garter belt and stockings in an attempt to arouse Corrado's jealousy. She proves that she, not the men

24. Corrado (Mastroianni) meets his match in Antonietta (Loren) in
La fortuna di essere donna (1956). Courtesy of Photofest.

and women above her in the hierarchy of the fashion and film commu-
nities, controls her body, and she uses that body to get what she wants:
in this case both a career and a husband, with sexual insinuations as
well (the film suggests that Antonietta sleeps with Corrado after the
towel photo session). His callous treatment of her after their liaison is
what fuels her revenge and drives her to pelt him with rocks at the film's
end, screaming at him, "Tell me you love me or I'll break your head."

Threats are not Antonietta's only tools of verbal manipulation used
to tame Corrado's bachelor ways and make him conform to heterosexual
norms. She revisits the sites of his mischief—his studio, the restaurant
—and flaunts feigned tales of her sexual exploits. She turns the very
lines he initially uses on her to induce his jealous rage. She throws
back Corrado's "progressive" discourse on marriage and sexual freedom
when she returns to his studio after being with the count. In exacting
her revenge, Antonietta takes the typical male verbal tools of seduction
and twists them around, proving that the unruly woman's body is not
the only instrument of her success.

Unlike *Peccato,* however, in which the main characters were all working class, in *Fortuna* Antonietta must hide her working-class origins as she passes from shopgirl to starlet. This metamorphosis is accomplished on both the iconic and verbal level. Her look changes: she goes from shapely and provocatively dressed in bright colors and loud prints to a thinner and more demure "woman"—she is in fact told by the manager of the fashion house Fontanesi (perhaps based on the popular Sorelle Fontana atelier) to lose ten pounds and dress only in black, advice she follows rigorously. Her long hair and wild curls are neatly coiffed into fashionable mink hats and headdresses. The count aids in remaking her image, counseling her on how she should walk, talk, and present herself to the public. Antonietta, however, ultimately rejects this class discourse. Her return to her untamed working-class roots comes at the end of the film. Inspired by Elena, the count's wife, and her departing words—"you've displayed real spirit—you're a wonderful person"— Antonietta realizes that class comes from within, not without. In the film's final scene, as she bombards Corrado with her anger (and stones), her hair has once again become as wild as her demeanor, a signifier of the unruly woman's untamed ways. As if to reinforce her riotous nature, she screams: "Don't forget I'm of peasant stock and I'm going to plow you under!" This ending is typical of the 1950s *commedia all'italiana*'s tendency toward a privileging of working-class life over the vacuous inclinations of the upper class, represented here by the phony count, and the profit-mongering and lecherous film industry. The intent, however, is not the subversion of authority by the working class, as was a common topos of the carnivalesque and the grotesque. Rather, it involves the recognition of the excessive materiality and emptiness of the industrial ruling class.

In both Blasetti films, the endings, although typical of romantic comedy, fail to imply the conversion to a desexualized, maternal femininity that traditionally characterizes the battle between the unruly woman and her male "victim." Whereas both Lina and Antonietta are calmed into submission by a passionate kiss, there is little proof that the women are tamed of their wild ways. In fact, both characters retain their exaggerated femininity, flaunting it to the very last frame. Ultimately, while Paolo and Corrado succeed in getting the girl and creating the couple, the hidden power of the unruly woman never quite disappears, and thus has important consequences for the representation of masculinity. While the man may be brought in line with social norms (as Corrado is cured of his pretentious, bachelor ways), he is unable to disempower the unruly woman completely. Her primary tool, her body, is never de-sexualized and still remains iconographically privileged at the films' conclusions. In each film, some sign of unruliness prevails, be it Antonietta's wild hair or Lina's physical and verbal insubordination. Thus the male character as incarnated by Mastroianni has proven himself inept at the taming of the shrew.

The 1960s: Belly Laughter

When asked to comment on their successful working relationship, De Sica, Mastroianni, and Loren have all pointed to their Neapolitan heritage as one of the primary reasons for their onscreen chemistry. Their genealogical roots, however, were anchored more to the rural area surrounding Naples than to the city itself. Loren was born in the town of Pozzuoli, just south of the city, and Mastroianni in Fontana-Liri, which, at the time of his birth, was situated in the province of Caserta in the Campania region (the home of Naples), but only three years later was redistricted to the province of Frosinone in Lazio. Although De Sica was born in Sora, a town southeast of Rome, he identified himself as Neapolitan: "My mother and father . . . were Neapolitan. And my family was very Neapolitan [neapolitanissma], the entire genealogical tree."[27] Loren attributes the "spark" among the three of them to the overall character of Neapolitan life: "the three of us were united in a kind of complicity that the Neapolitans always have among themselves. The same sense of humor, the same rhythms, the same philosophies of life, the same natural cynicism."[28]

In the 1960s, the trio made three films together, with De Sica behind rather than in front of the camera: two comedies—*Ieri, oggi e domani,* a three-episode film with Mastroianni and Loren playing different roles in each, and *Matrimonio all'italiana,* based on Eduardo de Filippo's famous play, *Filumena Marturanu*—and one drama, *I girasoli* (Sunflower, 1970), set in post-war Russia. De Sica's Neapolitan films can be seen, in many ways, as a cinematic love song to his heritage, and his films capture the city's chaotic nature in all its beauty. As De Sica himself put it, the Neapolitans are "a great people, unique in the world, with many defects, some of which are the consequence of their secular misery and undernourishment, and with noble heart and spirit like no one else."[29] Moreover, his picture of Neapolitan life is decidedly working class, as it takes its point of departure from the de Filippo sources. De Filippo wrote both the treatment and the screenplay (along with his wife Isabella Quarantotti) for the first episode of *Ieri, oggi, domani* entitled "Adelina of Naples." And, although de Filippo's class analysis aims more toward a dramatic exposition of the trials and tribulations of this sector of the population, De Sica is more concerned with the celebration of the Neapolitan spirit, rather than, in a departure from his neorealist production, a social exposé of its grave problems.

The first De Sica-Loren-Mastroianni collaboration set in Naples was not in fact directed by De Sica but by Mario Camerini. *La bella mugnaia* (The Miller's Beautiful Wife, 1955), a remake of Camerini's 1936 *Il capello a tre punti* (The Three-Pointed Hat), departs from the contemporaneous Blasetti films in that (1) it features Loren and Mastroianni already coupled as husband and wife; and (2) it is a historical comedy filmed in lush Technicolor Cinemascope, an extremely popular technique of the Hollywood productions being filmed in Italy at that time. Set in 1682, Mastroianni plays Luca, a scheming miller who uses his beautiful wife Carmela (Loren) to incur favors with the intrusive local government, headed by a corrupt governor (De Sica), whose principle desire is to sleep with Carmela. Through a series of comic mishaps and assumed identities, both men learn their appropriate lessons: the governor to govern fairly and to be faithful to his wife; and Luca to be a proper citizen and to covet, not flaunt, his wife's physical attributes. This scenario fits more closely to the model of the Hollywood romantic comedies, in that the unruly woman tames the male and subsumes him into the patriarchal order, thus enabling her to tone down her own sexuality as well. In fact, at the film's end, Carmela eschews her previously risqué style of dressing (tight bodices, bare arms, deep cleavage) for a more covered although still skin-tight look. Mastroianni and Loren's 1960s films continue to privilege the domestic situation, but the focus shifts from the romance itself to how the unruly woman negotiates the power struggles in both the public and the private sphere.

Culturally, Naples has many links to the figure of the unruly woman. As Giuliana Bruno has shown in her research on early film culture in Naples, the very nature of the public Neapolitan woman connotes unruliness. Although the division between public and private collapses in Neapolitan everyday life, that collapse is attributed mostly to men, who dominate the public sphere while relegating women to the private, domestic one. Consequently, men can walk the streets, while women are "streetwalkers."[30] The anthropologist Thomas Belmonte, in his study on Naples in the 1970s, observes that although Neapolitan culture is "mother-centered," women are still bound by patriarchal law, particularly in the division between public and private:

The women of southern Italy are powerful only in the sense that they perform "powerfully" the innumerable tasks and chores which men and children set for them. Women as wives are extolled, and women as mothers are deified, but women as women do not count for much in southern Italy. Men refer to them, as they pass in the street, synechdochically—a part of the body suffices to identify any female who is not immediately recognizable as wife or mother.[31]

The unruly woman as incarnated by Sophia Loren in the De Sica films challenges the division between public and private. Following in the tradition of the heroines of many Notari films, she proudly occupies that public space and reclaims it as her own, simultaneously bringing the private domestic sphere into the public. In the case of Adelina, the maternal body in all its glory conquers the dominant male sphere of public space with her triumphant *passeggiata*. Filumena, by contrast, relies on her mind, specifically the joke or *beffa*, as a means of attaining what she wants. In the end, the Neapolitan male, far from controlling his environment, is subsumed into the dominant unruly woman's space.

Yesterday, Today, and Tomorrow, as conceived by Carlo Ponti and financed by the American producer Joseph E. Levine, intended to play off the trio's popular 1950s comedies as well as their recent successes in the United States: De Sica and Loren from *Two Women* (La ciociara, 1960) and Mastrioanni in *Divorce—Italian Style* (see chapter 3). Ponti's idea was to direct the films toward the commercial rather than art-house market.[32] Both *Yesterday, Today, and Tomorrow* and *Marriage—Italian Style* were immediately dubbed into English and had very wide releases in non–art-house theaters in the United States, where the latter's title was intentionally changed from the de Filippo original to reference Germi's film. In keeping with its popular slant, the filmmakers of *Yesterday, Today, and Tomorrow* relied on the tripartite structure of the sketch, which evokes the popular variety-theater tradition and exploited a popular trend in Italian filmmaking of the 1950s and 1960s: De Sica had in fact made two previous sketch films, the above-mentioned *The Gold of Naples*, in which he directed all the episodes, and one episode ("La riffa," the raffle) in *Boccaccio '70* (1962). The sketch also has roots in the Neapolitan culture of the *sceneggiata*, in which a popular song was translated narratively into either a theatrical sketch or a short film and was often drawn from recent events covered in the *cronaca nera* (the darker side of the news).[33] The "Adelina" episode, although more a humorous feature than a dark tale, was actually inspired by the true story of Concetta Muccardo, a woman who resorted to a series of pregnancies in order to avoid being jailed, and who, at one point, threatened to shut down the production unless she received compensation (which she did).[34] The film adaptation did not deviate much from its real-life inspiration: Adelina Sbaratti (Loren) is about to be incarcerated for not paying a fine for selling black-market cigarettes, a fact complicated further by her and her husband Carmine's (Mastroianni) open flaunting of the law. She soon learns from a lawyer (Domenico Verace, played by Agostino Salvietti) that she cannot be thrown in prison while pregnant. The savvy Adelina then calculates just how long she will have after the birth of this, her second child, before she has to produce another one in order to avoid incarceration (she gets an additional six months for breastfeeding). She then proceeds to have a total of seven children, literally squeezing one on top of the other in their one room apartment. Trouble arrives when Carmine, exhausted from his familial duties, is unable to produce another offspring in time to keep Adelina out of jail. After a doctor's visit and a desperate turn to her friend Pasquale, Adelina decides that the only option left for her is to begin serving her sentence. Her neighborhood soon rallies behind her, imposing a "tax" on every purchase (*tassa d' 'a multa*) to help Adelina pay off the fine. An astute Verace also alerts the press to her plight, and soon she is given a presidential pardon. She triumphantly returns to her neighborhood and her family as a local celebrity.

De Sica's objective in bringing the story to the screen was to soften the non-cinematic style of de Filippo's film script by adding exterior shots to the interior ones, in order that "Naples be ever-present and the Neapolitans function like a Greek chorus."[35] In order to capture the reality of Naples, De Sica returned, at least stylistically, to his neorealist roots, filming mostly on location (some interior shots were done in Rome) and using non-professional actors in supporting roles and as extras. The episode is filled with unique touches of Neapolitan life and culture: its language (it was written and delivered in heavy Neapolitan dialect), its songs, and even its superstitions: at one point, Adelina calls in a sorcerer to help chase away the evil spirits that impede Carmine from performing his sexual duties. What emerges is a portrait of a community in which solidarity reigns above self-interest, revealing the beneficial side of the fusion of the public and the private in contemporary urban life.

Once again, Loren's body is at the center of the film. This fusion of public and private is written on the unruly female body, as Adelina uses her reproductive capacity to escape rather than conform to patriarchal law. Loren's first appearance on screen parodies the traditional presentation of the female body, as the camera pans to her legs and then tilts up to reveal the rest of her body as she sits behind her table selling cigarettes. She subsequently stands with her back to the camera

then quickly turns to reveal her pregnant belly, both playing with classical iconography and the spectator's expectations. Moreover, Adelina
proudly flaunts the unruliness of her motherly curves, particularly in
one of the film's most elaborately filmed sequences. After the lawyer
Verace has informed Carmine and Adelina that the latter's pregnancy
impedes her incarceration—*tene 'a panza*, literally translated as "she's
got the belly"—news spreads quickly throughout the streets. The scene
culminates in Adelina's triumphant parade around the neighborhood, as
she proudly displays her protruding belly, swinging her arms and hips
as she holds her head high. The accompanying music crescendos into a
loud, vivacious march with horns and drums, deliberately referencing
her infamous parade as the *pizzaiola* in *The Gold of Naples*. The sequence is filmed mostly in medium-long and long shots so as to capture
both the body and the environment (i.e., the public and the private)
within the same frame, integrating the performative display of the female body with an essential component of Neapolitan culture: the *passeggiata*. I have already discussed how the *passeggiata* signaled the moment of display and performance of masculinity for the *bella figura* (see
chapter 1). Adelina appropriates those very conventions for femininity
by parading its most visible sign—her belly—within the context of the
bella figura's very public display of the private self on the streets of
Naples.

This association between the city and the maternal body echoes another important text in Neapolitan culture: Matilde Serao's *Il ventre di
Napoli* (The Belly of Naples, 1884), a series of articles that Serao, an
accomplished author of fiction and journalism, intended as a response
to Prime Minister Agostino Depretis's declaration that "Naples must be
gutted" (the Italian word is *sventrare*) after the recent cholera epidemic.
The Italian word *ventre*, from the Latin *venter*, has several meanings,
from the generic "belly" or "stomach" to the more female-specific
"uterus" or "womb." *Il ventre di Napoli*, in line with what Laura Salsini
has called Serao's "realist revisions," aims to elucidate Naples's social and economic problems rather than smooth them over into a typical tourist-like vision of the city: to remake (*rifare*) rather than gut
(*sventrare*) the so-called underbelly of Naples.[36] In order to render the
horror of turn-of-the-century proletarian Neapolitan life, Serao often
refers to the plight of its female population. But, rather than just delin-
eate its miserable state, she also recounts tales of solidarity, particularly
in relation to motherhood and the female/maternal body: how one nursing mother, for example, helped feed the child of another mother whose
milk had dried up; and how one woman would bring a friend's baby to
her to be nursed at work.[37] The maternal body for Serao is seen as a site

25. Adelina (Loren) peddles her wares in the first sequence of Vittorio De Sica's *Yesterday, Today, and Tomorrow* (1963). From the author's private collection.

of hope for the future of Naples, through female solidarity and the restorative powers of the lactating female body in light of the indifference displayed by the dominant (read patriarchal) order.

The lactating female body also enables Adelina's rebellion against authority. When the police patrol the street where she sells her stolen wares, she defiantly declares, showing her baby attached to her breast, "I still have five more months." Demonstrating her insubordination with both speech and body, Adelina appropriates the traditional tools of female domestication as a means of her own empowerment. Rowe notes how Bakhtin and others have aligned the maternal body with the grotesque, and thus marginalized it in terms of its transgressive power (33–34). The unruly woman, however, uses this monstrous body precisely as a source of power, with Adelina constituting the perfect example of how the maternal body, so central to the preservation of social order, can subvert that very authority.

In the face of this power, Carmine, like the law itself, is left powerless. Already metaphorically castrated by his inability to find work, Carmine assumes the traditionally feminine position from the beginning: it is he, as much if not more than Adelina, who is seen taking care of the children, even when she is not in prison. His weakened status is further

26. The lactating female body enables Adelina's rebellion. Courtesy of Photofest.

threatened by his inability to impregnate Adelina for an eighth time. Thus, the sole proof of his masculinity—his ability to sire children— disappears. This emphasis on and preoccupation with paternity also plays a significant part in *Marriage—Italian Style,* as Mastroianni's character, Domenico Soriano, becomes a pawn in Filumena's plans to give her illegitimate sons a name. In this De Sica film, Filumena Marturano, a former prostitute, tricks her long-time lover Domenico into marrying her as she pretends to be on her deathbed. Flashbacks explicate their twenty-year relationship, focusing on how Domenico has taken advantage of Filumena: how he set her up in her own apartment (only to cheat a deserving family out of it), persuaded her to run his bakery business and care for his demanding elderly mother, all the while leaving her for long stretches of time and cheating on her with a series of cashiers at his café. When an outraged Domenico refuses to accept their marriage and moves to have it legally annulled, Filumena informs him that she has secretly been supporting three illegitimate sons, and that one of them is in fact his, but she will not tell him which one. Domenico then becomes obsessed with ascertaining paternity, approaching each of the boys secretly to establish who most resembles him. Ultimately, he confronts Filumena, who keeps him guessing as to which one is his offspring. A frustrated Domenico physically attacks her, but his violent grasp soon becomes romantic, and the film concludes with their marriage, attended by the three sons, still without the revelation of paternity.

Marriage—Italian Style differs from its original source play in two significant ways. First, Sophia Loren plays the lead instead of the actress for whom the role was originally written and with whom it was most identified: the author's sister, Titina de Filippo, who had recently passed away and to whom the film is dedicated. Although clearly designed to be a Loren vehicle (Ponti even insisted to De Sica at one point that Loren have more close-ups than Mastroianni), Titina de Filippo's ghost weighed heavily on the production, particularly in its sense of theatricality that De Sica tried at all costs to purge from what he intended to be a purely cinematic story.[38] Second, using precisely the language of cinema, De Sica incorporated flashbacks in order to flesh out the backstory of the relationship between Filumena and Domenico. And, although the film preserves the strong Neapolitan anchoring of the play (yet tempering Domenico's use of dialect), it mutes its social criticism of the plight of illegitimacy (a subject of importance to the illegitimate de Filippo) in favor of a rosier American-style romantic comedy.[39]

The film's narrative pivots around the trick Filumena plays to entrap Domenico in marriage: Filumena is being carried up the stairs of her apartment building in a chair, so close is she to death's door. Instead of calling a doctor, she asks Domenico to summon a priest, and much to his surprise he soon finds himself kneeling on the floor with the priest blessing their marriage *in extremis*. Once the marriage is a fait accompli, Domenico telephones his fiancée Diana to inform her of Filumena's impending demise. Standing screen right in front of a deep red curtain, he is soon interrupted by a resurrected Filumena, who angrily reveals her deception. She then proceeds to the kitchen to eat and celebrate her triumph, unleashing twenty years of anger at Domenico for taking advantage of her "situation"—the fact that her past as a prostitute prevents her from ever becoming an honest woman. Loren's disheveled appearance in this scene reinforces her status as unruly woman: in a major departure from the traditional iconography of the *maggiorata fisica,* she appears to wear no makeup, is dressed in an unflattering nightgown, and has unkempt hair. Her movements, as she screams at Domenico while shoving food in her face, betray the unleashing of the shrew's wrath. The combination of anger and food links the mouth with the unruly woman's excess: the gluttonous and the garrulous. The color red,

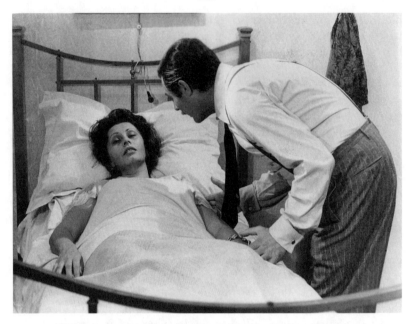

27. Filumena (Loren) pretends to be on death's door to trick Domenico
(Mastroianni) into marriage in *Marriage—Italian Style* (1964).
From the author's private collection.

long associated with the feminine, figures prominently in the mise-en-
scène: in the curtain as well as the robe Filumena wears on her first
morning as Signora Soriano, highlighting the power of the unruly woman
as she revels in her triumph.

Thus Domenico, like Snàporaz before him, becomes the object of the
female-manipulated Boccacian *beffa* (see chapter 4), which assumes a
more subversive nature because of the infusion of anger in its configuration. For Rowe, anger combines with the joke to form "transgressive
laughter," whereby "women both initiate the joke and complete it with
their laughter" (17). The unruly woman becomes what Boccaccio might
call the *beffatrice* (female joker), using *ingegno* to obtain what she wants:
here, a father for her sons. Even though Domenico succeeds in having
the marriage annulled, Filumena cunningly transforms the *beffa*/joke
into the riddle of his paternity, strategically feeding him clues but then
contradicting herself. Yet Domenico never learns which son is his, despite a futile interrogation of the three before the wedding. The wedding scene itself, recounted as a series of semi-still frames designed to
evoke a wedding album, reinforces Domenico's lack of certainty: three

28. Food and anger fuel the unruly woman's wrath in *Marriage—Italian Style.* Courtesy of Photofest.

"photographs" have him looking at each of the boys, trying to discern similarities. Thus, by remaining in control of both the joke, and, consequently, the narrative, Loren as unruly woman succeeds again in both subsuming Mastroianni's character into the patriarchal order and preserving her status as the woman on top.

Underlying this power shift is the gradual emergence of the woman in the 1960s as increasingly independent, preceding what Paul Ginsborg has called the era of collective action from 1968 to 1973.[40] Both Adelina and Filumena, more than Lina and Antonietta, occupy public space in a progressively assertive way: Adelina by bringing the maternal and the domestic into the public, and Filumena as working woman who leaves her prostitute days behind in favor of legitimate hard work to provide for her illegitimate children. The repercussions of this public emergence in the historically masculine sphere, particularly within the context of Southern Italy, speak to a threatened masculinity, evident in these Mastroianni *inetti:* both Carmelo's inability to perform sexually and Domenico's inability to solve the riddle of paternity, forsake, especially in the latter's case, the traditional mechanisms of narrative closure and the restoration of patriarchal order. Moreover, the unruly woman comes to dominate the male through an increasingly desexualized body. The exaggerated body of the *maggiorate fisiche* has become the downright dowdy body of the middle-aged woman: the unruly

29. Domenico attempts to ascertain which of Filumena's sons is his.
From the author's private collection.

woman has forsaken her position as sexualized object of the gaze in favor of an inversion of both the social and economic order. Loren and
Mastroianni's most critically successful film of the subsequent decade
would further exploit this de-iconicization, as it simultaneously dis-
tanced itself from and relied on the unruly woman/*inetto* coupling.

The 1970s: *A Special Day* and
the Woman on Top

In the 1970s, filmmakers hoping to capitalize on the previous successes
of the Loren/Mastroianni coupling released several films which were
intended for both national and international audiences: Dino Risi's *La
moglie del prete* (The Priest's Wife, 1970), with Loren as a singer and
Mastroianni as a priest with whom she falls in love; Giorgio Capitani's
La pupa del gangster (The Gangster's Moll, 1975), in which she played
another ex-prostitute and he the gangster; and Lina Wertmüller's *Fatto
di sangue fra due uomini per causa di una vedova—si sospettano motivi poli-
tici* (Blood Feud, 1979), about, as the Italian title explains, two men who
fall in love with a widow. While some of these films played well at the

box office, most were critical failures. Their most significant collaboration of this period in terms of critical praise and international success, Ettore Scola's *A Special Day*, radically departs from the romantic comedy formula set above: like the Wertmüller film, it is a drama set during the Fascist period, with Loren as a frumpy Mussolini-loving housewife and Mastroianni as a gay anti-Fascist radio announcer. What is interesting about this film is how it nevertheless draws on the codes and conventions established in the unruly woman comedies described above, particularly in the film's "climactic" sexual resolution.

A Special Day takes place on May 6, 1938, during Hitler's visit to Rome. It tracks the encounter of two people who do not attend the occasion's parades and spectacles: Antonietta (Loren), an uneducated mother and housewife, and an avid supporter of the Fascist regime; and Gabriele (Mastroianni), a well-educated gay radio announcer opposed to Fascism. Scola's film efficiently implodes the gender mythologies through which the Fascist regime attempted to impose cultural and political conformity, with Antonietta as the quintessential *donna madre* (maternal woman) as opposed to the materialistic, sterile *donna crisi* (crisis woman).[41] Antonietta is mother to six healthy children, fulfilling her "innate feminine" calling as well as her public duty as proper Fascist citizen. In her extended conversation with Gabriele, she proudly comments that if she has one more child, she is eligible for a government prize during the Mother's and Child's Day celebration in Rome, initiated in 1933 in order to propagandize the regime's demographic politics. Her life, however, does not provide the rewarding fulfillment of the regime's conceptualization of female subjectivity. Antonietta's family resources are stretched beyond their limits. The filmmakers' effective camera work visually reveals the burden of Antonietta's familial responsibilities. Our first introduction to the family is a two-minute, one-shot sequence as the camera follows Antonietta's movements and actions as she wakes her husband and her children on the morning of the parade. As she weaves her way in and out of the tiny rooms and the makeshift room dividers, we discover one child after another hiding among the apartment's cracks and crevices.

Antonietta had blindly accepted the gender and sexual constructions expected of her. Gabriele, by contrast, is forced to consciously assume them in order to escape persecution. Little ambiguity existed during the Fascist period in the cultural configuration of the deviant. The negative other, assigned to the category of the degenerate, included hermaphrodites, androgynes, masturbators, criminals, lesbians, and homosexuals. Sodomy in particular came to symbolize the confusion of the sexes and sexual excess; it was perceived as a conspiratorial secret practice the consequences of which were depopulation, disease, and political subversion.[42] Specific legislation reinforced the regime's social and sexual fear of the degenerate homosexual threat: in 1926 the government imposed the infamous bachelor tax—a punitive tax on those adult males who were not yet married—and in 1931 all homosexual acts were officially outlawed. As opposed to the regime in Nazi Germany, however, the Italian government did not set out on a programmed elimination of homosexuals. Rather, as Ruth Ben-Ghiat has recently argued, the government aimed to sequester and reform those labeled as deviants in an effort to cure Italy of degeneracy. For Ben-Ghiat, this project of *bonifica* (reclamation) was integral to the Fascist project of national regeneration and the restoration of international prestige through colonial expansion, cultural practices, and modernist visions.[43]

What ultimately dooms Gabriele in *A Special Day* is his inability to successfully recite the role of the happy, healthy heterosexual. Scola employs the figure of the homosexual not as a means of vilifying or demonizing Fascism, as is the case, for example, with Roberto Rossellini's *Roma, città aperta* (Open City, 1945) or Bernardo Bertolucci's *Il conformista* (The Conformist, 1970), but, rather, as a means of demystifying the Fascist myth of virility which formed the basis for much of the movement's rhetorical power. Unlike most post-war depictions of the era, here the homosexual is neither a Fascist, nor does he possess any of the traditional, iconic signs associated with cinematic representations of homosexuality, such as excessive femininity, exaggerated flamboyance, or "perversion." Scola appears to counter this negative tendency by means of what Richard Dyer sees as the shift from the act of homosexuality to characterization: in other words, by showing that homosexuals are, in fact, like everyone else.[44]

The irony of *A Special Day* rests in the fact that a man who is far from the virile image that Fascism and Mussolini attempted to project sexually satisfies the ideal Fascist woman. By contrast, the sexual union draws on both traditional cinematic constructions and extra-cinematic expectations. In the classical paradigm, the heterosexual coupling/union constitutes the natural form of closure to the text as it resolves the gender conflicts raised in the film's narrative. The audience assumes Mastroianni's and Loren's characters will become romantically involved, because of the actors' long history of collaboration in the romantic comedies analyzed above. Each had come to symbolize Italian eroticism for both a national and international audience. In fact, the promotional copy in the American newspaper advertisements played on this very ex-

30. Gabriele (Mastroianni) comforts Antonietta (Loren) in Ettore Scola's *A Special Day*. From the author's private collection.

pectation. It reads "Loren and Mastroianni together again in a very special movie."

The climactic love scene, while seeming to departing from the traditionally romanticized Loren/Mastroianni couplings in its style, nevertheless physically incorporates the idea of the "woman-on-top," as it is Antonietta who assumes the traditionally masculine position as initiator of the sexual act. What destabilizes this sexual inversion is that, unlike unruly women such as Mae West or Marlene Dietrich, Loren does not possess signs of masculinity, such as West's husky voice or Dietrich's cross-dressing. Despite the fact that the filmmakers purposely tried to make Sophia Loren look unattractive to counter her star persona—she wore little or no makeup to accentuate the bags under her eyes and dressed in ragged clothes—she still exudes femininity and, in this scene, uncontrolled female sexuality. Shot predominantly as a series of close-ups and medium shots, the sequence underscores Antonietta's awakening passion in contrast to Gabriele's physically rigid passivity: as she takes the lead in their love-making, low-angle shots emphasize her libidinous power, while Gabriele's facial expression subliminally relays both pain and pleasure. And, although Gabriele eventually succumbs to sexual arousal, his is devoid of the cathartic release that Antonietta experiences. The homosexual, although heterosexually competent, remains the sexual *inetto* in traditionally masculine terms, dominated by the woman on top.

Part of a spate of 1970s films which examined Italy's Fascist legacy, *A Special Day* both draws on and departs from the cinematic paradigms established in earlier Loren/Mastroianni collaborations. The film succeeds in examining and dismantling the Fascist constructions of male sexuality and in countering representational stereotypes of homosexuality. The counterpoint sound of patriotic Fascist music, which had been blaring throughout the film but reaches its crescendo during the sex scene, further destabilizes the heterosexual ideal in its departure from the traditional string symphonies accompanying the classic coupling. It fails to give Antonietta the happy end of her (heterosexual) romantic fantasies: Gabriele is led off into internal exile, and Antonietta returns to her role as Fascist mother and wife. Homosexuality, although not converted, is contained and re-inscribed along heterosexual lines by the figure of the unruly woman, but those very lines in the long run are ambiguous at best.

Because Mastroianni and Loren proved to be a successful commercial pairing on both a national and international level with even mediocre films, one wonders what would have happened had one project proposed to them gotten off the ground: the film adaptation of Shakespeare's *The Taming of the Shrew*, which eventually starred Elizabeth Taylor and Richard Burton. Franco Zeffirelli, the film's director, approached Loren about teaming with Mastroianni, but the latter declined the role, citing his poor English.[45] Shakespeare's comedy, in reality, might have been a perfect fit for the pair. First, the text, like the Mastroianni/Loren films, takes a realistic middle-class setting as the point of departure for a social commentary on the constructed nature of gender and the social order. Second, for Coppélia Kahn, Shakespeare's play satirizes the male urge to control women by showing that patriarchal authority is authenticated by female subjugation to it, in this case Kate's seemingly complete devotion and submission to Petruchio's will.[46] Similarly, the Mastroianni/Loren films, through the carnivalesque figure of the unruly woman who inverts the gender hierarchy, reveal the *inetto* behind the mask of Italian patriarchal masculinity. Finally, as Kate merely plays the role of dutiful wife, the play literally "plays" with the very notion of "play" itself. This idea of playing a part in the social order, reinforced by the many self-reflexive elements in the drama and by the unruly woman's use of ironic speech and performance in the Mastroianni/Loren films, furthers the notion of the world turned upside-down by the ever-increasing public presence of women and the repercussions for traditional constructions of Italian masculinity.

Mastroianni's and Loren's final appearance on screen together in Robert Altman's *Prêt-à-Porter* (1994), the second of only two American films that Mastroianni would make in his career, proves an important transitional text, because it takes the Loren/Mastroianni comedic formula and introduces a factor which characterizes the production of Mastroianni's final films: aging and masculinity. A parody of the fashion world with an ensemble cast, the film, in a rather unbelievable subplot humorously referencing *Sunflower,* features Mastroianni as a fervid young Italian communist (Sergio) who had left his young wife Isabella (Loren) to go to Moscow in the 1950s, but lost touch with her in the confusion after Stalin's death. She went on to marry Olivier de la Fontaine, the current chairman of the French fashion council, whom she has now come to despise because of his extra-marital affairs. Sergio returns forty years later to find Isabella, first by arranging a meeting with her husband, who suddenly chokes on his ham sandwich and dies. De la Fontaine's chauffeur accuses Sergio of strangling him, and Sergio flees. Sergio, furtively hiding in clothes stolen from various hotel rooms, finally finds Isabella, and they agree to meet. They retreat to another one of Sergio's purloined rooms, and while Isabella seductively begins to remove her clothing, an exhausted Sergio falls asleep.

Altman's use of Loren and Mastroianni in his critique of the vacuity and ridiculousness of haute couture is, like many of the actors' films examined in this study, highly self-referential. The fashion industry plays an integral role in its representation: the film features designers playing themselves (Christian Lacroix, Sonia Rykiel, and Jean-Paul Gautier, among others) and showcasing their collections, and those designers played by actors had their collections created by fashion houses such as Nino Cerruti and Vivienne Westwood.[47] The presence of Loren and Mastroianni references their status as icons of Italian style: she for her patronage of high fashion (her long associations with Christian Dior, Gianfranco Ferre, and Giorgio Armani) as well as her own foray into the accessories world with her line of eyeglasses, and he, as discussed in chapter 2, for his association with the new Italian men's fashion which emerged in the late 1950s and early 1960s. In addition, Altman wanted them to recreate a scene from one of their earlier films, but it had to be something with which an international audience would be familiar.[48] They chose the third episode of *Yesterday, Today, and Tomorrow,* in which Loren plays Mara, one of the many cinematic incarnations of the prostitute with the golden heart, who promises to take a vow of celibacy for one week if she can convince her young neighbor

31. The famous striptease sequence from the third episode of
Yesterday, Today, and Tomorrow. Courtesy of Photofest.

(Umberto, played by Gianni Ridolfi) to return to the seminary and reject the impure world. As her loyal client on a visit from Bologna, Mastroianni's character (Augusto Rusconi) is the victim of frustrated desire
three times: after Mara is insulted by Umberto's grandmother; after the
grandmother begs Mara's forgiveness and asks for her help; and when,
during a provocative striptease to the popular song from the 1960s "La
luce blu," she remembers her vow and forces Augusto to pray rather
than lay with her.

In the De Sica film, Loren as unruly woman frustrates the male's
desire, and he is powerless in the face of her decision. In Altman's version, it is the unruly woman's sexuality that remains unsatisfied by the
aging *inetto* man. Altman recreates the scene to its very last detail: Mastroianni's position on the bed, his animal sounds of pleasure at the spectacle of the striptease, "La luce blu," and Loren's black-lace bustier and
garter belt (albeit this time over a body stocking). The fact that Sergio
has fallen asleep in the face of such an open display of female sexuality
speaks to two important themes that run through the final decades of
Mastroianni's career. First, unlike his American contemporaries, Mastroianni never made any attempts to counter the effects of aging in

32. Loren recreates the striptease in Robert Altman's *Prêt-à-Porter* (1994). From the author's private collection.

his appearance. In *Prêt-à-Porter* (and other films), he appears as the seventy-year-old man he was, in contrast to Sophia Loren, who consistently takes pains to appear as young as possible in her films. Second, by turning to a past text for inspiration, one associated with Mastroianni's younger years, *Prêt-à-Porter* evokes a sense of nostalgia for a time gone by. This nostalgia for the past is a common theme in Mastroianni's final films, one that evokes simpler times, when the world was not turned upside down by the unruly woman and changing gender roles.

6

Remembrance of
Films Past

Mastroianni and the Aging Male Body

In Ettore Scola's 1982 film *Il mondo nuovo* (The New World, released in the United States under the French title *La Nuit de Varennes*), Marcello Mastroianni plays an aging Giacomo Casanova, who, along with several notables, including the American Thomas Paine (Harvey Keitel) and the French novelist Restif de la Breton (Jean-Louis Barrault), reflects on the changing world as the French monarchy prepares to tumble. With his overly powdered face, eloquent wig, and heels, Casanova appears as a parody of his former self, simultaneously acknowledging the effects of aging while clinging to an image of spectacle and elegance. In one scene at a pub where he has stopped along his journey, Casanova begins to publicly recount one of his sexual exploits to de la Breton. As he enters into his discourse, he sees an elderly woman staring into space. When he is about to launch into the encounter's graphic details, he looks at the woman and abruptly stops. The shots then oscillate between close-ups of the old woman and Casanova reacting to her blank stare. Excerpts of "The Catalogue of Women" from Mozart's opera *Don Giovanni* play in the background. As de la Breton applauds, Casanova sits down and returns to their conversation under much more intimate terms.

This scene is revealing for two important reasons. First, it shows that Mastroianni, unlike most actors in their late fifties and early sixties, was unafraid to take on roles which physically aged him even further. Second, it illustrates the traditional paradigm of the representation of aging in film. The male protagonist denies the aging process by first masking his own aging and then projecting his anxiety about growing old onto

140

33. Mastroianni as
the aging Casanova in
Ettore Scola's *La Nuit
de Varennes* (1982).
Courtesy of Photofest.

the female body. In Scola's film, however, that façade recedes. The elderly woman becomes Casanova's mirror of truth, despite his attempts to mask his age through an extravagant toilette. Casanova's youthfulness as masquerade in *Il mondo nuovo,* to paraphrase Kathleen Woodward's pioneering article in the field of age studies, inevitably fails.[1]

The role of the maturing Casanova is typical of those Mastroianni would play as he himself aged. As opposed to other stars who disappeared from the screen as they grew older, Mastroianni in his last five years was more prolific than ever, appearing in approximately twenty films. Always a welcome participant of international productions, in the 1990s Mastroianni made films all over the world with prominent directors, including the Chilean Raoul Ruiz, the Argentinian María Luisa Bemberg, the Portuguese Manoel de Oliveira, the French Agnés Varda, and, in a first for the actor, two American films. Mastroianni's choice of roles was inevitably affected by the slow-down of the Italian cinema in the 1980s and 1990s. Not only did the industry's revenue decline (despite a gradual rise in ticket sales) and Italy's share of the pot decrease, but theaters also closed down, with the number halved between 1985 and 1998, as television became the dominant medium of cultural dissemination.[2] Nevertheless, Mastroianni continued to work with up-and-coming Italian directors, including Giuseppe Tornatore, Francesca Archibugi, and Roberto Faenza.

This diverse array of films provides a unique opportunity for a cross-cultural comparison of the representation of aging masculinity in the cinema. For Woodward, aging, "like other markers of social difference" is "socially constructed," with the differences produced by discursive formations, social practices, and material conditions.[3] The topic of aging is particularly relevant for contemporary Italy, a country which tradi-tionally has venerated the elderly. Over the past decades, the average age of the population has increased dramatically. It has been predicted that by the year 2020 the number of citizens over 65 will jump from 15 per-cent (1992) to 23 percent. Even the aged are aging: recent studies expect that the percentage of people over eighty will double by that same year.[4]

This chapter interrogates the image of aging that Mastroianni pro-jected on screen, and how that changed with respect to different na-tional cinemas. What emerges is that unlike in the Hollywood para-digm, in which aging is denied, Mastroianni's characters brought aging masculinity unabashedly onto the screen, confronting it in all its con-tradictions, examining the tension between biological and experienced age; the dialectic in Christian culture between decline (death) and re-demption; and the nostalgia for the past in the face of inevitable death. Once again, Mastroianni's roles reflect an unstable rather than iconic masculinity, embodying the figure of the *inetto:* here the aging man out of touch with a world in which he no longer has a place. Moreover, his is a globalized, aging male body that cross-culturally acknowledges rather than disavows the effects of age.

With a myriad of films to choose from in the last decade of Mas-troianni's career, this chapter, perhaps more than the others in this study, suffers from the fate of omission. Some choices presented them-selves easily: Beeban Kidron's American production *Used People* (1992) and María Luisa Bemberg's *De eso no se habla* (I Don't Want to Talk about It, 1993) directly tackle the Hollywood paradigm of the older man/younger woman by pairing Mastroianni, in the first instance, with a middle-aged woman, and in the second case, with a dwarf. The Italian films under analysis are Tornatore's *Stanno tutti bene* (Everybody's Fine, 1990), with its portrayal of the aging male against the backdrop of a changing national landscape, and Fellini's *Ginger and Fred* (1986), which, while not made during the last years of Mastroianni's life, never-theless addresses the nostalgic longing for the past, the emptiness of the present, and the fear of the imminent future.[5]

Aging, Masculinity, and Italian Cinema

Old age as a separate life phase is a modern phenomenon, one linked, in Western culture, to the growth of the welfare state in the nineteenth and twentieth centuries. According to Christoph Conrad, three particular areas of socio-economic change led to its development: (1) the redistribution of time spent in education, at work, and at leisure; (2) the advent of retirement as a social institution, with the creation of pension funds and mandatory retirement ages; and (3) cultural shifts, which saw a gradual movement away from a preoccupation with the eternal to a more secular and individualistic sense of self.[6] More people began to pass into this stage of life, as advances in medical care and better sanitation resulted in longer average-life expectancy. No longer needing to work until death, they had more leisure time with which to spend their increasing disposable income. Furthermore, the theologically ingrained idea that old age was a time during which the individual attained a greater wisdom and spirituality, as the old body, now weak, functioned as symbol of material transience, began to evaporate. As modernity encroached on the twentieth century, the traditional Catholic emphasis of the moral and the spiritual over the material and the corporeal, leading to the privileging of inner fulfillment as opposed to outward decay, seemed out of sync with a society that stressed scientific and economic "perfection" over resignation and self-transcendence.[7]

Much of the theoretical work that has been done on aging and representation has focused on women from two perspectives: the idea of aging as trauma, and the idea of aging as a masquerade and/or performance. E. Ann Kaplan sees the trauma of aging as revolving around time: simultaneously being in time and being unable to escape it. For women, this trauma is intensified, because, as the traditional object of the gaze, they experience the culturally constructed traumatic effects of aging to a much greater degree.[8] Thus, the representation of the female body bears the burden not only of her aging but that of all of patriarchal society, which denies white male aging. A classic example in Italian literature is Luigi Pirandello's often-cited example of his theory of *umorismo:*

> I see an old lady whose hair is dyed and completely smeared with some kind of horrible ointment; she is all made-up in a clumsy and awkward fashion and is all dolled-up like a young girl. I begin to laugh. I *perceive* that she is *the opposite* of what a respectable old lady should be. Now I could stop here at this initial and superficial

comic reaction: the comic consists precisely of this *perception of the opposite*. But if, at this point, reflection interferes in me to suggest that perhaps this old lady finds no pleasure in dressing up like an exotic parrot, and that perhaps she is distressed by it and does it only because she pitifully deceives herself into believing that, by making herself up like that and by concealing her wrinkles and gray hair, she may be able to hold the love of her much younger husband—if reflection comes to suggest all this, then I can no longer laugh at her as I did at first, exactly because the inner working of reflection has made me go beyond, or rather enter deeper into, the initial stage of awareness: from the beginning of the *perception of the opposite*, reflection has made me shift to a *feeling of the opposite*. And herein lies the precise difference between the comic and humor.[9]

What is interesting about the Pirandello passage is the language he uses to describe the old woman's appearance: "clumsy," "awkward," "horrible" in his original perception and "pitifully" deceived in his later state of awareness. The difference in the expressive means by which the author aims to convey meaning reveals a deep-seated anxiety about growing old, and how the male author projects his own and patriarchal society's anxiety about aging onto the representation of the ludicrous and grotesque female body.

The makeup that Pirandello's old woman adorns functions as the overt sign of an attempt to mask the effects of aging. Woodward, in her above-mentioned article as well as in her larger study *Aging and Its Discontents*, observes how masquerade, while possible at any age, is in old age a denial of that stage of life. The masquerade is the result of a clash between the external and the internal: that while it is possible to hide the outward effects of aging, it is impossible to ward off the inevitable aging process within.[10] Woodward's theoretical orientation owes much to Freud, for whom aging results in a collapse of the sexes, and thus the return of the other gender. Thus, in Woodward's words, "youthfulness as a masquerade in women may *sometimes* serve as a defense which reveals—not the fear of losing one's femininity, as we might expect— but rather the denial of a desire for masculinity."[11] The relevant question for this study is the converse: Is a man's masquerade, to paraphrase, "a denial of a desire for femininity"? For men, there is an extremely visible internal sign of the decline of manhood, which manifests itself externally: impotence. Male aging is associated physically with loss in the penis's muscle tone, a decrease in the skin's elasticity, and less pliable vasculature. Older men take longer to achieve an (often weaker) erection which does not last as long and occurs less frequently.[12] In Western culture, which equates the penis with the phallus, and thus sexual power with symbolic power, this fear of aging may not necessarily entail a "denial of desire for femininity" but, rather, a *denial of a loss of masculinity.* Jeff Hearn, in one of the few studies to examine the representation of masculinity and aging, concentrates precisely on this issue of power.[13] The denial of desire for the feminine does not enter into the equation for aging masculinity—rather, it entails a negation and masking of the loss—physical, economic, and social—which aging affects.

In several films—*La Nuit de Varennes, Everybody's Fine,* and *Ginger and Fred*—Mastroianni, already in his sixties, allows himself to appear even older. In a time when, as Vivian Sobchack has noted, cinema functions as cosmetic surgery by using special effects to repair the ravages of time, how does one theorize the representation of a masculinity that allows itself to age unabashedly? And what about Mastroianni's star image as "Latin lover"?[14] Jodi Brooks, in her work on stars and aging, observes how the representation of aging female stars is necessarily contrasted with their youthful images, particularly in films that self-referentially call attention to their status as actresses. Thus, the aged star nostalgically references her younger apparition, whereby the former functions as fossil—the representation of loss—and the latter as souvenir—the remembrance of the now forgotten and discarded. The discarded female star, as represented on the screen, "attempts to refuse her status as the discarded by freezing time," by masquerading as a young woman.[15]

Federico Fellini's 1987 film *Intervista,* his self-reflexive homage to Cinecittà on its fiftieth anniversary, illustrates the fossil/souvenir dichotomy with respect to stars and images. Several films within a film, the pseudo-documentary recounts a Japanese film crew following Fellini as he embarks on several endeavors: a cinematic "memory" about his first visit to Cinecittà, and the pre-production of his intended film version of Kafka's *Amerika.* One episode relates Fellini's surprise visit to the home of Anita Ekberg while accompanied by the film crew and the actor who plays the young Fellini in the Cinecittà memory (Sergio Rubini). Mastroianni, who had been filming a commercial at Cinecittà in costume as Mandrake the magician, comes along for the ride.[16] The entire scene, according to Mastroianni, was improvised—he had no idea where Fellini was taking him.[17] Initially skeptical of Fellini's intentions, Ekberg at first reluctantly but then wholeheartedly welcomes the group into her country home. Ekberg, who had been seen on screen infrequently since the late 1960s, appears much like Pirandello's old woman or the typical Fellinian female grotesque: overly made-up, with the same mane of thick, blond hair for which she was famous, but overweight, dressed in what appears to be a bed sheet wrapped around her body.[18] Despite the fact that all the men in the scene reassure her that she is still as beautiful as ever, the camera speaks the truth, reinforced by a very unattractive low-angle shot which exaggerates her transformation from Rubinesque to blatantly heavy. For Ekberg, the loss is conscious and palpable, and is made all the more painful by the deliberate apparition of the souvenir image: Marcello/Mandrake magically makes a screen appear, with the incantation of returning to "the old times of the past." As he and Anita begin dancing behind the screen to Nino Rota's score from La dolce vita, their shadows fade to black and a scene from the film appears, in which Marcello and Sylvia dance at the Caracalla spas and then wade into the Trevi Fountain (see chapter 2). Ekberg is clearly both moved and disturbed by what she sees on the screen, crying with her back to the camera as she jokes with Mastroianni about his silly request for schnapps. But Mastroianni's emotional response comes out when he looks at the present-day Ekberg as well as his own image. The actor is also visibly moved by what he sees within the frame. Spectatorial reaction shots of Ekberg and Mastroianni as they watch their much younger selves on the screen reveal the burden of the past on the present, or the effect of the image of the souvenir on the fossil. Far from projecting his own anxieties about aging onto the female body, Mastroianni recognizes them in himself. Nicola Piovani's soulful adaptation of Nino Rota's original film score, which accompanies the Trevi Fountain scene rather than its original dialogue, underscores the melancholic effect.

In Intervista and other films, Mastroianni's characters call into question several traditional paradigms in the representation of masculinity and the cinema: (1) the immortality of phallic power; (2) the denial of the effects of time on the male body; and (3) the idea of life as a journey toward moral and spiritual fulfillment. His roles uncover the many tensions and conflicts involved in the aging process: between decline and redemption, between absence and presence, between outward decay and inner desire. In the case of Italian cinema, the idea of loss in the present and nostalgia for the past assumes a double meaning. The films under discussion—Tornatore's Everybody's Fine and Fellini's Ginger and Fred, both made during a period of decline in production in the Italian film industry, self-consciously address its waning in both popularity and prestige on a national and international stage. Aging masculinity in these films comes to symbolize loss on a personal as well as a national/cultural level.

Italian Cinema as Fossil

Everybody's Fine, in its portrait of an aging pensioner, is a film about loss on several different levels: the loss of the traditional Italian family structure, the loss of interpersonal relationships, a loss of spirituality, and, ultimately, a longing for the past glories of Italian cinema. In the post-war years, the typical Italian family, despite decreasing in size and being more "individualized" (that is, individual members carving their own identities for themselves), nevertheless remained interconnected, with the elderly predominantly cared for at home by a son or a daughter.[19] Furthermore, the elderly were often important economic contributors to the household. The solid pension system and the labor unions' dogged protection of workers, both old and young, strengthened the economic usefulness of the retired members of the family unit.[20] In recent years, however, this traditional structure has begun to change. Tensions have arisen between the generations, as more money is spent on the pension system than on any other sector of the welfare state.[21] In addition, the demands of greater economic development, including increasing patterns of internal migration, have resulted in the disintegration of the established family structure. As a result, more and more elderly are not being cared for at home by a son or a daughter.[22] This phenomenon is brought to light in Tornatore's film, which chronicles the travels of a Sicilian widower whose children are scattered all over Italy, and whose lives fail to include him.

The film tells the story of Matteo Scuro, a Sicilian pensioner whose five children never materialize for their annual summer visit to their hometown. Instead, Matteo takes it on himself to pay a surprise visit to each of them. The genesis of the film came while Tornatore was sitting in his usual restaurant in Rome, particularly despondent over the initial lack of success of *Nuovo Cinema Paradiso* (1988), his second feature film and first major release. There he saw an old man with a suitcase dining by himself. When he asked the waiter who the diner was, the waiter responded, "He seems to be someone who travels." Tornatore constructed the story of *Everybody's Fine* based on the image of this elderly, solitary traveler.[23] Rather than an expedition that unites the family and resolves geographic and emotional distance, this film ultimately reinforces the growing divide. Moreover, this journey at the end of life leads not to the promised moral and spiritual completion but, rather, to disillusionment and self-deception.

The image Tornatore presents of Italy as Matteo visits his children in its principle cities—Naples, Rome, Florence, Milan, and Turin—is much like the one Gianni Amelio would present one year later in his "road movie," *Il ladro di bambini* (Stolen Children, 1992): far from the idyllic, romantic settings of Merchant-Ivory's *A Room with a View* (1986), these Italies are crowded, polluted, mean-spirited, and decidedly lacking any form of compassion.[24] Tornatore stated that it was his intention to paint a portrait of Italians as "disillusioned and disenchanted," as souls caught in the limbo of Purgatory.[25] One scene in each city features Matteo lost in a crowd of people: in Naples at the university in a fruitless search for Alvaro; hitchhiking alone on the highway; the lone human face on a Roman bus caught in a major traffic jam; and amid the pollution of Milan's crowded sidewalks. These episodes are often shot in either extreme long or bird's-eye shots, with Matteo's physical distance from the camera mirroring his sense of isolation.

When asked at one point by a policeman, who has requested Matteo's identification papers, if he is Sicilian, Matteo responds: "E' grave?" This question can mean both "Is it a serious offense?" and "Is it serious?" as in a fatal illness. Sicily itself stands as an important leitmotif throughout the film. Matteo's isolation is indicative of Sicily's geographic and metaphoric positioning on Italy's margins (see chapter 3). Moreover, as it is seen as backward in comparison to the more industrialized North, it is, in a certain sense, perceived as a fossil, a relic of an older Italy, out of touch with the modern ways and resistant to change. Matteo's isolation from the fast-paced, technologically oriented world around him is indicative not only of generational shifts which have resulted in the segregation of the elderly from contemporary society but also of Sicily's marginalization as a vestige of a former era.

Throughout the film, however, Matteo hides his growing despondency under a mask of happiness. His joie de vivre, expressed through various exchanges with the strange cast of characters he meets during his journey, underscore both his naïveté and his persistence in believing that "everybody's fine." While these quips provide some much-needed comic relief to Matteo's disillusions and delusions, they are few and far between. Most human communication in the film is forced and deceitful. Matteo's children lie to him about their perceived failure to live up to their father's high expectations. Guglielmo is a timpanist in the symphony who fakes a European tour in order to avoid spending time with his father; Alvaro is employed at the university but, unbeknown to Matteo, a suicide; Norma is an operator rather than an executive at the Italian phone company who fakes a happy marriage; Tosca is an "actress" who in reality is a lingerie model and mother to an illegitimate son; and Canio is a regional undersecretary, rather than secretary, of the Communist Party. They take this deception to even greater heights, by conspiring not to inform Matteo of their brother Alvaro's death. The fact that each son and daughter has names evoking great characters of Italian opera—Matteo is a self-described "fanatic" of lyric opera—underscores the theatricalization of the reality in which Matteo lives.[26]

In the extra-familial sphere, conversation, particularly intergenerational, is almost non-existent, exposing the ever-growing gap between the old and the young in contemporary Italy. Caught in an increasingly egocentric world, Matteo must both seek out and initiate interpersonal exchange, and the result is often either incomprehensibility (as with the German tourist who takes his photo on the boat to the mainland), polite disinterest, or total rejection. Typical of his often desperate need for human contact are the interactions on his various train rides in which he passes around a photograph of his children dressed up as their operatic namesakes. These moments are often painful. Matteo frequently interrupts his fellow passengers' tranquility and does not know when to stop. The lone exception is when he encounters a group of pensioners on an organized vacation tour together, and discovers a distinct connection with one woman. Matteo accompanies them on their trip to a dreary, empty Rimini. Ironically, Matteo rejects the one person with whom he has a real connection in the entire film. The unnamed woman's truthfulness in acknowledging the loneliness of old age—she lives in a rest home, and her children do not even recognize her voice on the telephone anymore—is too much for the self-deceiving Matteo to bear. The telephone is an important symbol in the film: it functions as an ironic reinforcement of the lack of communication in the post-modern, technological age.[27]

The interlude with the pensioners concludes with one of many references to Italian cinema in the film: a homage to Rimini's famous resident Federico Fellini. Quoting from the opening dream sequence in *8½*, in which Guido is trapped in his car and those on the bus are unable to help him, Matteo says goodbye to the woman while the other pensioners stare at him from their bus, as if frozen in time.[28] An additional Fellinian touch is the sound of the wind and the leaves blowing all around, further emphasizing the dream-like atmosphere. Similarly, Matteo's entire journey, much like the structure of *8½* (see chapter 4), is consistently interrupted by dreams and visions of the past, as he imagines talking to his sons and daughters as children, uncorrupted by the constraints of modern society and still preserving their innocence. Rather than illuminating the protagonist's psyche, these visions serve to reinforce Matteo's growing dementia and approaching senility, as he often believes them to be real.

Fellini's specter hangs over the film in another scene: at the Trevi

34. Mastroianni as Matteo in Giuseppe Tornatore's *Everybody's Fine* (1990).
Courtesy of Photofest.

Fountain in Rome.[29] While in Rome, Matteo stands with a multitude of other tourists behind glass. They watch the workers who have drained the fountain sweep away the mounds of dead birds which, as they fly over the city, "lose their sense of orientation" and plunge to their death.[30] The image, while symbolic of Matteo's own fruitless journey, simultaneously cannot help but evoke for the viewer familiar with Mastroianni and the history of Italian cinema the Trevi Fountain scene in *La dolce vita* (see chapter 2), in which Marcello the journalist attempts to embrace an impulsive, sensual view of life embodied in Sylvia's invitation to join her in the revitalizing waters of the fountain. The implied contrast is between the youthful Mastroianni of over thirty years ago and the overly aged Matteo Scuro—Mastroianni wears thick glasses, false teeth, a completely white head of hair, and unflatteringly unfashionable clothes. Tornatore's film reinforces rather than negates the passage of time, compelling the spectator to confront rather than deny the effects of aging on the male body, a fact underscored by the presence of the dead birds. An actor who worked on this scene noted the profound sense of melancholy Mastroianni exuded during filming, recalling Ekberg's reaction to the same sequence in *Intervista*.[31]

For Matteo Scuro at the end of his literal and life journey, there is no moral transcendence or spiritual redemption. The audience learns, however, that self-deception has in fact been a way of life for Matteo. Many scenes, including the opening one, feature the protagonist's direct address to the camera, with Matteo ostensibly speaking to his wife Angela, whom the spectator neither sees nor hears. At the end of the film, the audience finally sees the object of his direct address: his wife, or rather her gravestone, as she is dead. Just as Matteo has been deceived by his children, Matteo has been deceiving both himself and the spectator throughout the film: about his wife, his children, and his own inevitable death. Clues to Matteo's ill-health appear throughout the film: his need to bring his pills "just in case," his being easily winded while dancing in Rimini, and his subsequent hospitalization near the end of the film, the only event which brings his family together. While in Rome, Matteo had had faith that the lost birds he saw flying over the Trevi Fountain would save themselves. In the end, that faith is lost, and the image of his wife's tombstone, as well as the knowledge of Alvaro's suicide, only serves to reinforce rather than mask his own impending demise. Much like the illusion of fireflies that his grandson created over Milan's cathedral, in a homage to an Italian film classic, Vittorio De Sica's *Miracolo a Milano* (Miracle in Milan, 1950), all that Matteo had believed to be true has turned out a lie, and his choice is either the painful acknowledgment of loss or the continuation of self-deception.

Fellini's *Ginger and Fred* also engages film history, with the nostalgic focus on American cinema of the 1930s, an era that has always held a special fascination for the director. The film recounts the reunion of Amelia Bonetti and Pippo Botticella, dance partners in the 1930s and 1940s under the stage name and style of Ginger (Rogers) and Fred (Astaire). They are invited to participate in the Christmas variety-show special, *Ed ecco a voi* (We are proud to present), thirty years after their last performance together. Originally, the project was envisioned as an episode for a television series starring Giulietta Masina, with additional installments to be directed by Michelangelo Antonioni, Franco Zefferelli, and others. When it became too costly, Alberto Grimaldi, one of many producers attached to the project, suggested that Fellini make it into a feature film, which he in turn would produce.[32] It was Masina who suggested Mastroianni to portray the aging, out-of-shape dancer. This time Fellini did not make Mastroianni lose the usual ten kilograms as he did before his other films. Instead, he thinned out and completely grayed his hair, leaving Mastroianni with the fear that it would never grow back (which it did); and he asked him tone down his dancing, so as to make it appear as if he was a mediocre dancer.[33] Mastroianni was in fact a talented musical performer, starring in, among

35. Fellini alters Mastroianni's appearance as Fred in *Ginger and Fred* (1987). From the author's private collection.

other shows, *Ciao, Rudy,* a musical based on the life of Rudolph Valentino. Mastroianni and others have noted how Fred resembled Fellini himself: his desire to "evade responsibility and maturity," or, in Mastroianni's own words "the swindler who knows how to get by, a big talker, presumed artist who is at bottom extremely fragile."[34] Masina as Amelia, by contrast, continues in her role as Fellini's projection of triumphant yet wounded innocence, from the child-woman Gelsomina in *La strada* (1954) and the likeable prostitute in *Le notti di Cabiria* (The Nights of Cabiria, 1956), to the frustrated and unfulfilled housewife in *Giulietta degli spiriti* (Juliet of the Spirits, 1966). In *Ginger and Fred,* Fellini examines the cinematic images of his most preferred actors as they grow old and as they come to reflect the director's own worries, fears, and denials of old age.[35] They are the Ginger Rogers and Fred Astaire that Hollywood never allowed the audience to see.

Millicent Marcus, in a recent essay on *Ginger and Fred,* observes how the film is in reality a meshing of two different story lines: the (never-acted-on) love story between Amelia and Pippo, and a meditation on the disingenuousness and the ultimate vacuity of the television industry and postmodern culture.[36] Fellini was never shy, nor did he ever waver, in his pronouncements on the depravity of television, despite appearing to bite the hand that fed him: in addition to *Fellini: A Director's Notebook* (for

NBC) and *The Clowns* (1972), he also directed several commercials in the 1980s, a form which receives particular criticism in this film.[37] Television, according to Fellini, is omnipresent in present-day Italy (rarely is there a scene in the film without a television set) and has lost its connection to Italian culture. The state-run television agency, RAI, which today still controls three television channels (RAI 1, RAI 2, and RAI 3), initially envisioned itself an instrument of cultural promotion from the largest cities to the smallest towns.[38] Fellini sees the medium as now catering to the audience's lowest common denominator. The variety show in which Amelia and Pippo participate, as opposed to drawing on its long tradition in Italian culture of songs, dances, and circus-like acts, has become a grotesque freak show, featuring a parade of convicts, transvestites, dancing dwarfs, look-a-likes, and psychics. The fact that the show takes place on Christmas Day comments on television's status as the new religion in contemporary Italian culture.[39]

For Marcus, this attack on television and postmodern culture intersects with the love story through the idea of hyperfilm, which she defines as "the unitary, ongoing creative project that links the artist's biography to his cinematic corpus at a relatively high level of abstraction and in which the author's life in filmmaking comes to coincide with the film of his life."[40] In Fellini's case, the director consistently "recycles" motifs from his own cinematic past: not only the circus and variety show motifs, but also the actors Masina, Mastroianni, and Franco Fabrizi, who plays the insipid host of *Ed ecco a voi* and who appeared most prominently in Fellini's *I vitelloni* (1953) and *Il bidone* (The Swindle, 1955). Hyperfilm's self-consciousness also references not only other Fellini films, but also the onscreen images of Mastroianni and Masina throughout their careers. The first appearance of Mastroianni in the film contrasts with the viewer's traditional expectations: he is disheveled, balding, and dirty, both hoarse and drunk. The images of the aging Mastroianni and Masina cannot help but recall their younger selves. Highly infused with a nostalgia for the innocence of the 1930s and 1940s, the film also mourns the passage of time with respect to these two actors and all that they came to represent for a national cinema now a fossil of its former self.

From its opening credits, *Ginger and Fred* expresses a yearning for a previous era, for a more provincial Italy and the "enchanted and seductive" image of a "free America, rich and happy," that Italians embraced through American films.[41] After the above-the-title credits for Grimaldi and Fellini, the film begins with a gradual fade to a still publicity photograph of Amelia and Pippo from their dance act with the film's title superimposed on it. The image of a young Mastroianni and Masina in matching tuxedos and top hats against the backdrop of a fake (presumably American) skyscraper-filled skyline, their legs raised in classic tap-dance mode and their faces lit up by enigmatic smiles, invokes Fellini's view of American popular culture in the Italian imaginary. The credits unfold to an overture of motifs from classic American songs from the 1930s, including "Tea for Two," "Cheek to Cheek," and "The Continental," as arranged by Nicola Piovani and to which Amelia and Pippo perform their dance routine. This mood immediately clashes with the chaotic sequence at the Rome train station, as Amelia descends into a cacophony of advertisements, billboards, promotions, television images, and, in a clear metaphoric commentary, garbage. Amelia herself is a relic from another era, wearing a tweed cape and matching suit, a red fedora hat, and white fur throw, and sporting a stylish luggage set. She is clearly a fish out of water as she awaits Pippo in the alienating, Antonioni-esque landscape of her antiseptic hotel room, complete with a fabulous view of the monstrously large television tower and piles of garbage outside the hotel's entrance. The hotel staff is more interested in watching the televised soccer game than in helping her get settled. When in her room, which features a large mirror, she looks at herself, first as she dances, then, with a somewhat disgusted face, as she attempts to lift up her sagging chin and smooth out her wrinkles, ultimately shaking her head and her hands in frustration at the effects of aging.

In this scene and in many others, Amelia contemplates her reflection in the mirror. This idea of the double appears throughout the film in the guise of the many look-a-likes who figure prominently in the variety-show broadcast as an indictment of television's preference for reproduction over authenticity.[42] For Amelia and Pippo, however, the mirror does not lie, whether they peer at themselves or at the other aging characters who serve as their metaphoric doubles: the moribund admiral who must be helped by two attendants in order to appear on the show; the seven oldest wind musicians whose total age adds up to 620; and the woman who has visited the renowned German plastic surgeon to have a series of eight-hour operations over a period of four months to alter her face. Whereas Amelia is clearly preoccupied with her aging image, constantly questioning her decision to make a spectacle out of herself "at her age," Pippo, as typical of the representation of aging masculinity in classical cinema, constantly denies his fears and anxieties by attempting to demonstrate his vitality: by lifting Amelia several times in succession as they rehearse their routine, and by making lewd jokes about his sexual potency and inventing dirty rhymes.

Fellini here unmasks the denial of aging masculinity, and nowhere is that better revealed than in the dance sequence Amelia and Pippo perform as Ginger and Fred during the televised variety show.[43] On stage, where the magic of spectacle can fabricate almost anything in the Fellinian world, the truth of the aging *inetto* is revealed. As Fred, Pippo forgets his steps, can't keep time to the music, gets a cramp, almost sneezes from a feather in Ginger's costume, and barely makes it through the routine, collapsing at its end. The sequence is composed of a mix of long, extreme long, and medium shots, which expose moments of real pathos, the most pathetic of which occurs midway during the act when Pippo falls while dancing solo. Pippo's gaff perfectly elucidates Pirandello's "feeling of the opposite." He is literally carried away by his own bravura as he attempts to show off during the solo. The audience's reaction is a mix of horrified gasps and amused laughter. Like Pirandello's old lady who attempts to mask the effects of age, Pippo's masquerade ultimately proves illusory. What is so innovative and significant about this scene, which did not appear in the original treatment for the television episode,[44] is that it is aging masculinity, rather than femininity, which becomes the spectacle. Just as in his previous films, Fellini allows the older Mastroianni to address his own fears and anxieties about masculinity, rather than deny them (see chapter 4). Here, as in Tornatore's *Everybody's Fine*, it is about an aging male who, as fossil of both his former self and of an Italy past, nostalgically evokes a period of film history to present a postmodern culture dominated by a superficial rather than an authentic visual medium. The film's final scene at the train station, where Amelia leaves Pippo as she returns to her life running the family business and attending to her grandchildren, attests to this distance: Pippo calls to Amelia as the train whistle "blows," but unlike Ginger who runs into Fred's arms, Amelia shrugs and walks off. In Fellini's cinematic world, there is no happy ending for the aging man.

I Don't Want to Talk about It and *Used People:* Problematizing the Hollywood Paradigm

In classic Hollywood cinema, the older woman, when present at all, has come to be seen as a reflection of male fears of aging. For the older male actor, by contrast, films mask the effects of aging by romantically pairing him with a much younger woman. Such is the case, as Chris Holmund has argued, with Clint Eastwood, an iconic symbol of American male sexuality. An examination of Eastwood's long and prolific career both in front of and behind the camera exposes how Hollywood masks male aging in order to legitimize white male power and potency, both sexual and otherwise. Eastwood's couplings are most often with

36. Ginger (Giulietta Masina) and Fred in their big performance.
From the author's private collection.

younger women such as Renee Russo in *In the Line of Fire* (1993). When co-starring with middle-aged women, such as Meryl Streep in *The Bridges of Madison County* (1995), as the famously seductive photographer Robert Kincaid, he leaves no doubt as to his sexual prowess, reinforced through onscreen performance.[45]

Mastroianni's career choices consistently challenged those models, engaging, to paraphrase Hearn, the "ambiguities between social meaning (i.e., men = power) and the physical aging body."[46] Even the films in which he appears with younger women, Alberto Lattuada's *Così come sei* (Stay As You Are, 1979) and Francesca Archibugi's *Verso sera* (Toward Evening, 1991), challenge the masking of aging via the younger woman. In Lattuada's film, Nastassja Kinski plays Francesca, a sexually confident twenty-year-old woman who is attracted to her dead mother's former lover, the married architect Giulio (Mastroianni). When Giulio learns that Francesca may be his daughter, he is torn between his own lust and the taboo of incest, as well as his own relationship with his troubled, pregnant teenage daughter. Giulio's difficulty in dealing with both young women's liberated ideas on female sexuality and social mores serves to undermine rather than glorify the image of the sexual, older male. In *Verso sera*, Mastroianni's rigid, old-fashioned retired professor

37. Giulio (Mastroianni) falls in love with the much younger Francesca
(Nastassja Kinski) in Alberto Lattuada's *Stay As You Are* (1979).
From the author's private collection.

(Ludovico) becomes caregiver to his granddaughter Papere and, soon, to
his attractive daughter-in-law Stella. Generational conflict between the
old political left and the new leads to sexual tension, with no happy
resolution, sexual or otherwise: Stella and Papere leave, and the eventually happy chaos they had brought to his neatly compartmentalized life
disappears.

I Don't Want to Talk about It, the sixth and final feature film in the
all-too-short career of the Argentinian filmmaker María Luisa Bemberg
(1922–95), further complicates the older man/younger woman paradigm by injecting an element of magical realism into the equation.
Born into a prominent and wealthy Argentinian family, Bemberg came
to the film world late in life. She began making documentaries about the
Argentinian women's movement and initiated her career in feature films
as a scriptwriter. Always concerned with gender issues, she has written
and directed films about famous and infamous women: *Camila* (1984) is
based on the true story of Camila O'Gorman, who was executed in
1848 for eloping with her priest lover, and *Yo, la peor de todas* (I, Worst
of All, 1990) recounts the life of Sor Juana Inés de la Cruz. An Italian-
Argentinian co-production, *I Don't Want to Talk about It* narrates the

story of Doña Leonor Bacigalupo (Luisina Brando), a fiercely over-protective mother to Carlota/Charlotte, an *enana* (a dwarf, played by Alejandra Podestà) in a provincial Argentinian town during the 1930s or 1940s, judging by the characters' fashions. As Charlotte grows up educated at home in arts and letters, Ludovico D'Andrea (Mastroianni), a Venetian of mysterious origin, realizes that he is in love with her, and asks Doña Leonor for Charlotte's hand in marriage. The whole town celebrates the nuptials, despite the fact that the mayor dies during the festivities, and soon d'Andrea becomes mayor of the town. One day, Doña Leonor hears the circus approach and begs d'Andrea not to let Charlotte see it. Charlotte, however, sneaks off in the night, and the next morning leaves with the other circus dwarfs, riding the white horse on which she sat when Ludovico first realized his passion for her. Doña Leonor, her worst fears manifested, closes herself in her home, never, as the voice-over recounts, to show her face again.

The film is in many ways emblematic of Bemberg's cinematic opus, as it deals with questions of power and its authoritarian abuse, with Doña Leonor as, in Bemberg's own words, a metaphor for repression and intolerance.[47] Doña Leonor's incongruous laugh at Charlotte's wedding to Ludovico, as she watches the couple proceed down the aisle, represents the release of repression that overwhelms the story. Charlotte's condition, the subject that "one does not talk about"—the correct English translation of the title—is laid bare for all to see. Rather than an ironic Pirandellian "feeling of the opposite," Doña Leonor's laugh divulges her to be the one person in the town for whom Charlotte's identity was completely defined by her condition and who could ultimately not accept her difference.[48]

Bemberg and Jorge Goldenberg, her co-screenwriter, take many liberties in their adaptation of Julio Llinás's short story for the screen. Doña Leonor, a decidedly more humanized character in the film, supposedly had a one-night stand with a visiting circus dwarf (hence, in the film, a more personal reason to fear the circus). The white horse is a significant addition to the story, as both symbol of Charlotte's inner spirit and an image of freedom in contrast to the stifling repression of the provincial town. Two significant changes affected the character of Ludovico in the transformation from page to screen image: in the story he is around fifty years old, while in the film he looks decidedly older (no effort was made to mask the effects of age on the Mastroianni's almost seventy-year-old body). In addition, the filmmakers added several scenes in a brothel, where Ludovico and other men go to satisfy their repressed sexual urges.[49] Jason Wilson sees how the brothel serves to differentiate Ludovico's carnal sexuality from his attraction to and passion for Charlotte. In the film it also solidifies the fact that, even as an old man, Ludovico can perform sexually, and, as the shot of the prostitutes' weeping at the wedding suggest, perform magnificently. In another testament to Ludovico's appeal, the other women in the town, including Doña Leonor, revel in his worldly charm, as when he sings a love song accompanied by Charlotte on the piano during one of their many evening soirées. Doña Leonor even mistakenly believes that Ludovico, when he asks for a private meeting with her, is going to ask for her hand in marriage, not Charlotte's. Thus his marriage to Charlotte is not a masquerade of sexual inadequacy, for his sexual urges, and his sexual appeal, are real.

Like Charlotte, Ludovico, from his first appearance on screen, appears as somewhat different himself. The sequence involves Ludovico getting dressed to go out. The care with which he shaves, puts on his cravat and his jacket, and perfumes himself references Mastroianni's image as the Latin lover in the importance of making a *bella figura*, as well as the importance of appearances for the townspeople. Before leaving, however, Ludovico adds one odd accessory: his pet monkey, which sits calmly on his shoulder as they prepare to exit his home. The scene is filmed in a sepia-toned haziness with infusions of bright, natural light entering from the windows, in contrast with the sharp, bright colors of the town's exteriors. The voice-over narration adds an additional note of magical realism, in citing that no one knows for sure exactly when he settled in the town, and local gossip thought him to be a spy, a political refugee, or an eccentric millionaire. The future is foreshadowed by the sequence's final image: a shot of a bust of a white circus horse, similar to the one on which he would see Charlotte and fall under her spell. In that scene, as he watches Charlotte ride, Ludovico is overcome by his own sexual urges, a change once again signaled by the lighting: both he and Charlotte are infused with a deep blue hue, which, like the slow-motion image of the galloping horse, reinforces the profound and magical effect of this image on Ludovico. His urges send him first to drink and then to sexual gratification: when his preferred prostitute Myrna is not available, he takes instead the brothel's head mistress, whom he ravages on top of the pool table. Unable to deny his passion, he returns after a long absence, accepting his desire for Charlotte. His longing for the younger woman is configured, in the tradition of Latin American magical realism, as both absurd and normal, real and surreal: absurd and surreal in its departure from normalcy, but yet normal and real because of the genuine feelings which motivate it. When placed within the context of Mastroianni's opus, Bemberg's film is consistent with the actor's challenges of traditional representations of masculinity.

Infused with a romantic nostalgia from its sepia-toned opening credits, Beeban Kidron's *Used People* (1992), by contrast, both conforms to and rebels against the various representational paradigms in Hollywood's images of aging. Cast as the wildly romantic Joe Meledandri, who has harbored a secret love for Pearl Berman (Shirley MacLaine) for twenty-three years, Mastroianni's character, like Ludovico, evokes the cultural construction of the Latin lover, but with a twist: he is now old. Joe had met Pearl's husband Jack (Bob Dishy) twenty-three years ago at his bar, on the night that Jack was about to abandon his family. Joe convinces him to return to his wife, and when he follows Jack home and sees Pearl in the window, he immediately falls in love. A man respectful of family, Joe waits over two decades until Jack dies, when he appears at Jack's funeral to ask Pearl out on a date. Reluctant but nevertheless intrigued, Pearl vacillates between her own desire and mourning propriety. The love story is framed against the backdrop of Pearl's troubled relationship with her two daughters, Bibby (Kathy Bates), an overweight divorcee searching for her own identity, and Norma (Marcia Gay Harden), a woman so distraught over the loss of her baby from Sudden Infant Death Syndrome that she assumes the persona of others—Barbara Streisand, Anne Bancroft in *The Graduate*—to mask her own pain. Norma's son Sweet Pea, reacting to his mother's crisis and the death of his beloved grandfather, takes on his own neurosis: he is convinced that his grandfather's angel protects him from harm, and consistently puts himself in dangerous situations as a test. The film's conclusion, which culminates in Joe and Pearl's wedding, resolves many of the characters' conflicts with each other: Bibby returns from California and makes peace with Pearl, and Norma and Sweet Pea vow to heal their wounds together.

Used People treats the issue of an older man's sexuality, albeit from a lighthearted point of view, without resorting to the traditional mechanisms of rejuvenation by legitimating his sexual attraction with a younger woman. Nor does it negate older women's sexuality, by acknowledging Pearl's sexual dissatisfaction in her previous marriage and her search for fulfillment in her next. Moreover, it reverses a pattern that Jean Kozlowski refers to as the "Sousatzka-ing" of older actresses in Hollywood cinema. The term references a previous Shirley MacLaine role as the eccentric piano teacher Madame Sousatzka in the eponymous film directed by John Schlesinger (1988). Kozlowski contends that as traditional, romantic lead actresses pass into middle age, they are relegated to character roles, as menopause signals the end of their "productivity":

"their 'Sophie's choice' is between fading into early retirement or accepting unglamorous, eccentric, prematurely elderly roles (which, gen-
erally unflattering, are in turn insulting to real-life elderly women)."[50]
In traditional Hollywood film, leading men are not "neutralized" in
this fashion—Kozlowski cites MacLaine's brother, Warren Beatty, as
a prototypical example—for their fertility is not age-designated, and
"pairing him with a woman who's his equal in terms of life experience
is tantamount to holding up a mirror to reveal his own mortality" (10).
MacLaine was fifty-eight when *Used People* was released, which contrasted with Mastroianni's sixty-eight at the time, a relatively negligible
age difference by Hollywood standards.

If any character can be labeled a Sousatzka, it is Mastroianni's Joe.
But, rather than pejoratively coding his eccentricities as old-age oddi-
ties, they serve to revitalize him, playing off Mastroianni's Latin lover
image despite his age. This recourse to star persona comes as no surprise, since Mastroianni's image in the United States has always been
tied to the Latin lover mystique (see chapter 2). From his first onscreen
appearance, as he emerges at Jack's funeral to ask Pearl out to coffee, he
is marked by a magical romanticism. Much as in *I Don't Want to Talk
about It*, Mastroianni's character is well-groomed: he appears at the
door fashionably dressed in an elegant brown tweed suit and dapper hat,
setting him apart from the dourly dressed funeral crowd. On their first
"date," Joe explains to Pearl that he helped save her marriage by teaching her husband how to dance, "to breath new life into an empty heart."
A flashback shows Joe teaching Jack exactly how to dance with her: he
takes Jack's hand and they dance cheek to cheek. Completely coded as
heterosexual, this scene reveals how Joe resembles the first Latin lover
Rudolph Valentino's woman-made-man and the role dance played in his
persona (see chapter 2). As the man who knows what women want, Joe
instructs Jack on how to romance his way back into Pearl's heart. Joe's
own persistence in pursuing Pearl involves waiting under her window
for three weeks, and composing and singing a song he wrote for her, all
things typically associated with Italian culture. He spouts quotes from
Shakespeare and Octavio Paz, recounts his many foreign travels and
speaks to Pearl in both French and Italian, bringing the mystique of
internationality to Pearl's sheltered life. He literally sweeps her off her
feet in the middle of a wading pool in front of her family and friends,
magically weakening her resolve to preserve a proper sense of mourning
decorum.

Mastroianni, whom the screenwriter Todd Graff had in mind when
he wrote the role of Joe, took on his first American screen appearance
because of the actresses with whom he would appear: MacLaine, Jessica

38. Mastroianni, ever
stylish, as Joe Meledandri
in *Used People* (1992).
From the author's private
collection.

Tandy, who plays Pearl's octogenarian mother Freida, and Sylvia Sydney
as her best friend Becky. Clearly in Souzatzka roles themselves—they
spend much of their screen time bickering over money, arguing over
silly subjects like whether one can freeze Tupperware, or trying to best
one another with their various physical ailments—they also serve, as is
typical of the aged female in Hollywood cinema, as the projections of
the male anxiety of aging, for only they are forced to confront those
very issues. Concerned about where they will live out the rest of their
lives, they debate between moving to Florida or settling into the nearby
Deepdale nursing home. The home itself is presented as a futuristic,
antiseptic modern structure, complete with mobile walkways, stark-
white minimalist bathrooms, artificial trees (as opposed to Freida's visions of Florida's real ones), and empty, alienating hallways. Freida
comes face to face with her own mortality when she happens upon a
water rehabilitation room and a group of wheelchair-bound elderly taking a rudimentary French lesson. Freida's visit to Deepdale becomes a
life lesson for Pearl, when the mother tells the daughter not to wait until
she's eighty "to realize how precious life is," and encourages her to shun
propriety and marry Joe. Thus, Pearl, the middle-aged woman, is saved

39. Freida (Jessica Tandy,
standing) and Becky (Sylvia
Sidney, *seated*) bear the
burden of aging in *Used
People*. From the author's
private collection.

from the anxieties of aging and is free to develop herself sexually, while
Freida and Sylvia assume the burden of age. Yet, even the representation
of Pearl's sexuality is decidedly tame: she wants to sleep with Joe before
they are married not because she wants to, as Joe's brother Paolo assumes, "check out the merchandise," but to see if she can sleep com-
fortably with him. They spend their first night together buried under
the covers rather than making passionate love. The representation of
middle-age sexuality in Hollywood cinema still has its limits.

Clearly modeled on the more successful *Moonstruck* (1988)—one
promotional photograph has all the main characters gathered around a
moon with the New York skyline underneath—*Used People*, while seeming a departure from the older man/younger woman paradigm, still resorts to the traditional representation of aging in Hollywood cinema. In
its reliance on the stereotypes of the Latin lover and Italian and Jewish
cultures, it seals its romantic ending with the marriage kiss. The message is, like *Moonstruck*, that romance cures all ills, and that yes, it may
find you in middle age, but still with the price of the aging woman, as
opposed to the aging man, being encumbered with the sole duty of confronting mortality on screen. In Mastroianni's last two films, Manoel

40. Joe and Pearl (Shirley MacLaine) find romance. From the author's private collection.

de Oliveira's *Viagem ao princípio do mundo* (Voyage to the Beginning of the World, 1997), and Anna Maria Tatò's *Marcello Mastroianni: Mi ricordo, sì io mi ricordo* (Marcello Mastroianni: I Remember, Yes, I Remember, 1997), that is precisely what the actor does. These films also serve as a fitting conclusion to this study. Released after the actor's death, both films self-referentially and silently tackle the issue of death in relation to memory, nostalgia, and the film medium itself.

Conclusion
*Cinema, Memory, and a Voyage
at the End of Life's Journey*

Marcello Mastroianni's last two films—Manoel de Oliveira's *Viagem ao
princípio do mundo* (Voyage to the Beginning of the World, 1997), and
Anna Maria Tatò's *Marcello Mastroianni: Mi ricordo, sì io mi ricordo*
(Marcello Mastroianni: I Remember, Yes, I Remember, 1997)—both contain abundant images of travel. One is fashioned by an aging director—
de Oliveira was eighty-eight when he made the film—and one self-
fashioned by an aging actor—the original title of the film was *Autoritratto,*
meaning self-portrait.[1] They are thematically and iconographically unified in their use of cinema as a way of remembering the past and of
pointing to the certain and all-too-proximate future. The former has as
its premise an aging director, Manoel (Mastroianni), and his return to
the land of his youth, and, perhaps not so coincidentally, the birthplace
of the Portuguese nation. Joining him on his journey are three actors
from the film he is presently shooting, one of whom, Afonso (Jean-Yves
Gautier), will be reunited with the aunt he has never met. Much of the
film takes place in the car that takes them to their various destinations
and features reoccurring tracking shots of the landscape: as the characters explore their various stops, and out of the rear and side windows of
the moving car. *I Remember,* a documentary about the actor's career, was
shot while Mastroianni was filming *Voyage,* and the surrounding landscape plays a significant role in that film's iconology as well. The appearance of these moving shots cinematically reinforces a major theme
that runs through both films: the idea of life as a journey which is now
coming to an end. When Mastroianni made these films, he was dying
of pancreatic cancer. In keeping with his reluctance to create a physical

165

façade of youthfulness in his previous films, Mastroianni does not hide the effects of the illness on his body. The difference between his appearance on screen only one year before in such films as *Trois vies & une seule mort* (Three Lives and Only One Death, 1996) and *Sostiene Pereira* (Pereira Declares, 1996), is drastic: he is gaunt, ash-toned, extremely thin, and either sitting or walking with a cane, what Manoel refers to as the "deterioration of the wrapping," in the film's opening dialogue. This dialectic between sound mind—what one of his traveling companions, the attractive actress Judite (Leonor Silveira), calls his "penetrating wit" and "gift for analysis"—and deteriorating body is explicitly thematicized from the film's opening sequence.

The film revolves around the concept of memory: memories of Manoel's past, Afonso's memories of his difficult father, and the latter's aunt's memories of her brother. De Oliveira, a Portuguese director who has made most of his recent films in French, interjects two important terms into their discussions: the French verb *souvenir*—literally the act of remembering and recalling as opposed to the function of the brain (*mémoire*) and memorizing (*mémoriser*)—and the Portuguese *saudade*. *Saudade* is akin to the concept of nostalgia, perhaps best defined as a nostalgic longing for something that is lost, or something in the past. It is a melancholy feeling, but one that also enables you to keep on living through an intolerable present.[2] The souvenir in its English meaning—defined by the Oxford English Dictionary online as a "remembrance," "a memory," "a slight trace of something," or "a token of remembrance"—while already integral to the representation of aging on screen, takes on additional meaning in the context of these two films. Cinema functions as a mirror of the present and the past, presence and absence, and life and death. Manoel as incarnated by Mastroianni appears as cinematic alter ego to de Oliveira: the aging director confronting his life and his imminent death. In this case, it is a two-way mirror, a fact underscored by the conflation of settings between *Voyage* and *I Remember.* Just as de Oliveira faces his aging reflection in the former, Mastroianni in *I Remember* constantly evokes memories of his younger self. The film translates words into images, with the presence of the souvenir as Jodi Brooks defines it in film clips and stills of Mastroianni as a much younger man (see chapter 6). The older Mastroianni, like Manoel, is a fossil of his former self.

In *I Remember,* Mastroianni recounts the memories of his youth, his experiences with particular directors (Fellini, Monicelli, Ferreri), and his work in the theater, among other topics. The film's structure reinforces the disjunctive nature of memory—the film reads as a series of disconnected sequences evoking different episodes in Mastroianni's

41. Mastroianni talks about his life in *Marcello Mastroianni: I Remember,
Yes, I Remember* (1997). Courtesy of Photofest.

life and career. Interspersed between these remembrances are extended
film clips of some of his more famous roles, such as Professor Sinigaglia
in Monicelli's *The Organizer* (1963), as well as some rare clips from Elio
Petri's *Todo Modo* (1976) and a number from the musical *Ciao, Rudy.*
Although intended primarily as a celebration of the actor's life and career, included in these images are two sequences that cannot help but
evoke his death, as the film was released posthumously: a view into
Mastroianni's apartment in Paris, and his seventy-second—and last—
birthday celebration. The first sequence, which appears in a section of
the film devoted to his favorite cities, Rome and Paris, consists of a series of fifteen shots, beginning with the Eiffel Tower and interconnected by dissolve transitions, of Mastroianni and Tatò's well-appointed
Paris penthouse apartment. On the soundtrack is a musical love duet
sung by Mastroianni and Monica Vitti from Ettore Scola's 1970 film
Dramma di gelosia—Tutti i particolari in cronaca (Drama of Jealousy—
All the Details in the News), another rarely seen film highlighted several times in the documentary. What is striking about the images is the
way in which they capture life and death. The abundant plants and flow-
ers, as well as photographs and "souvenirs" of Mastroianni's past, contrast with the lack of human presence in the apartment: it is at the same
time full and empty, alive in the present but a relic of the past, like the
ruins of the Grand Hotel that Manoel visits in *Voyage.* The birthday
party sequence, one of the few non-film clips to actually feature others
besides Mastroianni in front of the camera (and the only actual shot of

Tatò in the film), shares much of the same contradictory tone as the shots of the Paris apartment. While it is a celebration of the actor's life, a fact clear from the actor's modest glee during the festivities, at the same time it cannot but help but invoke death, since Mastroianni, as the spectator would know, died less than three months later.

The film concludes with Mastroianni citing Franz Kafka's short story "The Next Village," in which the journey between two towns serves as a metaphor for life and death. In *I Remember,* Mastroianni reflects on the brevity of his voyage: how life goes by so fast, and that the next village is in fact "so close." Much as *Voyage* invokes the beginning of one journey (of Afonso and his reunited family) and the end of another (the impending death of the director), *I Remember* commemorates the journey itself, rather than its ending. What is lacking from these films is any kind of sentiment of spiritual and moral redemption in old age. Decidedly materialist in their outlook, both films negate the traditional Catholic ideal of the afterlife, instead preferring memory as embodied in the immortality of the cinematic image against the inevitable expedition to the end of the world.

In *I Remember,* Mastroianni alludes to a role he always wanted to play—Tarzan as an old man:

> Why not? A funny film but with a melancholic tone, because it's the drama of the problems of the "third age," of this gentle hero about whom nobody speaks anymore. Today, heroes are those with machine guns, kicks in the groin, shots in the mouth. And Tarzan —no one cares about him anymore. . . . I would have liked to have made a film like this one, a little bit crazy. But in reality it's not really too, too crazy.[3]

The choice of Tarzan is a revealing one, for it encapsulates the argument put forth in this study, perhaps better than any other concluding remarks. Tarzan, as a hero, represents, in many ways, the consummate twentieth-century *inetto:* unable to assimilate into civilized society, he chooses a primitive life away from the alienating confines of the modern world. Like Mastroianni's various incarnations of the *inetto*—the impotent man, the cuckold, and the unruly woman's victim, among others— the aging Tarzan is in conflict with representational norms for cinematic masculinity. The fact that Mastroianni wanted to play him not in the prime of his youth but rather as an old man is consistent with many of the roles for which the Italian actor was famous. Marcello, Guido, Antonio, and others do not conform to but rather evoke, challenge, and problematize traditional constructs of post-war Italian masculinity and the male body across a wide variety of genres and national cinemas. So much of the suave, sexy image of Italian masculinity depended on visual representation—in fashion, in design, and in the movies. The image of an elderly, poorly dressed Tarzan, like Mastroianni's characters in Federico Fellini's films, would bare the artificiality of that construction. One could even imagine this film directed by Fellini and the humorous approach he might take, playing off against the Mastroianni star image to parody his own insecurities and anxieties.

The possibilities are endless, but unfortunately Mastroianni was unable to bring them to fruition. The legacy he left, however, is a rich and varied one, and this study has only scratched the surface of his cinematic production. What is clear, however, is that the image of Italian masculinity he presented on screen is a complex and contradictory one, one that differentiates between classical post-war Italian cinema and its representation of gender and the dominant Hollywood model. Mastroianni's many onscreen incarnations challenged those paradigms, particularly that of the Latin lover, by turning the lens on itself, self-consciously exposing the reality behind the myth and through humor laughing at it outright.

Notes

──────────

Introduction

1. Valerio Marchetti, "Fissazioni e transizioni," in *Genere e mascolinità: Uno sguardo storico,* ed. Sandro Bellassai and Maria Malatesta (Rome: Bulzoni, 2000), 89–129, here 89–91.

2. *Genere: La costruzione sociale del femminile e del maschile,* ed. Simonetta Piccone Stella and Chiara Saraceno (Bologna: Il Mulino, 1996).

3. David D. Gilmore, *Manhood in the Making: Cultural Concepts of Masculinity* (New Haven, Conn.: Yale University Press, 1990).

4. Some noteworthy contributions include Aaron Baker and Juliann Vitullo, "Screening the Italian-American Male," in *Masculinities: Bodies, Movies, Culture,* ed. Peter Lehman (New York: Routledge, 2001), 213–26; Fred Gardaphè, "Italian American Manhood," in *American Masculinities: A Historical Encyclopedia,* ed. Bret Carroll (New York: The Moschovitis Group, 2003); Gigliola Gori, "Model of Masculinity: Mussolini, the 'New Italian' of the Fascist Era," *International Journal of the History of Sport* 16, no. 4 (1999): 27–61; Jeff Hearn et al., "Critical Studies on Men in Ten European Countries: (1). The State of Academic Research," *Men and Masculinities* 4, no. 4 (Apr. 2002): 380–408; Michel Huysseune, "Masculinity and Secessionism in Italy: An Assessment," *Nations and Nationalisms* 6, no. 4 (Oct. 2000): 591–610; Marcia Landy, *Italian Film* (Cambridge: Cambridge University Press, 2000), 309–43; Marina deBellagente LaPalma, "Meditations on Masculinity: *Accattone* and *Midnight Cowboy,*" *Italian Culture* 10 (1992): 217–25; George L. Mosse, *The Image of Man: The Creation of Modern Masculinity* (New York: Oxford University Press, 1998); Ellen Nerenberg, "Tartar Control: Masculinity and *Impegno* in Buzzati's *Il deserto dei tartari,*" *Italica* 74, no. 2 (Summer 1997): 217–34; and Barbara

171

Spackman, *Fascist Virilities: Rhetoric, Ideology, and Social Fantasy in Italy* (Minneapolis: University of Minnesota Press, 1996).

5. Donald Dewey, *Marcello Mastroianni: His Life and Art* (New York: Birch Lane, 1993).

6. Michel Foucault, *The History of Sexuality, Volume I: An Introduction* (New York: Vintage Books, 1978); David Halperin, *One Hundred Years of Homosexuality and Other Essays on Greek Love* (New York: Routledge, 1990), 9; and George L. Mosse, *Nationalism and Sexuality: Respectability and Abnormal Sexuality in Modern Europe* (New York: Howard Fertig, 1985).

7. Kathleen Rowe, *The Unruly Woman: Gender and the Genre of Laughter* (Austin: University of Texas Press, 1995).

8. Manuela Gieri, *Contemporary Italian Filmmaking: Strategies of Subversion —Pirandello, Fellini, Scola, and the Directors of the New Generation* (Toronto: University of Toronto Press, 1995).

1. In the Beginning

1. Marcello Mastroianni, *Mi ricordo, sì, io mi ricordo*, ed. Francesco Tatò (Milan: Baldini and Castoldi, 1997), 57. All translations in the text are mine unless otherwise noted.

2. Gilmore, *Manhood in the Making*, 30–36.

3. Gloria Nardini, *Che Bella Figura! The Power of Performance in an Italian Ladies' Club in Chicago* (Albany: SUNY Press, 1999), 15. Although Nardini focuses on women in her analysis of the *bella figura* in Italian-American culture, the *bella figura* is a phenomenon which crosses gender lines.

4. Baldassare Castiglione, *The Book of the Courtier*, trans. Charles Singleton (Garden City, N.Y.: Anchor, 1959), 44 (Book 26).

5. Harry Berger, Jr., in his recent work on *sprezzatura*, sees it as a learned behavior, and one that reveals an anxiety or, rather, a performance anxiety, which masks the vulnerability of the threat of disempowerment. *Sprezzatura* is thus "a source and sign of manly inner strength rather than effeminacy." Harry Berger, Jr., *The Absence of Grace: Sprezzatura and Suspicion in Two Renaissance Courtesy Books* (Stanford, Calif.: Stanford University Press, 2000), 11.

6. Niccolò Machiavelli, *The Prince*, trans. Peter Bondanella and Mark Musa (Oxford: Oxford University Press, 1979), 59–60. All further citations will appear in the text.

7. For Ellen Moers, "the ideal of the dandy is cut in cloth. . . . His independence, assurance, originality, self-control and refinement should all be visible in the cut of his clothes." Ellen Moers, *The Dandy: Brummell to Beerbohm* (Lincoln: University of Nebraska Press, 1960), 21. See also Joanne Finkelstein, *The Fashioned Self* (Philadelphia: Temple University Press, 1991), 113–14.

8. Giuliana Bruno, *Streetwalking on a Ruined Map: Cultural Theory and the City Films of Elvira Notari* (Princeton, N.J.: Princeton University Press, 1993), 43–48.

9. Keith Tester, "Introduction," and Bruce Mazlish, "The *Flâneur:* From Spectator to Representation," in *The Flâneur,* ed. Keith Tester (London: Routledge, 1994), 1–21, 43–60.

10. Rhonda K. Garelick, *Rising Star: Dandyism, Gender and Performance in the Fin de Siècle* (Princeton, N.J.: Princeton University Press, 1998).

11. Donald Pitkin notes how Italians, as opposed to their more European counterparts, have privileged and idealized the urban over the rural space, and that that very public space has been "domesticated," thus blurring the distinction between public and private. Donald S. Pitkin, "Italian Urbanscape: Intersection of Private and Public," in *The Cultural Meaning of Urban Space,* ed. Robert Rotenberg and Gary McDonogh (Westport, Conn.: Bergin and Garvey, 1993), 95–101.

12. Kaja Silverman, *Male Subjectivity at the Margins* (New York: Routledge, 1993), 42–48. Peter Lehman argues that the representation of the penis is itself filled with anxiety for men. "Crying Over the Melodramatic Penis: Melodrama and Male Nudity in the Films of the 90s," in *Masculinities: Bodies, Movies, Culture,* ed. Peter Lehman (New York: Routledge, 2001), 25–41, here 27.

13. David D. Gilmore, "Introduction: The Shame of Dishonor," in *Honor and Shame and the Unity of the Mediterranean,* ed. David D. Gilmore (Washington, D.C.: American Anthropological Association, 1987), 16–17.

14. This is not unique to the Italian situation. There are, in fact, a number of cultures with which Italy shares this phenomenon. Gilmore's work alone reflects fieldwork done in Africa, East and Southeast Asia, and Brazil, among other places. With respect to effeminacy, Gilmore finds similarities in Mediterranean, Jewish, and Indian cultures. *Manhood in the Making,* 11–12, 127–28, 183–84. Stanley Brandes's work reveals how male sexual ideology betrays a powerlessness at the root of Spanish masculinity in the face of the feminine. Stanley Brandes, "Like Wounded Stags: Male Sexual Ideology in an Andalusian Town," in *Sexual Meanings: The Cultural Construction of Gender and Sexuality,* ed. Sherry B. Ortner and Harriet Whitehead (Cambridge: Cambridge University Press, 1981), 216–39, and *Metaphors of Masculinity: Sex and Status in Andalusian Folklore* (Philadelphia: University of Pennsylvania Press, 1985).

15. Lee Edelman, "Minding the Body: Queer Theory in the Flesh," lecture delivered at SUNY at Stony Brook, November 18, 1998.

16. Gilmore, "Introduction: The Shame of Dishonor," 10–13.

17. Pinsker relies on the *Universal Jewish Encyclopedia* for his precise definition of the *schlemiel.* Sanford Pinsker, *The Schlemiel as Metaphor: Studies in Yiddish and American Jewish Fiction,* rev. and enlarged ed. (Carbondale: Southern Illinois University Press, 1991), 2.

18. Gian Paolo Biasin, *Montale, Debussy, and Modernism* (Princeton, N.J.: Princeton University Press, 1989), 69–107.

19. Italo Svevo, *La coscienza di Zeno* (Milan: Dall'Oglio, 1976 [1923]), 479. Translated as *The Confessions of Zeno*, trans. Beryl de Zoete (New York: Alfred A. Knopf, 1930), 410.

20. Flaminio Scala, *Scenarios of the Commedia dell'arte: Flaminio Scala's Il teatro delle favole rappresentative*, trans. Henry F. Salerno (New York: Limelight, 1989), 47–54. See also Robert Erenstein, "The Humour of the *Commedia dell'arte*," in *The Commedia dell'arte from the Renaissance to Dario Fo*, ed. Christopher Cairns (Lewiston, Me.: Mellen Press, 1988), 118–40.

21. Luigi Pirandello, *L'umorismo* (Milan: Mondadori, 1986), 105–12, 129–68. It is interesting to note that Pirandello, at the end of his essay, cites the *schlemiel* as one of the precursors of the humoristic character.

22. Luigi Pirandello, *Il fu Mattia Pascal* (Milan: Mondadori, 1933 [1904]), 133.

23. Biasin, *Montale, Debussy, and Modernism*, 78.

24. Christopher Lasch, *The Culture of Narcissism: American Life in an Age of Diminishing Expectations*, 2nd ed. (New York: W. W. Norton, 1991), 10, 36–38, 50–51; Freud, "On Narcissism: An Introduction," *Standard Edition of the Complete Psychological Works of Sigmund Freud*, Vol. 14 (London: Hogarth Press, 1963), 73–102; and Otto Kernberg, *Borderline Conditions and Pathological Narcissism* (New York: Jason Aronson, 1975). A good summary of narcissism and its relation to cinema can be found in Glen Gabbard and Krin Gabbard, *Psychiatry and the Cinema*, 2nd ed. (Washington, D.C.: American Psychiatric Press, 1999), 233–75.

25. Freud's concept of innate bisexuality of the human subject lies at the crux of Dennis Bingham's work on stardom and masculinity. For Bingham, the deconstruction of the masculine persona reveals "man's identification with his repressed femininity." Dennis Bingham, *Acting Male: Masculinities in the Films of James Stewart, Jack Nicholson, and Clint Eastwood* (New Brunswick, N.J.: Rutgers University Press, 1994), 9.

26. The following overview is an extremely brief and schematic analysis into Italian film history. Certainly, a much more in-depth study is needed on the representation of masculinity in Italian cinema. My project, while focusing only on the cinematic production of Mastroianni, aims to address some of these issues and provoke further discussion.

27. Mosse, *The Image of Man*, in particular, 5–7, 45, 50, 52–53.

28. Other figures in the Strong Man cycle include Sansone, played by Luciano Albertini; Aiax (Carlo Aldini); and in one case a woman, Astrea. Gian Piero Brunetta, *Storia del cinema italiano*, 4 vols. (Rome: Riuniti, 1993), vol. I, pp. 317–20.

29. Richard Dyer, *White* (London: Routledge, 1998), 164–65. The series continued in the late 1950s and 1960s with the popularity of the peplum film, historical epics featuring ancient musclemen such as Hercules in various situations designed to show off the sculpted male body.

30. Piero Meldini, *Sposa e madre esemplare: Ideologia e politica della donna e della famiglia durante il fascismo* (Rimini-Firenze: Guaraldi, 1975), 35–39.

31. As Alexander De Grand notes, "The regime was quick to use the conservative influence of the church to support its economic and social policies and the Vatican seized its opportunity to condition the ideology of the Fascist state." De Grand, "Women under Italian Fascism," *Historical Journal* 19, no. 4 (1976): 956–57. See also Lucia Chiavola-Birnbaum, *Liberazione della donna: Feminism in Italy* (Middletown, Conn.: Wesleyan University Press, 1986), 34–37.

32. Cited in Elisabetta Mondello, *La nuova italiana: La donna nella stampa e nella cultura del ventennio* (Rome: Riuniti, 1987), 27.

33. Tracy H. Koon, *Believe, Obey, Fight: Political Socialization of Youth in Fascist Italy* (Chapel Hill: University of North Carolina Press, 1985), 16.

34. For more on male sexuality during Fascism, see Mosse, *Nationalism and Sexuality*, 156–57; and Barbara Spackman, "The Fascist Rhetoric of Virility," *Stanford Italian Review* 8, no. 1–2 (1990): 81–101. For a related study of Nazism and masculinity, consult Klaus Theweleit, *Male Fantasies, Volume I: Women, Floods, Bodies, History*, trans. Steven Conway et al. (Minneapolis: University of Minnesota Press, 1987).

35. Gori, "Model of Masculinity."

36. For an example of how cultural production rebelled against these dominant masculine and feminine constructions, see Carole Gallucci, "Alba de Céspedes's *There's No Turning Back*: Challenging the New Woman's Future," in *Mothers of Invention: Women, Italian Fascism, and Culture*, ed. Robin Pickering-Iazzi (Minneapolis: University of Minnesota Press, 1995), 200–19; Nerenberg, "Tartar Control," 217–34; Robin Pickering-Iazzi, *Politics of the Visible: Writing Women, Culture, and Fascism* (Minneapolis: University of Minnesota Press, 1997); and Jacqueline Reich, "Reading, Writing, and Rebellion: Collectivity, Specularity, and Sexuality in the Italian Schoolgirl Comedy, 1934–43," in *Mothers of Invention: Women, Italian Fascism, Culture*, ed. Robin Pickering-Iazzi (Minneapolis: University of Minnesota Press, 1995), 220–51.

37. Liliana Elena's work also has focused on the plurality of representations of masculinity in the cinema of the Fascist era, looking at the variations in different film genres. Liliana Elena, "Mascolinità e immaginario nazionale nel cinema italiano negli anni trenta," in *Genere e mascolinità: Uno sguardo storico*, ed. Sandro Bellassai and Maria Malatesta (Rome: Bulzoni, 2000), 243–64.

38. Mino Argentieri, *Risate di regime: La commedia italiana, 1930–1944* (Venezia: Marsilio, 1991); Gian Piero Brunetta, *Cinema italiano fra le due guerre* (Milan: Mursia, 1975); David Forgacs, *Italian Culture in the Industrial Era, 1880–1980: Cultural Industries, Politics and the Public* (Manchester: Manchester University Press, 1990); Jean Gili, *Stato fascista e cinematografia: Repressione e promozione* (Rome: Bulzoni, 1981); James Hay, *Popular Film*

Culture in Fascist Italy: The Passing of the Rex (Bloomington: Indiana University Press, 1986); Marcia Landy, *The Folklore of Consensus: Theatricality in Italian Cinema, 1930–1943* (Albany: SUNY Press, 1998); *Re-viewing Fascism: Italian Cinema, 1922–1943,* ed. Jacqueline Reich and Piero Garofalo (Bloomington: Indiana University Press, 2002); and Francesco Savio, *Ma l'amore no: Realismo, formalismo, propaganda e telefoni bianchi nel cinema italiano di regime (1930–43)* (Milan: Sonzogno, 1975).

39. Landy, *Folklore of Consensus,* 140–60, 170–71. Other films in this genre include Augusta Genina's *Squadrone bianco* (White Squadron, 1936), and Goffredo Alessandrini's *Luciano Serra, pilota* (Luciano Serra, Pilot, 1938).

40. Cited in Gianfranco Casadio, *Il grigio e il nero: Spettacolo e propaganda nel cinema italiano degli anni trenta (1931–1943)* (Ravenna: Longo, 1989), 104.

41. Paul Ginsborg, *A History of Contemporary Italy: Society and Politics, 1943–1988* (London: Penguin, 1990), 72–120.

42. Terri Ginsburg, "Nazis and Drifters: The Containment of Radical (Sexual) Knowledge in Two Italian Neorealist Films," *Journal of the History of Sexuality* 1, no. 2 (Oct. 1990): 241–61.

43. Millicent Marcus, *Italian Film in the Light of Neorealism* (Princeton, N.J.: Princeton University Press, 1986), 60–61.

44. Films in this series include Carlo Ludovico Bragaglia's *Totò cerca moglie* (Totò Searches for a Wife, 1950) and Camillo Mastrocinque's *Totò all'inferno* (Totò in Hell, 1954), among many others.

45. Brunetta, *Storia del cinema italiano,* vol. III, pp. 592–93.

46. Rowe, *The Unruly Woman.*

47. Peter Bondanella, *Italian Cinema from Neorealism to the Present,* 3rd ed. (New York: Continuum, 2001), 145. These films, through the mask of laughter, were often but not always able to escape the Andreotti censorship laws that discouraged the blatant social criticism of many neorealist dramas.

48. As quoted in *Comedy, Italian Style: 1950–1980,* ed. Adriano Aprà and Patrizia Pistagnesi (Torino: Edizioni Rai, 1986), 66.

49. Manuela Gieri notes the affinities between Fellini's various *vitellone* characters and Pirandello's Mattia Pascal, particularly in light of both the director's and the author's reliance on the serio-comic, or the "humoristic" in portraying modern male subjectivity. Gieri, *Contemporary Italian Filmmaking,* 125.

50. A few episodes from "Moraldo" survive in *La dolce vita:* notably, the visit of Marcello's father, as well as, more indirectly, the figure of Steiner. Franca Faldini and Goffredo Fofi, *L'avventurosa storia del cinema italiano raccontato dai suoi protagonisti 1960–1969* (Milan: Feltrinelli, 1981), 3–4. Dino de Laurentiis, the first producer associated with the film, originally wanted Paul Newman to play the role of Moraldo/Marcello.

51. Bingham, *Acting Male;* Steven Cohan, *Masked Men: Masculinity and the*

Movies in the Fifties (Bloomington: Indiana University Press, 1997); Richard de Cordova, *Picture Personalities: The Emergence of the Star System in America* (Urbana: University of Illinois Press, 1990); Chris Holmund, *Impossible Bodies: Femininity and Masculinity at the Movies* (London: Routledge, 2002); Paul Smith, *Clint Eastwood: A Cultural Production* (Minneapolis: University of Minnesota Press, 1993); Gaylyn Studlar, *This Mad Masquerade: Stardom and Masculinity in the Jazz Age* (New York: Columbia University Press, 1996); and Sharon Willis, *High Contrast: Race and Gender in Contemporary Hollywood Film* (Durham, N.C.: Duke University Press, 1997).

52. Richard Dyer, *Heavenly Bodies: Film Stars and Society* (New York: St. Martin's Press, 1986), 17. See also Dyer's *Stars*, new ed. (London: British Film Institute, 1998).

53. Studlar, *This Mad Masquerade*, 6–7.

54. Brunetta, *Storia del cinema italiano*, vol. III, pp. 247–63; and Vittorio Spinazzola, *Cinema e pubblico: Lo spettacolo filmico in Italia 1945–1965* (Rome: Bulzoni, 1985), 304–17. Stephen Gundle has written on the cultural significance of the beauty contest for post-war Italy, not only in terms of how the new national popular culture came to be written on the female body but also how the contests themselves reflected the political struggle for power between the Catholics and the Communists. Stephen Gundle, "Feminine Beauty, National Identity and Political Conflict in Postwar Italy, 1945–1954," *Contemporary European History* 8, no. 3 (1999): 359–78.

55. Stephen Gundle, "Fame, Fashion and Style: The Italian Star System," in *Italian Cultural Studies: An Introduction*, ed. David Forgacs and Robert Lumley (Oxford: Oxford University Press, 1996), 309–26.

56. Mastroianni, *Mi ricordo*, 22–23.

57. Gideon Bachmann, "Marcello Mastroianni and the Game of Truth," *Film Quarterly* 46 (Winter 1992–93): 2–7.

58. Gundle, "Fame, Fashion and Style," 312.

59. Alan Cowell, "Thousands of Italian Mourners File in Homage Past Fellini Bier," *New York Times* (November 3, 1993): D24; John Tagliabue, "Crowds in Rome Bid Farewell to Mastroianni, Artist of Film," *New York Times* (December 23, 1996): B11.

60. Dyer, *Heavenly Bodies*, 18.

61. Daniel Golden, "Pasta or Paradigm: The Place of Italian-American Women in Popular Film," *Explorations in Ethnic Studies: The Journal of the National Association of Interdisciplinary Ethnic Studies* (1978): 3–10; Giovanna Grignaffini, "Female Identity and Italian Cinema of the 1950s," in *Off-Screen: Women and Film in Italy*, ed. Giuliana Bruno and Maria Nadotti (London: Routledge, 1988), 111–23.

62. Brunetta, *Storia del cinema italiano*, vol. III, pp. 139–41. Similarly, Patrizia Carrano takes the position that Mastroianni represents the summa of Italian masculinity's defects. Patrizia Carrano, "Divismo," in *Schermi ed om-*

bre: Gli italiani e il cinema del dopoguerra, ed. Marino Livolsi (Firenze: La Nuova Italia, 1988), 229–47, here 241. Marcia Landy integrates the idea of performative masculinity into her assessment of Mastroianni's legacy. Landy, *Italian Film,* 331–34.

2. Undressing the Latin Lover

1. Mastroianni, *Mi ricordo,* 135.

2. Tullio Kezich, *Su La dolce vita di Federico Fellini: Giorno per giorno, la storia di un film che ha fatto epoca* (Venezia: Marsilio, 1996), 25. This is an updated edition of the journal Kezich kept during the making of the film, first published as *La dolce vita* (Capelli, 1960). For an excellent discussion of the film in light of these issues, see Stephen Gundle, "*La dolce vita,*" *History Today* (Jan. 2000): 29–35.

3. Mastroianni, *Mi ricordo,* 61–62.

4. Beverly Allen, introduction to *Revisioning Italy: National Identity and Global Culture,* ed. Beverly Allen and Mary Russo (Minneapolis: University of Minnesota Press, 1997), 3; John Dickie, "Imagined Italy," in *Italian Cultural Studies: An Introduction,* ed. David Forgacs and Robert Lumley (Oxford: Oxford University Press, 1996), 19–33.

5. John Agnew, "The Myth of Backward Italy in Modern Europe," in *Revisioning Italy: National Identity and Global Culture,* ed. Beverly Allen and Mary Russo (Minneapolis: University of Minnesota Press, 1997), 23–42.

6. Giannino Malossi, "Introduction: The Banality of the Latin Lover," in *Latin Lover: The Passionate South,* ed. Giannino Malossi (Milan: Charta, 1996), 19–24, here 24.

7. Basing their ideas on Judith Butler's analysis of the performative aspects of gender, Dennis Bingham (through a more psychoanalytic approach, focusing on the instability of male sexuality) and Steven Cohan (through a more materialist examination of the masquerades of 1950s normative masculinity) have foregrounded the way the film text self-consciously masks but nonetheless reveals the fragile nature of male identity. Bingham, *Acting Male;* and Cohan, *Masked Men.*

8. Luigi Settembrini, "The Passionate South: Holiday Fun," in *Latin Lover: The Passionate South,* ed. Giannino Malossi (Milan: Charta, 1996), 66.

9. Angelica Forti-Lewis, *Maschere, libretti e libertini: Il mito di Don Giovanni nel teatro europeo* (Rome: Bulzoni, 1992), 11–31.

10. Studlar, *This Mad Masquerade,* 150–98.

11. Alberto Panaro, "Mass-produced Valentinos: Rudolph Valentino's Doubles," in *Latin Lover: The Passionate South,* ed. Giannino Malossi (Milan: Charta, 1996), 95–113.

12. Luis Reyes and Peter Rubie, *Hispanics in Hollywood: An Encyclopedia of Film and Television* (New York: Garland, 1994), 9.

13. Ana M. López, "Are All Latins from Manhattan? Hollywood, Ethnography, and Cultural Colonialism," in *Unspeakable Images: Ethnicity and the Cinema*, ed. Lester Friedman (Urbana: University of Illinois Press, 1991), 404–24, here 409.

14. Reyes and Rubie, *Hispanics in Hollywood*, 430.

15. Ana M. López, "Of Rhythms and Borders," in *Everynight Life: Culture and Dance in Latin/o America*, ed. Celeste Frasier Delgado and José Esteban Muñoz (Durham, N.C.: Duke University Press, 1997), 310–44, here 315–17.

16. Chon A. Noriega, "Internal 'Others': Hollywood Narratives about Mexican Americans," in *Mediating Two Worlds: Cinematic Encounters in the Americas*, ed. John King et al. (London: British Film Institute, 1993), 52–66, here 61.

17. Even though Ava Gardner's character was Spanish in *The Barefoot Contessa*, her Hollywood glamour image was so ingrained in American popular culture that her "Americanness" was never in doubt, despite her admirable try at producing a Spanish lilt to her English.

18. Settembrini, "The Passionate South," 68. One article in *Life* notes that after the release of *Three Coins in the Fountain*, Brazzi received forty thousand love letters from American women. "Brazzi as a Heavy Lover," *Life* 39, no. 4 (July 25, 1955): 57.

19. Panaro, "Mass-produced Valentinos," 95–113, here 110.

20. Dewey, *Marcello Mastroianni*, 142–46.

21. On fashion and the Latin lover, see Carlo Romano, "Anarchy Hurt the Latin Lover: Fantasy, Decline and Eternal Fascination of the Latin Lover," in *Latin Lover: The Passionate South*, ed. Giannino Malossi (Milan: Charta, 1996), 60–63.

22. Allan Ellenberger, *Ramon Novarro: A Biography of the Silent Film Idol, 1899–1968* (Jefferson, N.C.: McFarland, 1999), 35.

23. "A Titre de Revanche: Rossano Brazzi conjure le mauvais sort en faisant à Hollywood une rentrée en beauté," *Cine Revue* (Aug. 1957), published in the original and in translation at The Rossano Brazzi International Network website, <http://www.neponset.com/brazzi/party.htm>. Accessed June 19, 2003.

24. Mastroianni, *Mi ricordo*, 61.

25. Vittorio Gassman, *Un grande avvenire dietro le spalle* (Milan: Longanesi, 1981), 85. Gassman's Hollywood filmography included a Mexican in *Sombrero* (Norman Foster, 1953), a non-specified European violinist in *Rhapsody* (Charles Vidor, 1954), and an Italian in *Mambo* (Robert Rossen, 1954), with his then-estranged wife Shelley Winters (their battles on the set were notorious). Gassman never adapted to the Hollywood way of life, especially the studio system: "[I had] the impression of being operated like a puppet, condemned to being a Valentino or not working at all" (*Un grande avvenire*, 109). He was originally offered the Rossano Brazzi part in *Three*

Coins in the Fountain, but by that time he was so sick of Hollywood that he begged Dino de Laurentiis and Carlo Ponti to cast him in *War and Peace* (King Vidor, 1956), to be shot in Italy.

26. Ginsborg, *History of Contemporary Italy,* 210–53; Michele Salvati, *Economia e politica in Italia dal dopoguerra a oggi* (Milan: Garzanti, 1984), 47–62; and Donald Sassoon, *Contemporary Italy: Economy, Society and Politics since 1945,* 2nd ed. (London: Longman, 1997), 26–41.

27. Penny Sparke has noted that the success of Italy's electrical domestic appliances and modern furniture designs was due to the fact that they were aimed at the bourgeois markets both at home and abroad. "'A Home for Everybody?': Design, Ideology and the Culture of the Home in Italy, 1945–1972," in *Culture and Conflict in Postwar Italy: Essays on Mass and Popular Culture,* ed. Zygmunt Baranski and Robert Lumley (London: Macmillan, 1990): 225–41.

28. David Forgacs, "Cultural Consumption, 1940s to 1990s," in *Italian Cultural Studies: An Introduction,* ed. David Forgacs and Robert Lumley (Oxford: Oxford University Press, 1996), 273–90.

29. Natalia Aspesi, *Il lusso e l'autarchia: Storia dell'eleganza italiana 1930–1944* (Milan: Rizzoli, 1982).

30. Ornella Morelli, "The International Success and Domestic Debut of Postwar Italian Fashion," in *Italian Fashion: The Origins of High Fashion and Knitwear,* ed. Gloria Bianchino et al. (Milan: Electa, 1985), 58–65.

31. Luigi Settembrini, "From Haute-Couture to Prêt-à-Porter," in *The Italian Metamorphosis, 1943–1968,* ed. Germano Celant (New York: Guggenheim Museum, 1994), 484–94.

32. Gloria Bianchino, *Italian Fashion Designing/Disegno della moda italiana 1945–1980,* with a translation by Bonizza Giordani Aragno (CSAC dell'Università di Parma, 1987), 20. Federica di Castro notes that Italian designers modified the new look to the peculiarities of the typical Italian female body, narrowing the width of the skirt to minimize wider hips. Federica di Castro, "Italian High Fashion," in *Italian Fashion: The Origins of High Fashion and Knitwear,* ed. Gloria Bianchino et al. (Milan: Electa, 1985), 212–25.

33. Morelli, "International Success," 60–62.

34. Beverly Allen, "The Novel, the Body, and Giorgio Armani: Rethinking National 'Identity' in a Postnational World," in *Feminine Feminists: Cultural Practices in Italy,* ed. Giovanna Miceli Jeffries (Minneapolis: University of Minnesota Press, 1994), 153–70.

35. Settembrini, "From Haute-Couture to Prêt-à-Porter," 485–87; Valerie Steele, "Italian Fashion and America," in *The Italian Metamorphosis, 1943–1968,* ed. Germano Celant (New York: Guggenheim Museum, 1994), 496–506.

36. Di Castro, "Italian High Fashion," 212–16.

37. Luigi Settembrini, "La regola estrosa: Cent'anni di eleganza maschile," in *La regola estrosa: Cent'anni di eleganza maschile italiana*, ed. Giannino Malossi (Milan: Electa, 1993), 13–33; Colin McDowell, *The Man of Fashion: Peacock Males and Perfect Gentlemen* (London: Thames and Hudson, 1997), 94–95, 137–40; Farid Chenoune, *A History of Men's Fashion*, translated by Deke Dusinberre, preface by Richard Martin (Paris: Flammarion, 1993), 241–50; and Farid Chenoune, *Brioni* (New York: Universe, 1998).

38. Steele, "Italian Fashion and America," 503. Cohan devotes an entire chapter to the gray flannel suit as both symbol and representation in *Masked Men*, 1–33.

39. Giorgio Triani, "Love Affairs in Romagna: The Sociology of Beach Boys," in *Latin Lover: The Passionate South*, ed. Giannino Malossi (Milan: Charta, 1996), 136–47.

40. Giuliano Accordi, "The Soundtrack of Seduction: The Latin Lover in Italian Songs," in *Latin Lover: The Passionate South*, ed. Giannino Malossi (Milan: Charta, 1996), 124–32.

41. Chenoune, *A History of Men's Fashion*, 241–50.

42. J. C. Flugel, *The Psychology of Clothes* (London: Hogarth, 1930), 110–13; Jennifer Craik, *The Face of Fashion: Cultural Studies in Fashion* (London: Routledge, 1994), 176–203, in particular 197.

43. Ted Polhemus, *Street Style: From Catwalk to Sidewalk* (New York: Thames and Hudson, 1994), 45.

44. Giannino Malossi, "La bella figura: Gli italiani e l'eleganza," in *La regola estrosa: Cent'anni di eleganza maschile*, ed. Giannino Malossi (Milan: Electa, 1993), 37–42.

45. Anne Hollander, *Sex and Suits* (New York: Knopf, 1995), 63–113.

46. Stella Bruzzi, *Undressing Cinema: Clothing and Identity in the Movies* (London: Routledge, 1997), 67–94.

47. Isabella Pezzini examines the idea of fashion as a mask of virility in terms of homosexuality in "L'ideologia virile e le sue trasgressioni: il dandy, il rebelle," in *Virilità e trasgressione* (Novara: Istituto Geografico De Agostini, 1992), 9–25.

48. As cited in Peter Bondanella, *The Cinema of Federico Fellini* (Princeton, N.J.: Princeton University Press, 1993), 134.

49. Arturo Carlo Quintavalle, "Fashion: The Three Cultures," in *Italian Fashion: The Origins of High Fashion and Knitwear*, ed. Gloria Bianchino et al. (Milan: Electa, 1985), 21–25.

50. Roberto Campari, "Film and Fashion," in *Italian Fashion: The Origins of High Fashion and Knitwear*, ed. Gloria Bianchino et al. (Milan: Electa, 1985), 198–211.

51. Chenoune, *Brioni*, 13.

52. *The Barefoot Contessa* also features a cameo by Enzo Staiola, Bruno of *The Bicycle Thief* fame, as a bus boy in the restaurant where Ava Gardner dances.

53. P. Adams Sitney also notes that while Fellini eschewed a political meaning to his films, *La dolce vita* nonetheless reflects the political climate of the late 1950s, in which the majority Christian Democrats formed an alliance with the neo-Fascist MSI (Movimento socialista italiano) in order to maintain their power. The result was a political climate which fed on scandal and violence, fueled by the growth of yellow journalism and, as it came to be known, after *La dolce vita*, the *paparazzi*, many of whom actually appear in the film. P. Adams Sitney, *Vital Crises in Italian Cinema* (Austin: University of Texas Press, 1995), 109–10.

54. There has been some dispute as to the origins of the term *paparazzo* in reference to its use in *La dolce vita*. According to the *Dizionario etimologico della lingua italiana* (Bologna: Zanicelli, 1985: 873–74), Fellini was reading George Gissing's *By the Ionian Sea* (1901), translated into Italian by Margherita Guidacci in 1957. In this memoir, the author describes a pleasant stay at a Catanzaro hotel owned by Coriolano Paparazzo. Fellini apparently liked the onomatopoeic flow of the last name. Ennio Flaiano corroborates this theory in *The Via Veneto Papers*, trans. John Satriano (Marlboro, Vt.: Marlboro Press, 1992), 10. I would like to thank Lori Repetti for her help in this etymological research.

55. Bondanella, *The Cinema of Federico Fellini*, 137–38; *Conversations with Fellini*, ed. Costanzo Costantini, trans. Sohrab Sorooshian (San Diego: Harvest, 1995), 58–59; *Fellini on Fellini*, trans. Isabel Quigley (New York: Delacorte, 1976), 75–81; Federico Fellini, *Comments on Film*, ed. Giovanni Grazzini, trans. Joseph Henry (Fresno: California State University Press, 1988), 131–39.

56. *Fellini on Fellini*, 67.

57. Sparke, "A Home for Everybody?" 230; see also Stephen Gundle, "From Neo-Realism to *Luci Rosse:* Cinema, Politics and Society, 1945–85," in *Culture and Conflict in Postwar Italy: Essays on Mass and Popular Culture,* ed. Zymunt Baranski and Robert Lumley (London: Macmillan, 1990), 195–224.

58. Bondanella, *The Cinema of Federico Fellini*, 143–44.

59. Barbara K. Lewalski, "Federico Fellini's Purgatorio," in *Federico Fellini: Essays in Criticism*, ed. Peter Bondanella (Oxford: Oxford University Press, 1978), 113–20, here 114.

60. Brunetta, *Storia del cinema italiano*, vol. III, pp. 514–16.

61. John Welle, "Fellini's Use of Dante in *La dolce vita*," *Studies in Medievalism* 2, no. 3 (Summer 1983), 53–66. For another essay which deals with the influence of Dante on *La dolce vita*, see Lewalski, "Federico Fellini's Purgatorio," 113–20.

62. Marcello's passivity and state of impotence has not gone unnoticed by critics. Frank Burke notes the character's inability to change throughout the film, which results in a creative negation, as opposed to the life-affirming ideology of Fellini's *Le notti di Cabiria* (The Nights of Cabiria,

1957). Frank Burke, *Fellini's Films: From Postwar to Postmodern* (New York: Twayne, 1996), 98–103.

63. Tester, introduction to The *Flâneur*, ed. Tester, 7, 14.

64. Stephen Neale, "Masculinity as Spectacle," in *Screening the Male: Exploring Masculinities in Hollywood Cinema*, ed. Steven Cohan and Ina Rae Hark (London: Routledge, 1993), 9–20.

65. Bondanella, *The Cinema of Federico Fellini*, 147. Sitney views this scene and others throughout the film as parodies of Catholic rites of passage. *Vital Crises*, 115–16.

66. Kezich, *Su* La dolce vita, 137.

67. Kezich, *Su* La dolce vita, 95.

68. The film was extremely well received critically, despite some mixed reviews in *Time* and *Newsweek*. *Time* (Apr. 21, 1961); *Newsweek* (Apr. 24, 1961).

69. National Legion of Decency Separate Classification, May 25, 1961. For a more detailed discussion, see James M. Skinner, *The Cross and the Cinema: The Legion of Decency and the National Catholic Office for Motion Pictures, 1933–1970* (Westport, Conn.: Praeger, 1993), 134–38.

70. *Details* magazine interview with Mastroianni (Nov. 1994), 100.

71. Craik, *The Face of Fashion*, 203.

72. Faldini and Fofi, *L'avventurosa storia del cinema italiano*, 17.

3. Masculinity, Sicilian Style

1. Sebastiano Aglianò, *Che cos'è questa Sicilia?* Introduction by Marzio Mazzara (Palermo: Sellerio, 1996). The study was first published in 1945.

2. Bondanella, *Italian Cinema from Neorealism to the Present*, 142–95. Three additional 1960s films, Fellini's *8½* (1963) and Mastroianni's two comedies with Sophia Loren directed by Vittorio De Sica—*Ieri, oggi e domani* (Yesterday, Today, and Tomorrow, 1963) and *Matrimonio all'italiana* (Marriage —Italian Style, 1964)—will be discussed in subsequent chapters, for they are best interpreted in light of the actor's collaborations with Fellini and Loren, respectively.

3. Leonardo Sciascia, *Nero su nero* (Torino: Einaudi, 1979), 141–44, here 143.

4. In a recent article, Michel Huysseune argues that in terms of political rhetoric, the South is feminized in comparison to the more masculine North. He traces this discourse from the nineteenth-century Lombrosian school of thought as embodied in the work of Alfredo Niceforo. The masculine North/feminine South has found its most recent incarnation in the secessionist position of the Lega Nord (the Northern League) and its founder Umberto Bossi. Huysseune, "Masculinity and Secessionism in Italy," 591–610.

5. Pasquale Verdicchio has argued that Northern Italy's relationship to Southern Italy could be construed as colonial in nature. "The Preclusion of Post-

colonial Discourse in Southern Italy," in *Revisioning Italy: National Identity and Global Culture,* ed. Beverly Allen and Mary Russo (Minneapolis: University of Minnnesota Press, 1997), 191-212, here 191.

6. The authors define cultural codes not as "quaint manifestations of stable and remote rural-agrarian past" but, rather, as "products of forces set in motion by core area expansion in the past" with the idea that "cultural codes are fashioned collectively by people who are responding to their changing natural and political environments." Jane Schneider and Peter Schneider, *Culture and Political Economy in Western Sicily* (New York: Academic Press, 1976), 2, 81-82.

7. Anton Blok, "Rams and Billy-Goats: A Key to the Mediterranean Code of Honor," *Man* 16, no. 3 (Nov. 1981): 427-40, here 432-33.

8. Constance Cronin, "Illusion and Reality in Sicily," in *Sexual Stratification: A Cross-Cultural View,* ed. Alice Schlegel (New York: Columbia University Press, 1977), 67-93, here 74.

9. Julian Pitt-Rivers defines honor in the Mediterranean context as "the value of a person in his own eyes, but also in the eyes of his society. It is his estimation of his own worth, his *claim* to pride, but it is also the acknowledgement of that claim, his excellence recognized by society, his *right* to pride." Julian Pitt-Rivers, "Honour and Social Status," in *Honour and Shame: The Values of Mediterranean Society,* ed. J. G. Peristiany (Chicago: University of Chicago Press, 1966), 19-77, here 21. The italics are those of the author.

10. Schneider and Schneider, *Culture and Political Economy,* 96.

11. Maureen J. Giovannini, "Female Chastity Codes in the Circum-Mediterranean: Comparative Perspectives," in *Honor and Shame and the Unity of the Mediterranean,* ed. David D. Gilmore (Washington, D.C.: American Anthropological Association, 1987), 61-74, here 67.

12. Maureen J. Giovannini, "Woman: A Dominant Symbol within the Cultural System of a Sicilian Town," *Man: The Journal of the Royal Anthropological Institute* 16, no. 3 (Nov. 1981): 408-26, here 409. All further citations will appear directly in the text.

13. Vitaliano Brancati, "Piaceri del gallismo," *Il tempo* (July 12, 1946), republished in *Il borghese e l'immensità: Scritti 1930-1954,* ed. Sandro de Feo and G. A. Cibotto (Milan: Bompiani, 1973), 148-51.

14. Vitaliano Brancati, *Diario romano,* ed. Sandro de Feo and G. A. Cibotto (Milan: Bompiani, 1961), 79.

15. Gilmore, *Manhood in the Making,* 40-41.

16. Aglianò, *Che cos'è questa Sicilia?* 127.

17. Vitaliano Brancati, *Don Giovanni in Sicilia* (Milan: Bompiani, 1999), 29. The novel was first published in 1941.

18. Leonardo Sciascia, "Don Giovanni a Catania," reprinted as the introduction to the 1999 edition of Brancati's *Don Giovanni in Sicilia.*

19. Aglianò, *Che cos'è questa Sicilia?* 49–50.

20. Landy, *Folklore of Consensus,* 169–236.

21. Millicent Marcus, *Filmmaking by the Book: Italian Cinema and Literary Adaptation* (Baltimore, Md.: Johns Hopkins University Press, 1993), 1–11. Marcus further elucidates the complex relationship between literature and film on a theoretical level, exploring the traditional interpretive dichotomies of story and discourse. She comes to the conclusion that "Literature and film cease to be fixed monolithic entities locked in eternal combat like the personified abstractions of a Psychomachia and reveal themselves instead to be fluid constellations of codes, subject to many of the same intertextual influences and ideological constraints" (22).

22. Vitaliano Brancati, *Il bell'Antonio* (Milan: Bompiani, 1965), 12–13. All further citations will appear directly in the text.

23. Vitaliano Brancati, *I fascisti invecchiano,* in *Opere 1932–1946,* ed. Leonardo Sciascia (Milan: Bompiani, 1987), 1135.

24. This view is supported by Tullio Kezich in his essay "Dalla pagina allo schermo," in Il bell'Antonio *di Mauro Bolognini: Dal romanzo al film,* ed. Lino Miccichè (Torino: Lindau, 1996), 73–76, here 75.

25. Gian Piero Brunetta, "Literature and the Cinema in the Works of Mauro Bolognini," in *Bolognini,* ed. Ministero degli Affari Esteri (Rome: Istituto Poligrafico dello Stato, 1977), 101–103.

26. Bolognini has said that he wanted to show how much of the mentality of the Fascist period regarding virility had remained pervasive some fifteen years later. Faldini and Fofi, *L'avventurosa storia del cinema italiano,* 164.

27. Bruno Torri, "*Il bell'Antonio* di Mauro Bolognini," and Vito Zagarrio, "La regia," in Il bell'Antonio *di Mauro Bolognini: Dal romanzo al film,* ed. Lino Miccichè (Torino: Lindau, 1996), 57–61 and 63–68, respectively.

28. The interiors appear, according to Vito Zagarrio, as more in the vein of a cold and distant still-life painting. "La regia," 63.

29. Although Bolognini insinuates that his choice was Delon or some other good-looking French actor, other sources confirm that it was Charière, who withdrew at the last minute out of concern for his own virile image. Bolognini called Mastroianni on the Thursday before the planned Monday commencement of shooting. Faldini and Fofi, *L'avventurosa storia del cinema italiano,* 164.

30. Ibid., 164–65.

31. Aglianò, *Che cos'è questa Sicilia?* 130.

32. Ginsborg, *History of Contemporary Italy,* 216, 229–33.

33. Giuseppe Tomasi di Lampedusa, *Il gattopardo* (Milan: Feltrinelli, 1958), 21.

34. Torri, "*Il bell'Antonio* di Mauro Bolognini," 60.

35. Dyer, *Heavenly Bodies,* 7–8.

36. Dyer, *Stars,* 126.

37. Andrew Sarris, "Pietro Germi: Idealist with No Illusions," and Mario Sesti, "Pietro Germi: Life and Films of a Latin Loner," in *Pietro Germi: The Latin Loner,* ed. Mario Sesti (Milan: Edizioni Olivares, 1999), 19–21 and 22–64, here 46, respectively. Much of Sesti's essay is adapted from Mario Sesti, *Tutto il cinema di Pietro Germi* (Milan: Baldini and Castoldi, 1997).

38. Faldini and Fofi, *L'avventurosa storia del cinema italiano,* 128.

39. Mario Sesti analyzes this opening sequence as well, but from a more formalistic and narrative-centered as opposed to socio-political point of view. *Tutto il cinema di Pietro Germi,* 228–34.

40. The 1970 law, which was backed by a popular referendum four years later, provided the specific grounds for divorce in four distinct areas: (1) if one of the spouses was convicted of a serious crime; (2) if the couple was legally separated for five uninterrupted years; (3) if one spouse was a foreign citizen and had obtained a divorce abroad; and (4) in an echo of *Il bell'Antonio,* an unconsummated marriage. Giovanni B. Sgritta and Paolo Tufari, "Italy," in *Divorce in Europe,* ed. Robert Chester, with the collaboration of Gerrit Kooy (The Hague: Netherlands Interuniversity Demographic Institute, 1977), 253–81; Martin Clark, *Modern Italy, 1871–1991,* 2nd ed. (London: Longman, 1996), 282, 381; and Ginsborg, *History of Contemporary Italy,* 328.

41. Warren G. Harris, *Sophia Loren: A Biography* (New York: Simon and Schuster, 1998), 100–20, 204–24.

42. Schneider and Schneider, *Culture and Political Economy,* 101.

43. *Seduced and Abandoned* features a similar scene, but one much more graphic and brutal in its depiction of the obsession with female chastity codes in Sicilian daily life.

44. Ironically, Germi was reluctant to cast Mastroianni as the Barone, a role that Mastroianni deliberately sought out and campaigned for, even coming to his audition with head shots of himself made up as the Barone. Dewey, *Marcello Mastroianni,* 120–22.

45. Mastroianni also claims that the tic was used as a "counterpart to the tensest, most dramatic junctures of the story." Ibid., 121.

46. Sesti notes the combination of frenetic camera movements with traditional fixed editing. *Tutto il cinema di Pietro Germi,* 238.

47. Schneider and Schneider, *Culture and Political Economy,* 10.

4. "Remember, It's a Comedy"

1. Charlotte Chandler, *I, Fellini* (New York: Random House, 1995), 117.

2. Federico Fellini, *Un regista a Cinecittà* (Milan: Mondadori, 1988), 50.

3. Costanzo Costantini, *Marcello Mastroianni: Vita, amori e successi di un divo involontario* (Rome: Riuniti, 1996), 89. Similarly, Mastroianni has com-

mented that their relationship was based on a "total, reciprocal faith," one also characterized in adolescent terms. He uses the Italian phrase *compagno di banco*—literally meaning one who shares your desk at school and with whom you always sit—to describe it. Mastroianni, *Mi ricordo,* 132; Enzo Biagi, *La bella vita: Marcello Mastroianni racconta* (Milan: Rizzoli, 1996), 95, 116; and Fellini, *Un regista a Cinecittà,* 68.

4. Deena Boyer, *The Two Hundred Days of 8½,* trans. Charles Lam Markmann (New York: Macmillan, 1964), 135.

5. *Ginger and Fred* and *Intervista* will be dealt with in greater detail in chapter 6.

6. Brandes, *Metaphors of Masculinity,* 7–8. Brandes, like David Gilmore in his work on Mediterranean masculinity, makes the argument that his findings on Andalusian culture have broad applications for other Mediterranean masculinities; he in fact cites Southern Italy by name (10). What differs is how each culture's folklore functions as the expression of unique "psychological dynamics" (9). I would like to thank Mia Fuller for introducing me to Brandes's research. All further citations will appear directly in the text.

7. Gieri, *Contemporary Italian Filmmaking,* 71–88, here, 78–79.

8. Tullio Kezich, *Fellini* (Milan: Rizzoli, 1987), 315.

9. Chandler, *I, Fellini,* 148–49. In a recent article, John C. Stubbs refers to this episode as Fellini's "Eureka! moment," part of Guido/Fellini's four stages of creative thought: preparation, incubation, the Eureka! moment, and verification. John C. Stubbs, "Fellini's Portrait of the Artist as Creative Problem Solver," *Cinema Journal* 41, no. 4 (Summer 2002): 116–31, here 119–20.

10. Kezich, *Fellini,* 322.

11. Kezich, *Fellini,* 331–32; and Ted Perry, *Filmguide to 8½* (Bloomington: Indiana University Press, 1975), 15.

12. Carolyn Geduld, "Juliet of the Spirits: Guido's Anima," in *Federico Fellini: Essays in Criticism,* ed. Peter Bondanella (New York: Oxford University Press, 1978), 137–51, here 144. Geduld takes a primarily Jungian track for her analysis, but Freud's work on dreams is also important here. For Freud, dreams are made up of thoughts that build up during the day and are incompletely dealt with. The "day's residue" is transformed into the "dreamwork" through compression and condensation and ultimately displacement. The final stage is what Freud terms "the regression of the dream-material, thus revised, to perception, in which form the dream becomes conscious" (204). Sigmund Freud, *Jokes and Their Relation to the Unconscious,* trans. and ed. James Strachey (New York: Norton, 1960). Further citations will appear directly in the text.

13. Faldini and Fofi, *L'avventurosa storia del cinema italiano,* 276.

14. Boyer, *Two Hundred Days of 8½,* 8; Mastroianni, *Mi ricordo,* 141; Kezich, *Fellini,* 319; and Federico Fellini, *8½,* ed. Camilla Cederna (Bologna: Capelli, 1965), 45 and 73.

15. For more on self-referentiality and *8½*, see Francesco Casetti, "L'autoreferenzialità nel cinema: *8½* di Fellini," *Versus: Quaderni di Studi Semiotici* 65–66 (May–Dec., 1993): 95–106; and Christian Metz, "Mirror Construction in Fellini's *8½*," in *8½, Federico Fellini, Director,* ed. Charles Affron (New Brunswick, N.J.: Rutgers University Press, 1987), 261–66.

16. Fellini, *8½*, 18–19, 64, 83.

17. Fellini, *8½*, 50. According to Deena Boyer, Brunello Rondi even screen-tested for a role (Boyer, 7), while Antonio Monda on the Criterion Collection DVD commentary says the character of Daumier was based on the film critic Guido Aristarco. The Criterion Collection, Federico Fellini's *8½*, DVD (2001).

18. Affron, *8½*, 6.

19. Peter Bondanella notes the importance of Pirandello's plays for understanding *8½*. Bondanella, *The Cinema of Federico Fellini,* 175–77.

20. Aldo Carotenuto, *Jung e la cultura italiana* (Rome: Astrolabio, 1977), 137–43; Bondanella, *The Cinema of Federico Fellini,* 151–54; Chandler, *I, Fellini,* 141–44; and Kezich, *Fellini,* 302–307.

21. Carl Jung, *The Archetypes and the Collective Unconscious,* 2nd ed., trans. R. F. C. Hull (Princeton, N.J.: Princeton University Press, 1968). Here, "The Archetypes of the Collective Unconscious," 5.

22. Jung, "The Concept of the Collective Unconscious," in *Archetypes,* 49.

23. Carl Jung, "Aion," in *The Portable Jung,* ed. Joseph Campbell, trans. R. F. C. Hull (New York: Penguin, 1971), 139–62, here 149. Bondanella and others center their Jungian analysis of Fellini's work on the *anima/animus* tension, as espoused in Jung's essay "Marriage as a Psychological Relationship" (anthologized in Campbell, ed., *Portable Jung,* 163–77). This essay focuses on the relationship between the man and the woman in the marriage, with the man as the "container" and the wife as the "contained." Conflict arises when the contained demands too much of the container: "The more the contained clings, the more the container feels shut out of the relationship." This container/contained friction finds its most perfect manifestation in Fellini's *Giulietta degli spiriti* (Juliet of the Spirits, 1965), in which the protagonist suffers through the mid-life crisis of her philandering husband (the container) while she struggles with her status as the contained. See Bondanella, *The Cinema of Federico Fellini,* 299–300; and Geduld, "Juliet of the Spirits," 138–40.

24. Fellini, *8½*, 26; Boyer, *Two Hundred Days of 8½,* 4, 175.

25. Bondanella, *The Cinema of Federico Fellini,* 168.

26. Even so, in order to conform to the rounded, large-bottomed figure that he wanted, Milo had to gain an additional eight kilograms. Fellini, *8½*, 21, 45.

27. For Affron, Cardinale was "part of the general cultural mythology of stardom shared by the viewers of *8½* in the 1960s." Affron, *8½*, 11.

28. As quoted in Ronald S. Librach, "Reconciliation in the Realm of Fantasy:

The Fellini World and the Fellini Text," *Film/Literature Quarterly* 15, no. 2 (1987): 85–98, here 90.

29. Librach, "Reconciliation in the Realm of Fantasy," 89.

30. Stubbs sees the harem sequence as Guido's attempt to create his film in his mind (incubation). Stubbs, "Fellini's Portrait of the Artist," 122.

31. The quotation is from the Affron translation of the screenplay in Affron, *8½*, 89.

32. Pier Marco De Santi, *La musica di Nino Rota* (Bari: Laterza, 1983), 74, 76.

33. Rota as cited in De Santi, *La musica de Nino Rota*, 115.

34. Bondanella contradicts the widely held notion that the final ending was in fact first envisioned as the film's trailer, citing a conversation he had with Tullio Pinelli. See p. 178, n. 49, of *The Cinema of Federico Fellini*.

35. Carl Jung, "The Psychology of the Child Archetype," in *Archetypes*, 161–78.

36. Gieri reads this spiritual evocation as emblematic of reoccurring obsessive images and phantoms which pervade Fellini's work. See Gieri, *Contemporary Italian Filmmaking*, 147–49.

37. Interview with Lietta Tornabuoni, *La stampa*, Mar. 29, 1980 (as reprinted on the liner notes of the DVD *City of Women*, 2001, New Yorker Video).

38. Even during production, the film created a stir in the feminist community, which had discovered that it might be the subject of a Fellini parody. It was a cinematic venture that took four years to get off the ground, going through many different producers, including Bob Guccioni, the publisher of *Penthouse*, who left the project after his demands for more graphic sex and more English and American names in the cast with greater box-office appeal went unfulfilled (he was also concerned about the film's escalating budget). Chandler, *I, Fellini*, 212; and Kezich, *Fellini*, 480.

39. Peter Brunette and Emanuel Levy add to this equation by noting that the film conflates male fantasy with male anxiety in three arenas: fear of female insatiability, fear of losing one's sexual potency, and fear of aging. *City of Women* DVD, 2001, New Yorker Video.

40. Several scholars have developed this idea of the film as a journey. Donald Costello, in "Fellini, Juliet, and the Feminists, or: What Does Fellini Think about Women?" *Michigan Academician* 15, no. 2 (Winter 1983): 293–300, sees it as a continuation of Juliet's journey in *Juliet of the Spirits*. Frank Burke, in *Fellini's Films*, connects the character's "psycho-symbolic journey" more to *8½* (238). Gaetana Marrone individuates three stages of ego-memories to Snàporaz's journey: a pre-conscious stage, a stage of subjective consciousness, and ultimately an awareness of a "dualistic stage of being." Gaetana Marrone, "Memory in Fellini's *City of Women*," in *Perspectives on Federico Fellini*, ed. Peter Bondanella and Cristina Degli Esposti (New York: G. K. Hall and Co., 1993), 240.

41. Freud, *Jokes*, 214–15. One striking difference between jokes and dreams rests in their relation to the social: while dreams constitute an "asocial

mental project" that seeks to avoid pleasure, jokes for Freud are the most social of all mental functions, and one that actively seeks out pleasure (222). Other citations appear directly in text.

42. J. Laplanche and J. B. Pontalis, *The Language of Psycho-analysis*, trans. Donald Nicholson-Smith (New York: W. W. Norton, 1973), 62–65.

43. Ironically, although Gieri enumerates many Fellini protagonists as humorists in the Pirandellian sense, she does not include Snàporaz in her analysis nor does she mention *City of Women* at all in her work. See Gieri, *Contemporary Italian Filmmaking*, 150.

44. Susan Basnett, *Feminist Experiences: The Women's Movement in Four Cultures* (London: Allen and Unwin, 1986), 91–131; Chiavola-Birnbaum, *Liberazione della donna*, 79–231; Mariella Gramaglia, "1968: Il venir dopo e l'andar oltre del movimento femminista," in *La questione femminile in Italia dal '900 ad oggi*, ed. G. Ascoli et al. (Milan: Franco Angeli Editore, 1979), 179–201; Renate Holub, "Towards a New Rationality? Notes on Feminist and Current Discursive Practices in Italy," *Discourse* 4 (Winter 1981–82): 89–107; and Robert Lumley, *States of Emergency: Cultures of Revolt in Italy from 1968 to 1978* (London: Verso, 1990), 313–36.

45. Franca Faldini and Goffredo Fofi, *Il cinema italiano d'oggi: 1970–1984. Raccontato dai suoi protagonisti* (Milan: Mondadori, 1984), 262–63.

46. Biagi, *La bella vita*, 118–19; Kezich, *Fellini*, 445–63. Bondanella sees many affinities between Fellini's previous film *Casanova* and *City of Women*. Bondanella, *The Cinema of Federico Fellini*, 318–26.

47. "The scene emphasizes the relationship between masculine sexual desire and the cinema, just as it depicts Fellini's belief (and that of contemporary feminist theorists) that the image of woman in the movies is not an authentic representation of women's reality but, instead, a projection of male sexual fantasies." Bondanella, *The Cinema of Federico Fellini*, 322.

48. Marie Jean Lederman, "Dreams and Vision in Fellini's *City of Women*," *Journal of Popular Film and Television* 9, no. 3 (Fall 1981): 114–22, here 118; and Bondanella, *The Cinema of Federico Fellini*, 319–20. Raffaele Monti has called attention to how the womb- and uterine-like characteristics of the train car as well as Snàporaz's fetal-like positioning within it, among other things, establish Snàporaz's "infantile" relationship with his new reality. Raffaele Monti, *Bottega Fellini*, La città delle donne: *Progetto, lavorazione, film* (Rome: De Luca Ed., 1981), 164–66.

49. Chandler, *I, Fellini*, 210.

50. Nina Auerbach, *Romantic Imprisonment: Women and Other Glorified Outcasts* (New York: Columbia University Press, 1985), 165. Lederman was the first to establish parallels between *8½* and *Alice in Wonderland*. Lederman, "Dreams and Vision in Fellini's *City of Women*," 115.

51. Monti underscores many affinities between Dante and *City of Women*, with the forest as Hell's anti-chamber and the feminist convention its first circle, as well as Donatella's role as a Beatrice-like figure. Monti, *Bottega*

Fellini, 168, 174. See also Christie Milliken, "Fair to Feminism? Carnivalizing the Carnival in Fellini's *City of Women*," *Spectator* (Spring 1990): 28–45, here 36–37.

52. Àine O'Healy, "Unspeakable Bodies: Fellini's Female Grotesques," *RLA: Romance Languages Annual* 4 (1992): 325–29. Mary Russo notes how various women's movements were often described in terms of the grotesque, such as: "shrieking sisterhood," "hags," and satanic "bra-burners." Mary Russo, *The Female Grotesque: Risk, Excess, and Modernity* (New York: Routledge, 1995), 14. Milliken sees the carnival, in particular its emphasis on spectacle and masquerade, as subversive of dominant, patriarchal discourse. Milliken, "Fair to Feminism?" 37–42. The carnival and its relationship to the representation of gender in Mastroianni's films are discussed in detail in chapter 5.

53. For Milliken, she is "a conflation of the four traditional female stereotypes of Virgin/Whore/Mother and Muse." Milliken, "Fair to Feminism?" 41.

54. Chandler, *I, Fellini*, 215. Marrone cites Bernardino Zapponi, Fellini's co-writer, as referring to Katzone as Marcello's "scurril" double—the vulgar part of himself. Marrone, "Memory in Fellini's *City of Women*," 243.

55. Brandes notes how jokes between men often revolve around, among other things, the quality and size of male genitalia, resulting from a fear of sexual inadequacy. Brandes, *Metaphors of Masculinity*, 99–113.

56. Milliken ties the child-like language to Lacanian pre-linguistic *jouissance*. Milliken, "Fair to Feminism?" 44–45.

57. Bondanella notes that at this point in the film, Snàporaz has begun to regress to a childhood populated by "castrating females." Bondanella, *The Cinema of Federico Fellini*, 321.

58. Frank Burke likens the toboggan ride to a uterine chute, further connecting memory with pre-Oedipal regression. Burke, *Fellini's Films*, 240.

59. Burke sees this encounter as revealing how Snàporaz's fear of women is often connected to homophobia. Burke, *Fellini's Films*, 243.

60. Valerio C. Ferme, "*Ingegno* and Morality in the New Social Order: The Role of the *Beffa* in Boccaccio's *Decameron*," *RLA: Romance Languages Annual* 4 (1992): 248–53, here 253. The above definition of the *beffa* is translated from Ferme's citation of the *Accademia della Crusca*'s terminology, 248. Salvatore di Maria notes that the *beffa* is characterized by "the agent's [*beffatore*] creation of a fictitious reality, which the victim [*beffato*] is persuaded to accept as factual," ultimately causing the *beffato*'s downfall. Salvatore di Maria, "Fortune and the *Beffa* in Bandello's *Novelle*," *Italica* 59, no. 4 (Winter 1982): 306–15.

61. Salvatore di Maria, "Structure of the Early Form of the *Beffa* in Italian Literature," *Canadian Journal of Italian Studies* 4, no. 3–4 (Spring-Summer 1981): 227–39.

62. For the American critical response to the film, see Fausto Pauluzzi, "*City of Women*: Fellini's Bothersome Judgment Day among U.S. Critics," in

National Traditions in Motion Pictures: Proceedings of the Third Annual Film Conference at Kent State University April 17, 1985, ed. Douglas Radcliff Umstead (Kent, Ohio: Kent State University Romance Languages Department, 1985), 43–53.

63. Bondanella also observes the "sense of complicity" between the women in this final scene. Bondanella, *The Cinema of Federico Fellini,* 324.

64. Àine O'Healy notes how many Fellini films, with their "textual ambivalence" in the self-reflexive exploration of femininity, result in "an unsettling viewing experience" for the female spectator. "Interview with the Vamp: Deconstructing Femininity in Fellini's Final Films (*Intervista, La voce della luna*)," in *Federico Fellini: Contemporary Perspectives,* ed. Frank Burke and Marguerite R. Waller (Toronto: University of Toronto Press, 2002), 208.

65. Chandler, *I, Fellini,* 212.

5. The *Inetto* versus the Unruly Woman

1. Rowe, *The Unruly Woman.* All further citations of Rowe's work will appear in the text.

2. In their analysis I break from my intention of only devoting my attention to films readily accessible in the United States. I do so because the Blasetti films are so fundamental to the development of both stars' careers as well as to the codes and conventions on which their later films draw.

3. Natalie Zemon Davis, *Society and Culture in Early Modern France* (Stanford, Calif.: Stanford University Press, 1975), 129. All further citations will appear directly in the text.

4. Rowe supports her adaptation of early modern female tropes to contemporary culture by noting that "if the rigid gender division and social symbolism Davis describes can no longer be found in industrialized Western countries, the oppression of women and the projection of the feminine as a symbolic category on vast areas of culture do, however, persist" (47). Mikhail M. Bakhtin, *Rabelais and His World,* trans. Helene Iswolsky (Bloomington: Indiana University Press, 1984); and Mary Russo, "Female Grotesques: Carnival and Theory," in *Feminist Studies, Critical Studies,* ed. Teresa de Lauretis (Bloomington: Indiana University Press, 1986), 213–29.

5. "Gender inversion can also set into motion a destabilization of the binary categories of gender, opening the way to more fluid forms of sexuality before the hero and heroine are reinscribed into the norms of a more conventionally figured heterosexuality." Rowe, *The Unruly Woman,* 118.

6. Jane Tylus, "Women at the Windows: *Commedia dell'arte* and Theatrical Practice in Early Modern Italy," *Theatre Journal* 49 (1997): 323–42. Barbara Spackman has noted that, while it is tempting to apply the notion

of the "woman on top" to the enchantress-turned-hag of macaronic literature of the Renaissance, the categorization does not necessarily work, for it serves more of a hermeneutic rather than a subversive purpose. Barbara Spackman, "*Inter musam et ursam moritur:* Folengo and the Gaping 'Other' Mouth," in *Refiguring Woman: Perspectives on Gender and the Italian Renaissance,* ed. Marilyn Migiel and Juliana Schiesari (Ithaca, N.Y.: Cornell University Press, 1991), 19–34. See also Antonella Ansani, "Beauty and the Hag: Appearance and Reality in Basile's *Lo cunto de li cunti,*" in *Out of the Woods: The Origins of the Literary Fairy Tale in Italy and France,* ed. Nancy L. Canepa (Detroit, Mich.: Wayne State University Press, 1997), 81–98.

7. Giancarlo Pretini, *Spettacolo leggero: Dal music-hall, al varietà, alla rivista, al musical* (Udine: Trapezio, 1997), 11–80; *Viene avanti, cretino! Storia e testi dell'avanspettacolo e del varietà,* ed. Nicola Fano (Rome, Naples: Edizioni Theoria, 1993), 11–19; Daniela Vanelli, *Teatro di varietà a Livorno tra il 1880 e il 1914* (Livorno: Editrice Nuova Fortezza, 1990), 9–17.

8. Robert C. Allen, *Horrible Prettiness: Burlesque and American Culture* (Chapel Hill: University of North Carolina Press, 1991), 96.

9. As cited in Angelo Olivieri, *Le stelle del varietà: Rivista, avanspettacolo e cabaret dal 1936 al 1966* (Rome: Gremese, 1989), 34. A testimonial on Magnani's stage persona reinforces her status as unruly woman, describing her as "exuberant, aggressive, arrogant, vulgar and a joker. And her jokes were impetuous" (58).

10. Pretini, *Spettacolo leggero,* 81–100.

11. Landy, *Folklore of Consensus,* 50.

12. Reich, "Reading, Writing, and Rebellion," 220–51.

13. Brunetta, *Storia del cinema italiano,* vol. III, pp. 586–90.

14. Simonetta Piccone Stella, *La prima generazione: Ragazze e ragazzi nel miracolo economico italiano* (Milan: FrancoAngeli, 1993); and Guido Crainz, *Storia del miracolo italiano: Culture, identità, trasformazioni fra anni cinquanta e sessanta* (Rome: Donzelli, 1996), 73–74, 83. Giovanni Grignaffini discusses how increasing female spectatorship contributed to the greater liberalization of cultural and social norms during the 1950s. Grignaffini, "Female Identity and Italian Cinema of the 1950s," 121–23.

15. Brunetta, *Storia del cinema italiano,* vol. III, pp. 591–93.

16. Mira Liehm, *Passion and Defiance: Film in Italy from 1942 to the Present* (Berkeley: University of California Press, 1984), 141.

17. Colleen Ballerino Cohen and Richard Wilk, with Beverly Stoeltje, "Introduction: Beauty Queens and the Global Stage," in *Beauty Queens and the Global Stage: Gender, Contests, and Power,* ed. Cohen and Wilk, with Stoeltje (New York: Routledge, 1996), 1–11, here 8.

18. Gundle, "Feminine Beauty, National Identity, and Political Conflict," 359–

78; and Brunetta, *Storia del cinema italiano,* vol. III, p. 258. This image contrasted with the desexualized *donna-madre* extolled by the previous Fascist government.

19. Marcus, *Italian Film in the Light of Neorealism,* 136.

20. Harris, *Sophia Loren,* 74.

21. Stephen Gundle, "Sophia Loren, Italian Icon," *Historical Journal of Film and Television* 15, no. 3 (1995): 367–85.

22. Ginsborg, *History of Contemporary Italy,* 187.

23. *Comedy, Italian Style,* ed. Aprà and Pistangesi, 22–23.

24. Suso Cecchi d'Amico, *Storie di cinema (e d'altro), Raccontate a Margherita d'Amico* (Milan: Garzanti, 1996), 115. Blasetti claimed that casting Loren was his idea. As quoted in Dewey, *Marcello Mastroianni,* 71.

25. According to Suso Cecchi d'Amico, one of the screenwriters, the story was inspired by the writer Ercole Patti's torturous affair with a woman nicknamed Nerone (Nero), on account of her appearance as well as her abusive demeanor. Cecchi d'Amico also claims that Patti had to flee to Sicily to get away from her. Cecchi d'Amico, *Storie di cinema (e d'altro),* 160, 196–97.

26. An actual magazine cover featured Loren covered only by a towel, much like the provocative photograph Corrado takes of Antonietta in his studio. Harris, *Sophia Loren,* 57. See also Gundle, "Sophia Loren, Italian Icon," 374–76.

27. Vittorio De Sica, "Gli anni più belli della mia vita," *Tempo* 16, no. 50 (Dec. 16, 1954): 18–22, as cited in *Tutti i De Sica,* ed. Orio Caldiron (Rome: Ernesto Carpintieri Editrice, 1984), 8.

28. Dewey, *Marcello Mastroianni,* 71.

29. Vittorio De Sica, *Lettere dal set,* ed. Emi De Sica and Giancarlo Governi (Milan: SugarCo, 1987), 124.

30. Bruno, *Streetwalking on a Ruined Map,* 50, 164–65.

31. Thomas Belmonte, *The Broken Fountain,* 2nd expanded ed. (New York: Columbia University Press, 1989), 92–93.

32. *Yesterday, Today, and Tomorrow* broke box-office records in Italy. Franco Pecori, *Vittorio De Sica* (Firenze: La Nuova Italia, 1980), 88.

33. According to Bruno, "The characters of the *sceneggiata* are the *popolo* [the people], members of the underclass or poor artisanal class, caught between the familial and a harsh confrontation with the social and institutional apparatus." Bruno, *Streetwalking on a Ruined Map,* 171.

34. De Sica, *Lettere dal set,* 155–56.

35. De Sica, *Lettere dal set,* 115. De Sica's intention in filming what ended up being over two thousand meters of film on this one episode was to capture the city and its residents as "real, open, human and lyric" (133).

36. Laura A. Salsini, *Gendered Genres: Female Experiences and Narrative Pat-*

terns in the Works of Matilde Serao (Madison, N.J.: Fairleigh Dickinson University Press, 1999), 69–72.

37. Matilde Serao, *Il ventre di Napoli* (Rome: Vito Bianco Editore, 1973 [1884]), 87–88.

38. De Sica, *Lettere dal set,* 196, 220. There had been another film adaptation of the play in 1952, directed by de Filippo and starring himself and his sister, Titina. De Filippo was reportedly very unsatisfied with the De Sica production, even though he collaborated on the screenplay with Renato Castellani, Tonino Guerra, Leo Benvenuti, and Piero de Bernardi. Mastroianni, by contrast, was thrilled to be working on the de Filippo text, and the following year appeared in two films with de Filippo as director: an episode of *Oggi, domani e dopodomani* (Today, Tomorrow and the Next Day, 1965), and *Spara forte più forte, non capisco* (Shoot Loud, Louder, I Don't Understand, 1966). Maurizio Giammusso, *Vita di Eduardo* (Milan: Mondadori, 1993), 195, 312.

39. Giuseppe Faustini, "*Filumena Marturano:* From Play to Film," in *Transformations, from Literature to Film.* Proceedings from the 5th International Conference on Film of Kent State University (Kent, Ohio: Kent State University Romance Languages Department: 1987), 55–62. For more on the play, see Mario B. Mignone, *Eduardo de Filippo* (Boston: Twayne, 1984), 78–90; and Anna Barsotti, *Eduardo drammaturgo: Fra il mondo del teatro e teatro del mondo* (Rome: Bulzoni, 1988), 201–20.

40. Ginsborg, *History of Contemporary Italy,* 298–347.

41. Victoria de Grazia, *How Fascism Ruled Women: Italy, 1922–1945* (Berkeley: University of California Press, 1992), 212.

42. Mosse, *Nationalism and Sexuality,* 140–47.

43. Ruth Ben-Ghiat, *Fascist Modernities: Italy, 1922–1945* (Berkeley: University of California Press, 2001), 3–6.

44. Two of Richard Dyer's collections of essays deal with this topic: *Now You See It: Studies in Lesbian and Gay Film* (London: Routledge, 1990), and *The Matter of Images: Essays on Representations* (London: Routledge, 1993).

45. Harris, *Sophia Loren,* 194. For more on the representation of homosexuality and Fascism, see Kriss Ravetto, *The Unmasking of Fascist Aesthetics* (Minneapolis: University of Minnesota Press, 2001), 87–95.

46. Coppélia Kahn, "Coming of Age: Marriage and Motherhood in *The Taming of the Shrew,*" in *William Shakespeare's The Taming of the Shrew,* ed. Harold Bloom (New York: Chelsea, 1988), 41–51.

47. Bruzzi, *Undressing Cinema,* 31–34.

48. Harris, *Sophia Loren,* 359.

6. Remembrance of Films Past

1. Kathleen Woodward, "Youthfulness as Masquerade," *Discourse* 11, no. 1 (Fall–Winter 1988–89): 109–42.

2. Bondanella, *Italian Cinema from Neorealism to the Present*, 425–26; and Millicent Marcus, *After Fellini: National Cinemas in the Postmodern Age* (Baltimore, Md.: Johns Hopkins University Press, 2002), 4–12.

3. Kathleen Woodward, introduction to *Figuring Age: Women, Bodies, Generations*, ed. Kathleen Woodward (Bloomington: Indiana University Press: 1999), x.

4. Stefania Maggi et al., "Italy," in *Aging in Europe*, ed. Johannes J. F. Schroots, Rocío Fernández-Ballesteros, and Georg Rudinger (Amsterdam: IOS Press, 1999), 73–80, here 73.

5. Because my aim is to discuss films which are readily available in the United States, this goal forces me to omit detailed discussion of two Italian films that address issues of aging and masculinity: Francesca Archibugi's *Verso sera* (Toward Evening, 1991) and Roberto Faenza's *Sostiene Pereira* (Pereira Affirms, 1996). For two excellent discussions of these films, see respectively Àine O'Healy, "Are the Children Watching Us? The Roman Films of Francesca Archibugi," *Annali d'Italianistica* 17 (1999): 121–36; and Millicent Marcus, "From Salazar's Lisbon to Mussolini's Rome by Way of France in Roberto Faenza's *Sostiene Pereira*," in *After Fellini*, 94–112.

6. Christoph Conrad, "Old Age in the Modern and Postmodern Western World," in *Handbook of the Humanities and Aging*, ed. Thomas R. Cole, David D. Van Tassel, and Robert Kastenbaum (New York: Springer, 1992), 62–95.

7. Stephen G. Post, "Aging and Meaning: The Christian Tradition," in Cole et al., *Handbook of the Humanities and Aging*, 127–46, here 127. See also Shulamith Shahar, "The Old Body in Medieval Culture," in *Framing Medieval Bodies*, ed. Sarah Kay and Miri Rubin (Manchester: Manchester University Press, 1994), 160–286.

8. Kaplan states: "fears about global aging are a condensation of existential fears of aging (both male and female) and of patriarchal repulsion of the specificity of female aging." E. Ann Kaplan, "Trauma and Aging: Marlene Dietrich, Melanie Klein, and Marguerite Duras," in *Figuring Age: Women, Bodies, Generations*, ed. Kathleen Woodward (Bloomington: Indiana University Press, 1999), 171–94, here 172.

9. Luigi Pirandello, *On Humor*, trans. Antonio Illiano and Daniel P. Testa (Chapel Hill: University of North Carolina Press, 1974), 113. Italics are those of the author.

10. Kathleen Woodward, *Aging and Its Discontents: Freud and Other Fictions* (Bloomington: Indiana University Press, 1991); and Mike Featherstone and Mike Hepworth, "The Mask of Ageing and the Postmodern Life

Course," in *The Body: Social Process and Cultural Theory*, ed. Mike Featherstone, Mike Hepworth, and Bryan S. Turner (London: Sage, 1991), 379–82.

11. Woodward, "Youthfulness as Masquerade," 130.

12. William Marsiglio and Richard A. Greer, "A Gender Analysis of Older Men's Sexuality: Social, Psychological, and Biological Dimensions," in *Older Men's Lives*, ed. Edward H. Thompson, Jr. (Thousand Oaks, Calif., and London: Sage, 1994), 122–40, here 128.

13. Jeff Hearn, "Imaging the Aging of Men," in *Images of Aging: Cultural Representations of Later Life*, ed. Mike Featherstone and Andrew Wernick (London: Routledge, 1995), 97–115, here 106.

14. Vivian Sobchack, "Scary Women: Cinema, Surgery, and Special Effects," in *Figuring Age: Women, Bodies, Generations*, ed. Kathleen Woodward (Bloomington: Indiana University Press, 1999), 200–11, here 208–209.

15. Jodi Brooks, "Performing Aging/Performance Crisis (For Norma Desmond, Baby Jane, Margo Channing, Sister George—and Myrtle)," in *Figuring Age: Women, Bodies, Generations*, ed. Kathleen Woodward (Bloomington: Indiana University Press, 1999), 232–47, here 234–44.

16. The character of Mandrake, based on an American comic strip from the director's youth, had always fascinated Fellini. At one point in the early 1970s he considered making a film about him with Mastroianni in the title role and Claudia Cardinale as Mandrake's wife, Narda. Mastroianni wanted Fellini to cast Catherine Deneuve, with whom he was romantically involved at the time, as Narda. Chandler, *I, Fellini*, 242.

17. Biagi, *La bella vita*, 115.

18. For Àine O'Healy, *Intervista* presents one of the most complex portraits of femininity in all of Fellini's opus, one that reflects a decidedly masculine anxiety: about postmodern culture, the decline of the auteur, and the anxiety of old age. O'Healy, "Interview with the Vamp," 210.

19. Ginsborg, *History of Contemporary Italy*, 414–15.

20. María Luisa Mirabile, "The Politics of Old Age in Italy," in *The Politics of Old Age in Europe*, ed. Alan Walker and Gerhard Naegele (Buckingham: Open University, 1999), 110–22, here 110–11.

21. Mirabile, "The Politics of Old Age in Italy," 113.

22. Maggi et al., "Italy," 73.

23. *Giuseppe Tornatore*, ed. Sergio Toffetti (Torino: Lindau, 1995), 28–29.

24. Bondanella parallels Matteo's journey from Sicily to the "continent" to the one undertaken by Rossellini in *Paisà*, with pessimistic rather than liberationist overtones. Bondanella, *Italian Cinema from Neorealism to the Present*, 458.

25. As quoted in Angela Baldassare, *The Great Dictators: Interviews with Filmmakers of Italian Descent* (Toronto: Guernica, 1999), 98.

26. Giacomo Manzoli argues that this pretense has disastrous consequences

for Matteo. Giacomo Manzoli, "Barocco siciliano," *Annali d'italianistica* 17 (1999): 95–106.

27. Patrick Rumble interprets Tornatore's films as rebelling against and as antidotes to post-modernism in their authentic sentimentality, which also explains their appeal to American audiences. Patrick Rumble, "Tornatore e L'America: Il cinema dell'anamnesi," in *Sicilia e altre storie: Il cinema di Giuseppe Tornatore*, ed. Valerio Caprara (Naples: Edizioni Scientifiche Italiane, 1996), 11–20.

28. In addition to Fellini, the director Ettore Scola's influence can be seen in Tornatore's use of time. Just as in *C'eravamo tanto amati* (We All Loved Each Other So Much, 1974), a film in which Mastroianni makes a cameo appearance as himself, the action around Matteo often stops, particularly when he is leaving fruitless messages on Alvaro's answering machine.

29. Several critics have noted how Tornatore incorporates Italian film history into his own films, the most obvious example being *Nuovo Cinema Paradiso*. Claudio Siniscalchi, "Il primato del racconto," in *Sicilia e altre storie: Il cinema di Giuseppe Tornatore*, ed. Valerio Caprara (Naples: Edizioni Scientifiche Italiane, 1996), 28; and Paolo D'Agostini, "Giuseppe Tornatore: Un siciliano alla corte del cinema," *Annali d'Italianistica* 17 (1999): 31–37. Brunetta sees Tornatore as the member of a younger generation of directors most influenced by post-war Italian cinema. *Storia del cinema italiano*, vol. IV, p. 567.

30. Thomas di Salvo discusses the symbolism of the birds and the telephone in his article "The Severed Cord: Solitude and Alienation in Giuseppe Tornatore's *Nuovo cinema paradiso* and *Stanno tutti bene*," *Il Veltro: Rivista di civiltà italiana* 40, no. 1–2 (Jan.–Apr. 1996): 94–98.

31. As quoted in Dewey, *Marcello Mastroianni*, 275.

32. Kezich, *Fellini*, 512.

33. Chandler, *I, Fellini*, 331–34.

34. Bondanella, *The Cinema of Federico Fellini*, 223; and Federico Fellini, *Ginger e Fred: Rendiconto di un film*, ed. Mino Guerrini (Milan: Longanesi, 1986), 48.

35. *Ginger e Fred*, 44–45.

36. Marcus, *After Fellini*, 181–98.

37. Bondanella, *The Cinema of Federico Fellini*, 223; and *Ginger e Fred*, 33–35.

38. Aldo Grasso, *Storia della televisione italiana* (Milan: Garzanti, 1992), 15–27.

39. Burke, *Fellini's Films*, 259.

40. Marcus, *After Fellini*, 182–83. For American viewers, this self-reflexivity appears even before the film begins, since MGM, the studio which produced so many Fred Astaire and Ginger Rogers musicals, distributed the film in the United States.

41. *Ginger e Fred*, 29.

42. Marcus, *After Fellini*, 192.

43. The dance is modeled, according to Marcus, on the Astaire and Rogers film *Follow the Fleet* (1936). *After Fellini,* 194.

44. *Ginger e Fred,* 19–30.

45. Holmund, *Impossible Bodies,* 152–53.

46. Hearn, "Imaging the Aging of Men," 109.

47. Kathleen Newman, "'Convocar tanto mundo': Narrativising Authoritarianism and Globalisation in *De eso no se habla,*" in *An Argentinian Passion: María Luisa Bemberg and Her Films,* ed. John King, Sheila Whitaker, and Rosa Bosch (London: Verso, 2000), 181–92, here 183. For Katharine Jenckes, *I Don't Want to Talk about It* features a female protagonist who, like Camila and Sor Juana, exists "within a social structure that tries to define and contain them, and which they resist and subvert in their individual ways." Katharine Jenckes, "Identity, Image, and Sound in Three Films by María Luisa Bemberg," in *Cine-Lit III: Essays on Hispanic Fiction and Film,* ed. George Cabello-Castelet, Jaume Martí-Olivella, and Guy H. Wood (Corvallis: Oregon State University, 1997), 61–67, here 61.

48. Newman, "Convocar tanto mundo," 184.

49. Jason Wilson, "María Luisa Bemberg's *De eso no se habla:* From Fiction to Film, Some Notes," in *An Argentinian Passion: María Luisa Bemberg and Her Films,* ed. John King, Sheila Whitaker, and Rosa Bosch (London: Verso, 2000), 174–80.

50. Jean Kozlowski, "Women, Film, and Midlife Sophie's Choice: Sink or Sousatzka?" in *Menopause: A Midlife Passage,* ed. Joan C. Callahan (Bloomington: Indiana University Press, 1993), 3–22, here 5. All further citations will appear in the text.

Conclusion

1. Mastroianni, *Mi ricordo,* 57.

2. Nostalgia and *saudade* are a constant presence in Oliveira's films. For João Bénard da Costa, the nostalgia for unity and harmony is linked to the *saudade* of the Garden of Eden. João Bénard da Costa, "Manoel de Oliveira: la magia del cine," *Revista de occidente* 163 (1994): 19–39, here 29. I would like to thank John Eipper and Robert Harvey for the linguistic assistance in Portuguese and French, respectively.

3. Mastroianni, *Mi ricordo,* 121–22.

Bibliography

"A Titre de Revanche: Rossano Brazzi conjure le mauvais sort en faisant à Hollywood une rentrée en beauté." *Cine Revue* (Aug. 1957).

Accordi, Giuliano. "The Soundtrack of Seduction: The Latin Lover in Italian Songs." In *Latin Lover: The Passionate South*, ed. Giannino Malossi, 124–32. Milan: Charta, 1996.

Aglianò, Sebastiano. *Che cos'è questa Sicilia?* Palermo: Sellerio, 1996.

Agnew, John. "The Myth of Backward Italy in Modern Europe." *Revisioning Italy: National Identity and Global Culture*, ed. Beverly Allen and Mary Russo, 23–42. Minneapolis: University of Minneapolis Press, 1997.

Allen, Beverly. "The Novel, the Body, and Giorgio Armani: Rethinking National 'Identity' in a Postnational World." In *Feminine Feminists: Cultural Practices in Italy*, ed. Giovanna Miceli Jeffries, 153–70. Minneapolis: University of Minnesota Press, 1994.

Allen, Beverly, and Mary Russo, eds. *Revisioning Italy: National Identity and Global Culture*. Minneapolis: University of Minnesota Press, 1997.

Allen, Robert C. *Horrible Prettiness: Burlesque and American Culture*. Chapel Hill: University of North Carolina Press, 1991.

Ansani, Antonella. "Beauty and the Hag: Appearance and Reality in Basile's *Lo cunto de li cunti*." In *Out of the Woods: The Origins of the Literary Fairy Tale in Italy and France*, ed. Nancy L. Canepa, 81–98. Detroit, Mich.: Wayne State University Press, 1997.

Aprà, Adriano, and Patrizia Pistagnesi, eds. *Comedy, Italian Style: 1950–1980*. Torino: Edizioni Rai, 1986.

Argentieri, Mino. *Risate di regime: La commedia italiana, 1930–1944*. Venice: Marsilio, 1991.

Aspesi, Natalia. *Il lusso e l'autarchia: Storia dell'eleganza italiana 1930–1944*. Milan: Rizzoli, 1982.

201

Auerbach, Nina. *Romantic Imprisonment: Women and Other Glorified Outcasts.* New York: Columbia University Press, 1985.

Bachmann, Gideon. "Marcello Mastroianni and the Game of Truth." *Film Quarterly* 46 (Winter 1992–93): 2–7.

Bagley, Christopher. "The Sweet Life of Marcello Mastroianni." *Details* (Nov. 1994): 100.

Baker, Aaron, and Juliann Vitullo. "Screening the Italian-American Male." In *Masculinities: Bodies, Movies, Culture,* ed. Peter Lehman, 213–26. New York: Routledge, 2001.

Bakhtin, Mikhail M. *Rabelais and His World.* Translated by Helene Iswolsky. Bloomington: Indiana University Press, 1984.

Baldassare, Angela. *The Great Dictators: Interviews with Filmmakers of Italian Descent.* Toronto: Guernica, 1999.

Baranski, Zymunt, and Robert Lumley, eds. *Culture and Conflict in Postwar Italy: Essays on Mass and Popular Culture.* London: Macmillan, 1990.

Barsotti, Anna. *Eduardo drammaturgo: Fra il mondo del teatro e teatro del mondo.* Rome: Bulzoni, 1988.

Basnett, Susan. *Feminist Experiences: The Women's Movement in Four Cultures.* London: Allen and Unwin, 1986.

Beecher, Donald A. "Intriguers and Tricksters: The Manifestations of an Archetype in the Comedy of the Renaissance." In *Comparative Critical Approaches to Renaissance Comedy,* ed. Donald Beecher and Massimo Ciavolella, 52–72. Ottawa: Dovehouse, 1986.

Bellassai, Sandro, and Maria Malatesta, eds. *Genere e mascolinità: Uno sguardo storico.* Rome: Bulzoni, 2000.

Belmonte, Thomas. *The Broken Fountain.* 2nd expanded ed. New York: Columbia University Press, 1989.

Ben-Ghiat, Ruth. *Fascist Modernities: Italy, 1922–1945.* Berkeley: University of California Press, 2001.

Berger, Harry, Jr. *The Absence of Grace: Sprezzatura and Suspicion in Two Renaissance Courtesy Books.* Stanford, Calif.: Stanford University Press, 2000.

Biagi, Enzo. *La bella vita: Marcello Mastroianni racconta.* Milan: Rizzoli, 1996.

Bianchino, Gloria. *Italian Fashion Designing/Disegno della moda italiana 1945–1980.* With a translation by Bonizza Giordani Aragno. Parma: CSAC dell'Università di Parma, 1987.

Bianchino, Gloria, Grazietta Butazzi, Alessandra Mottola Molfino, and Arturo Carlo Quintavalle, eds. *Italian Fashion: The Origins of High Fashion and Knitwear.* Milan: Electa, 1985.

Biasin, Gian Paolo. *Montale, Debussy, and Modernism.* Princeton, N.J.: Princeton University Press, 1989.

Bingham, Dennis. *Acting Male: Masculinities in the Films of James Stewart, Jack Nicholson, and Clint Eastwood.* New Brunswick, N.J.: Rutgers University Press, 1994.

Blok, Anton. "Rams and Billy-Goats: A Key to the Mediterranean Code of Honor." *Man* 16, no. 3 (Nov. 1981): 427–40.

Bondanella, Peter. *The Cinema of Federico Fellini.* Princeton, N.J.: Princeton University Press, 1993.

———. *Italian Cinema from Neorealism to the Present.* 3rd ed. New York: Continuum, 2001.

———, ed. *Federico Fellini: Essays in Criticism.* New York: Oxford University Press, 1978.

Bondanella, Peter, and Cristina Degli Esposti, eds. *Perspectives on Federico Fellini.* New York: G. K. Hall and Co., 1993.

Boyer, Deena. *The Two Hundred Days of 8½.* Translated by Charles Lam Markmann. New York: Macmillan, 1964.

Brancati, Vitaliano. *Il bell'Antonio.* Milan: Bompiani, 1965 [1949].

———. *Diario romano.* Edited by Sandro de Feo and G. A. Cibotto. Milan: Bompiani, 1961.

———. *Don Giovanni in Sicilia.* Milan: Bompiani, 1999 [1941].

———. *I fascisti invecchiano.* In *Opere 1932–1946,* ed. Leonardo Sciascia. Milan: Bompiani, 1987.

———. *Paolo il caldo.* Milan: Bompiani, 1955.

———. "Piaceri del gallismo." In *Il borghese e l'immensità: Scritti 1930–1954,* ed. Sandro de Feo and G. A. Cibotto, 148–51. Milan: Bompiani, 1973.

Brandes, Stanley. "Like Wounded Stags: Male Sexual Ideology in an Andalusian Town." In *Sexual Meanings: The Cultural Construction of Gender and Sexuality,* ed. Sherry B. Ortner and Harriet Whitehead, 216–39. Cambridge: Cambridge University Press, 1981.

———. *Metaphors of Masculinity: Sex and Status in Andalusian Folklore.* Philadelphia: University of Pennsylvania Press, 1985.

"Brazzi as a Heavy Lover." *Life* 39, no. 4 (July 25, 1955): 57.

Brooks, Jodi. "Performing Aging/Performance Crisis (For Norma Desmond, Baby Jane, Margo Channing, Sister George—and Myrtle)." In *Figuring Age: Women, Bodies, Generations,* ed. Kathleen Woodward, 232–47. Bloomington: Indiana University Press, 1999.

Brunetta, Gian Piero. *Cinema italiano fra le due guerre.* Milan: Mursia, 1975.

———. "Literature and the Cinema in the Works of Mauro Bolognini." In *Bolognini,* ed. Ministero degli Affari Esteri. Rome: Istituto Poligrafico dello Stato, 1977.

———. *Storia del cinema italiano.* 4 vols. Rome: Riuniti, 1993.

Bruno, Giuliana. *Streetwalking on a Ruined Map: Cultural Theory and the City Films of Elvira Notari.* Princeton, N.J.: Princeton University Press, 1993.

Bruzzi, Stella. *Undressing Cinema: Clothing and Identity in the Movies.* London: Routledge, 1997.

Burke, Frank. *Fellini's Films: From Postwar to Postmodern.* New York: Twayne, 1996.

Burke, Frank, and Marguerite R. Waller, eds. *Federico Fellini: Contemporary Perspectives.* Toronto: University of Toronto Press, 2002.

Caldiron, Orio. *Tutti i De Sica.* Rome: Ernesto Carpintieri Editrice, 1984.

Campari, Roberto. "Film and Fashion." In *Italian Fashion: The Origins of High Fashion and Knitwear,* ed. Gloria Bianchino, Grazietta Butazzi, Alessandra Mottola Molfino, and Arturo Carlo Quintavalle, 198–211. Milan: Electa, 1985.

Caprara, Valerio, ed. *Sicilia e altre storie: Il cinema di Giuseppe Tornatore.* Naples: Edizioni Scientifiche Italiane, 1996.

Carotenuto, Aldo. *Jung e la cultura italiana*. Rome: Astrolabio, 1977.

Carrano, Patrizia. "Divismo." In *Schermi ed ombre: Gli italiani e il cinema del dopoguerra*, ed. Marino Livolsi, 229–47. Firenze: La Nuova Italia, 1988.

Casadio, Gianfranco. *Il grigio e il nero: Spettacolo e propaganda nel cinema italiano degli anni trenta (1931–1943)*. Ravenna: Longo, 1989.

Casetti, Francesco. "L'autoreferenzialità nel cinema: *8½* di Fellini." *Versus: Quaderni di Studi Semiotici* 65–66 (May–Dec., 1993): 95–106.

Castiglione, Baldassare. *The Book of the Courtier*. Translated by Charles Singleton. Garden City, N.Y.: Anchor, 1959.

Celant, Germano, ed. *The Italian Metamorphosis, 1943–1968*. New York: Guggenheim Museum, 1994.

Chandler, Charlotte. *I, Fellini*. New York: Random House, 1995.

Cecchi d'Amico, Suso. *Storie di cinema (e d'altro): Raccontate a Margherita d'Amico*. Milan: Garzanti, 1996.

Chenoune, Farid. *Brioni*. New York: Universe, 1998.

———. *A History of Men's Fashion*. Translated by Deke Dusinberre. Paris: Flammarion, 1993.

Chiavola-Birnbaum, Lucia. *Liberazione della donna: Feminism in Italy*. Middletown, Conn.: Wesleyan University Press, 1986.

Clark, Martin. *Modern Italy, 1871–1991*. 2nd ed. London: Longman, 1996.

Cohan, Steven. *Masked Men: Masculinity and the Movies in the Fifties*. Bloomington: Indiana University Press, 1997.

Cohen, Colleen Ballerino, and Richard Wilk, with Beverly Stoeltje, eds. *Beauty Queens and the Global Stage: Gender, Contests, and Power*. New York: Routledge, 1996.

Cole, Thomas R., David D. Van Tassel, and Robert Kastenbaum. *Handbook of the Humanities and Aging*. New York: Springer, 1992.

Conrad, Christoph. "Old Age in the Modern and Postmodern Western World." In *Handbook of the Humanities and Aging*, ed. Thomas R. Cole, David D. Van Tassel, and Robert Kastenbaum, 62–95. New York: Springer, 1992.

Costantini, Costanzo. *Marcello Mastroianni: Vita, amori e successi di un divo involontario*. Rome: Riuniti, 1996.

Costello, Donald. "Fellini, Juliet, and the Feminists, or: What Does Fellini Think about Women?" *Michigan Academician* 15, no. 2 (Winter 1983): 293–300.

Cowell, Alan. "Thousands of Italian Mourners File in Homage Past Fellini Bier." *New York Times* (Nov. 3, 1993): D24.

Craik, Jennifer. *The Face of Fashion: Cultural Studies in Fashion*. London: Routledge, 1994.

Crainz, Guido. *Storia del miracolo italiano: Culture, identità, trasformazioni fra anni cinquanta e sessanta*. Rome: Donzelli, 1996.

Cronin, Constance. "Illusion and Reality in Sicily." In *Sexual Stratification: A Cross-Cultural View*, ed. Alice Schlegel, 67–93. New York: Columbia University Press, 1977.

da Costa, João Bénard. "Manoel de Oliveira: la magia del cine." *Revista de occidente* 163 (1994): 19–39.

D'Agostini, Paolo. "Giuseppe Tornatore: Un siciliano alla corte del cinema." *Annali d'Italianistica* 17 (1999): 31–37.

Davis, Natalie Zemon. *Society and Culture in Early Modern France.* Stanford, Calif.: Stanford University Press, 1975.

de Cordova, Richard. *Picture Personalities: The Emergence of the Star System in America.* Urbana: University of Illinois Press, 1990.

De Grand, Alexander. "Women under Italian Fascism." *Historical Journal* 19, no. 4 (1976): 956–57.

de Grazia, Victoria. *How Fascism Ruled Women: Italy, 1922–1945.* Berkeley: University of California Press, 1992.

De Santi, Pier Marco. *La musica di Nino Rota.* Bari: Laterza, 1983.

De Sica, Vittorio. *Lettere dal set.* Edited by Emi De Sica and Giancarlo Governi. Milan: SugarCo, 1987.

Dewey, Donald. *Marcello Mastroianni: His Life and Art.* New York: Birch Lane, 1993.

di Castro, Federica. "Italian High Fashion." In *Italian Fashion: The Origins of High Fashion and Knitwear,* ed. Gloria Bianchino, Grazietta Butazzi, Alessandra Mottola Molfino, and Arturo Carlo Quintavalle, 212–25. Milan: Electa, 1985.

di Maria, Salvatore. "Fortune and the *Beffa* in Bandello's *Novelle.*" *Italica* 59, no. 4 (Winter 1982): 306–15.

———. "Structure of the Early Form of the *Beffa* in Italian Literature." *Canadian Journal of Italian Studies* 4, no. 3–4 (Spring–Summer 1981): 227–39.

di Salvo, Thomas. "The Severed Cord: Solitude and Alienation in Giuseppe Tornatore's *Nuovo cinema paradiso* and *Stanno tutti bene,*" *Il Veltro: Rivista di civiltà italiana* 40, no. 1–2 (Jan.–Apr. 1996): 94–98.

Dickie, John. "Imagined Italy." In *Italian Cultural Studies: An Introduction,* ed. David Forgacs and Robert Lumley, 19–33. Oxford: Oxford University Press, 1996.

Dizionario etimologico della lingua italiana. Bologna: Zanicelli, 1985.

Dyer, Richard. *Heavenly Bodies: Film Stars and Society.* New York: St. Martin's Press, 1986.

———. *The Matter of Images: Essays on Representations.* London: Routledge, 1993.

———. *Now You See It: Studies in Lesbian and Gay Film.* London: Routledge, 1990.

———. *Stars.* New ed. London: British Film Institute, 1998.

———. *White.* London: Routledge, 1998.

Edelman, Lee. "Minding the Body: Queer Theory in the Flesh." Lecture delivered at SUNY at Stony Brook, Nov. 18, 1998.

Elena, Liliana. "Mascolinità e immaginario nazionale nel cinema italiano negli anni trenta." In *Genere e mascolinità: Uno sguardo storico,* ed. Sandro Bellassai and Maria Malatesta, 243–64. Rome: Bulzoni, 2000.

Ellenberger, Allan. *Ramon Novarro: A Biography of the Silent Film Idol, 1899–1968.* Jefferson, N.C.: McFarland, 1999.

Erenstein, Robert. "The Humour of the *Commedia dell'arte.*" In *The Commedia dell'arte from the Renaissance to Dario Fo,* ed. Christopher Cairns, 118–40. Lewiston, Me.: Mellen Press, 1988.

Faldini, Franca, and Goffredo Fofi. *Il cinema italiano d'oggi—1970-1984: Raccontato dai suoi protagonisti.* Milan: Mondadori, 1984.

———. *L'avventurosa storia del cinema italiano raccontato dai suoi protagonisti 1960-1969.* Milan: Feltrinelli, 1981.

Fano, Nicola, ed. *Viene avanti, cretino! Storia e testi dell'avanspettacolo e del varietà.* Rome, Naples: Edizioni Theoria, 1993.

Faustini, Guiseppe. *"Filumena Marturano: From Play to Film." Transformations, from Literature to Film.* Proceedings from the 5th International Conference on Film of Kent State University, 55–62. Kent, Ohio: Kent State University Romance Languages Department, 1987.

Featherstone, Mike, and Mike Hepworth. "The Mask of Ageing and the Postmodern Life Course." In *The Body: Social Process and Cultural Theory,* ed. Mike Featherstone, Mike Hepworth, and Bryan S. Turner, 379–82. London: Sage, 1991.

Fellini, Federico. *Comments on Film.* Edited by Giovanni Grazzini. Translated by Joseph Henry. Fresno: California State University Press, 1988.

———. *Conversations with Fellini.* Edited by Costanzo Costantini. Translated by Sohrab Sorooshian. San Diego: Harvest, 1995.

———. *8½.* Edited by Camilla Cederna. Bologna: Capelli, 1965.

———. *8½, Federico Fellini, Director.* Edited by Charles Affron. New Brunswick, N.J.: Rutgers University Press, 1987.

———. *Fellini on Fellini.* Translated by Isabel Quigley. New York: Delacorte, 1976.

———. *Ginger e Fred: Rendiconto di un film.* Edited by Mino Guerrini. Milan: Longanesi, 1986.

———. *Un regista a Cinecittà.* Milan: Mondadori, 1988.

Ferme, Valerio C. *"Ingegno* and Morality in the New Social Order: The Role of the *Beffa* in Boccaccio's *Decameron." RLA: Romance Languages Annual* 4 (1992): 248–53.

Finkelstein, Joanne. *The Fashioned Self.* Philadelphia: Temple University Press, 1991.

Flaiano, Ennio. *The Via Veneto Papers.* Translated by John Satriano. Marlboro, Vt.: Marlboro Press, 1992.

Flugel, J. C. *The Psychology of Clothes.* London: Hogarth, 1930.

Forgacs, David. "Cultural Consumption, 1940s to 1990s." In *Italian Cultural Studies: An Introduction,* ed. David Forgacs and Robert Lumley, 273–90. Oxford: Oxford University Press, 1996.

———. *Italian Culture in the Industrial Era, 1880-1980: Cultural Industries, Politics and the Public.* Manchester: Manchester University Press, 1990.

Forgacs, David, and Robert Lumley, eds. *Italian Cultural Studies: An Introduction.* Oxford: Oxford University Press, 1996.

Forti-Lewis, Angelica. *Maschere, libretti e libertini: Il mito di Don Giovanni nel teatro europeo.* Rome: Bulzoni, 1992.

Foucault, Michel. *The History of Sexuality, Volume I: An Introduction*. New York: Vintage Books, 1978.

Freud, Sigmund. *Jokes and Their Relation to the Unconscious*. Translated and edited by James Strachey. New York: Norton, 1960.

———. "On Narcissism: An Introduction." In *Standard Edition of the Complete Psychological Works of Sigmund Freud*. Vol. 14, 73–102. London: Hogarth Press, 1963.

Gabbard, Glen, and Krin Gabbard. *Psychiatry and the Cinema*. 2nd ed. Washington, D.C.: American Psychiatric Press, 1999.

Gallucci, Carole. "Alba de Céspedes's *There's No Turning Back:* Challenging the New Woman's Future." In *Mothers of Invention: Women, Italian Fascism, and Culture*, ed. Robin Pickering-Iazzi, 200–19. Minneapolis: University of Minnesota Press, 1995.

Gardaphè, Fred. "Italian American Manhood." In *American Masculinities: A Historical Encyclopedia*, ed. Bret Carroll. New York: The Moschovitis Group, 2003.

Garelick, Rhonda K. *Rising Star: Dandyism, Gender and Performance in the Fin de Siècle*. Princeton, N.J.: Princeton University Press, 1998.

Gassman, Vittorio. *Un grande avvenire dietro le spalle*. Milan: Longanesi, 1981.

Geduld, Carolyn. "*Juliet of the Spirits:* Guido's Anima." In *Federico Fellini: Essays in Criticism*, ed. Peter Bondanella, 137–51. New York: Oxford University Press, 1978.

Giammusso, Maurizio. *Vita di Eduardo*. Milan: Mondadori, 1993.

Gieri, Manuela. *Contemporary Italian Filmmaking: Strategies of Subversion—Pirandello, Fellini, Scola, and the Directors of the New Generation*. Toronto: University of Toronto Press, 1995.

Gili, Jean. *Stato fascista e cinematografia: Repressione e promozione*. Rome: Bulzoni, 1981.

Gilmore, David D. "Introduction: The Shame of Dishonor." In *Honor and Shame and the Unity of the Mediterranean*, ed. David D. Gilmore, 2–21. Washington, D.C.: American Anthropological Association, 1987.

———. *Manhood in the Making: Cultural Concepts of Masculinity*. New Haven, Conn.: Yale University Press, 1990.

———, ed. *Honor and Shame and the Unity of the Mediterranean*. Washington, D.C.: American Anthropological Association, 1987.

Ginsborg, Paul. *A History of Contemporary Italy: Society and Politics, 1943–1988*. London: Penguin, 1990.

Ginsburg, Terri. "Nazis and Drifters: The Containment of Radical (Sexual) Knowledge in Two Italian Neorealist Films." *Journal of the History of Sexuality* 1, no. 2 (Oct. 1990): 241–61.

Giovannini, Maureen J. "Female Chastity Codes in the Circum-Mediterranean: Comparative Perspectives." In *Honor and Shame and the Unity of the Mediterranean*, ed. David D. Gilmore, 61–74. Washington, D.C.: American Anthropological Association, 1987.

———. "Woman: A Dominant Symbol within the Cultural System of a Sicilian

Town." *Man: The Journal of the Royal Anthropological Institute* 16, no. 3 (Nov. 1981): 408–26.

Golden, Daniel. "Pasta or Paradigm: The Place of Italian-American Women in Popular Film." *Explorations in Ethnic Studies: The Journal of the National Association of Interdisciplinary Ethnic Studies* (1978): 3–10.

Gori, Gigliola. "Model of Masculinity: Mussolini, the 'New Italian' of the Fascist Era." *International Journal of the History of Sport* 16, no. 4 (1999): 27–61.

Gramaglia, Mariella. "1968: Il venir dopo e l'andar oltre del movimento femminista." In *La questione femminile in Italia dal '900 ad oggi*, by Giulietta Ascoli, Nadia Fusini, Mariella Gramaglia, Lidia Menapace, Sandra Puccini, Enzo Santarelli, 179–201. Milan: Franco Angeli Editore, 1979.

Grasso, Aldo. *Storia della televisione italiana*. Milan: Garzanti, 1992.

Grignaffini, Giovanna. "Female Identity and Italian Cinema of the 1950s." In *Off-Screen: Women and Film in Italy*, ed. Giuliana Bruno and Maria Nadotti, 117–23. London: Routledge, 1988.

Gundle, Stephen. "*La dolce vita*." *History Today* (Jan. 2000): 29–35.

———. "Fame, Fashion and Style: The Italian Star System." In *Italian Cultural Studies: An Introduction*, ed. David Forgacs and Robert Lumley, 309–26. Oxford: Oxford University Press, 1996.

———. "Feminine Beauty, National Identity, and Political Conflict in Postwar Italy, 1945–1954." *Contemporary European History* 8, no. 3 (1999): 359–78.

———. "From Neo-Realism to *Luci Rosse*: Cinema, Politics and Society, 1945–85." In *Culture and Conflict in Postwar Italy: Essays on Mass and Popular Culture*, ed. Zygmunt Baranski and Robert Lumley, 195–224. London: Macmillan, 1990.

———. "Sophia Loren, Italian Icon." *Historical Journal of Film and Television* 15, no. 3 (1995): 367–85.

Halperin, David. *One Hundred Years of Homosexuality and Other Essays on Greek Love*. New York: Routledge, 1990.

Harris, Warren G. *Sophia Loren: A Biography*. New York: Simon and Schuster, 1998.

Hay, James. *Popular Film Culture in Fascist Italy: The Passing of the Rex*. Bloomington: Indiana University Press, 1986.

Hearn, Jeff. "Imaging the Aging of Men." In *Images of Aging: Cultural Representations of Later Life*, ed. Mike Featherstone and Andrew Wernick, 97–115. London: Routledge, 1995.

Hearn, Jeff, Keith Pringle, Ursula Müller, Elzbieta Oleksy, Emmi Lattu, Janna Chernova, Harry Ferguson, Øystein Gullvåg Holter, Voldemar Kolga, Irina Novikova, Carmine Ventimiglia, Eivind Olsvik, and Teemu Tallberg. "Critical Studies on Men in Ten European Countries: (1) The State of Academic Research." *Men and Masculinities* 4, no. 4 (Apr. 2002): 380–408.

Hollander, Anne. *Sex and Suits*. New York: Knopf, 1995.

Holmund, Chris. *Impossible Bodies: Femininity and Masculinity at the Movies*. London: Routledge, 2002.

Holub, Renate. "Towards a New Rationality? Notes on Feminist and Current Discursive Practices in Italy." *Discourse* 4 (Winter 1981–82): 89–107.

Huysseune, Michel. "Masculinity and Secessionism in Italy: An Assessment." *Nations and Nationalisms* 6, no. 4 (Oct. 2000): 591–610.

Jenckes, Katharine. "Identity, Image, and Sound in Three Films by María Luisa Bemberg." In *Cine-Lit III: Essays on Hispanic Fiction and Film*, ed. George Cabello-Castelet, Jaume Martí-Olivella, and Guy H. Wood, 61–67. Corvallis: Oregon State University, 1997.

Jung, Carl. *The Archetypes and the Collective Unconscious.* 2nd ed. Translated by R. F. C. Hull. Princeton, N.J.: Princeton University Press, 1968.

———. *The Portable Jung.* Edited by Joseph Campbell. Translated by R. F. C. Hull. New York: Penguin, 1971.

Kahn, Coppélia. "Coming of Age: Marriage and Motherhood in *The Taming of the Shrew.*" In *William Shakespeare's The Taming of the Shrew*, ed. Harold Bloom. New York: Chelsea, 1988.

Kaplan, E. Ann. "Trauma and Aging: Marlene Dietrich, Melanie Klein, and Marguerite Duras." In *Figuring Age: Women, Bodies, Generations*, ed. Kathleen Woodward, 171–94. Bloomington: Indiana University Press, 1999.

Kernberg, Otto. *Borderline Conditions and Pathological Narcissism.* New York: Jason Aronson, 1975.

Kezich, Tullio. "Dalla pagina allo schermo." In Il bell'Antonio *di Mauro Bolognini: Dal romanzo al film*, ed. Lino Miccichè, 73–76. Torino: Lindau, 1996.

———. *Fellini.* Milan: Rizzoli, 1987.

———. *Su* La dolce vita *di Federico Fellini: Giorno per giorno, la storia di un film che ha fatto epoca.* Venice: Marsilio, 1996.

King, John, Sheila Whitaker, and Rosa Bosch, eds. *An Argentinian Passion: María Luisa Bemberg and Her Films.* London: Verso, 2000.

Koon, Tracy H. *Believe, Obey, Fight: Political Socialization of Youth in Fascist Italy.* Chapel Hill: University of North Carolina Press, 1985.

Kozlowski, Jean. "Women, Film, and Midlife Sophie's Choice: Sink or Sousatzka?" In *Menopause: A Midlife Passage*, ed. Joan C. Callahan. Bloomington: Indiana University Press, 1993.

Krutnik, Frank. *In a Lonely Street: Film Noir, Genre and Masculinity.* London: Routledge, 1991.

Landy, Marcia. *The Folklore of Consensus: Theatricality in Italian Cinema, 1930–1943.* Albany: SUNY Press, 1998.

———. *Italian Film.* Cambridge: Cambridge University Press, 2000.

LaPalma, Marina deBellagente. "Meditations on Masculinity: *Accattone* and *Midnight Cowboy.*" *Italian Culture* 10 (1992): 217–25.

Laplanche, J., and J.-B. Pontalis. *The Language of Psycho-analysis.* Translated by Donald Nicholson-Smith. New York: W. W. Norton, 1973.

Lasch, Christopher. *The Culture of Narcissism: American Life in an Age of Diminishing Expectations.* 2nd ed. New York: W. W. Norton, 1991.

Lederman, Marie Jean. "Dreams and Vision in Fellini's *City of Women.*" *Journal of Popular Film and Television* 9, no. 3 (Fall 1981): 114–22.

Lehman, Peter. "Crying Over the Melodramatic Penis: Melodrama and Male Nudity in the Films of the 90s." In *Masculinities: Bodies, Movies, Culture*, ed. Peter Lehman, 25–41. New York: Routledge, 2001.

——. *Running Scared: Masculinity and the Representation of the Male Body*. Philadelphia: Temple University Press, 1993.

——, ed. *Masculinities: Bodies, Movies, Culture*. New York: Routledge, 2001.

Lewalski, Barbara K. "Federico Fellini's Purgatorio." In *Federico Fellini: Essays in Criticism*, ed. Peter Bondanella, 113–20. Oxford: Oxford University Press, 1978.

Librach, Ronald S. "Reconciliation in the Realm of Fantasy: The Fellini World and the Fellini Text." *Film/Literature Quarterly* 15, no. 2 (1987): 85–98.

Liehm, Mira. *Passion and Defiance: Film in Italy from 1942 to the Present*. Berkeley: University of California Press, 1984.

López, Ana M. "Are All Latins from Manhattan? Hollywood, Ethnography, and Cultural Colonialism." In *Unspeakable Images: Ethnicity and the Cinema*, ed. Lester Friedman, 404–24. Urbana: University of Illinois Press, 1991.

——. "Of Rhythms and Borders." In *Everynight Life: Culture and Dance in Latin/o America*, ed. Celeste Frasier Delgado and José Esteban Muñoz, 310–44. Durham, N.C.: Duke University Press, 1997.

Lumley, Robert. *States of Emergency: Cultures of Revolt in Italy from 1968 to 1978*. London: Verso, 1990.

Machiavelli, Niccolò. *The Prince*. Translated by Peter Bondanella and Mark Musa. Oxford: Oxford University Press, 1979.

Maggi, Stefania, N. Minicuci, F. Grigoletto, and L. Amaducci. "Italy." In *Aging in Europe*, ed. Johannes J. F. Schroots, Rocío Fernández-Ballesteros, and Georg Rudinger, 73–80. Amsterdam: IOS Press, 1999.

Malossi, Giannino. "La bella figura: Gli italiani e l'eleganza." In *La regola estrosa: Cent'anni di eleganza maschile italiana*, ed. Giannino Malossi, 37–42. Milan: Electa, 1993.

——. "Introduction: The Banality of the Latin Lover." In *Latin Lover: The Passionate South*, ed. Giannino Malossi, 19–24. Milan: Charta, 1996.

——, ed. *Latin Lover: The Passionate South*. Milan: Charta, 1996.

——, ed. *La regola estrosa: Cent'anni di eleganza maschile*. Milan: Electa, 1993.

Manzoli, Giacomo. "Barocco siciliano." *Annali d'italianistica* 17 (1999): 95–106.

Marcus, Millicent. *After Fellini: National Cinemas in the Postmodern Age*. Baltimore, Md.: Johns Hopkins University Press, 2002.

——. *Filmmaking by the Book: Italian Cinema and Literary Adaptation*. Baltimore, Md.: Johns Hopkins University Press, 1993.

——. *Italian Film in the Light of Neorealism*. Princeton, N.J.: Princeton University Press, 1986.

Marrone, Gaetana. "Memory in Fellini's *City of Women*." In *Perspectives on Federico Fellini*, ed. Peter Bondanella and Cristina Degli Esposti, 240–47. New York: G. K. Hall and Co., 1993.

Marsiglio, William, and Richard A. Greer. "A Gender Analysis of Older Men's Sexuality: Social, Psychological, and Biological Dimensions." In *Older Men's Lives*, ed. Edward H. Thompson, Jr., 122–40. Thousand Oaks, Calif., and London: Sage, 1994.

Mastroianni, Marcello. *Mi ricordo, sì, io mi ricordo*. Edited by Francesco Tatò. Milan: Baldini and Castoldi, 1997.

Mazlish, Bruce. "The *Flâneur:* From Spectator to Representation." In *The Flâneur*, ed. Keith Tester, 43–60. London: Routledge, 1994.

McDowell, Colin. *The Man of Fashion: Peacock Males and Perfect Gentlemen*. London: Thames and Hudson, 1997.

Meldini, Piero. *Sposa e madre esemplare: Ideologia e politica della donna e della famiglia durante il fascismo*. Rimini-Firenze: Guaraldi, 1975.

Metz, Christian. "Mirror Construction in Fellini's *8½*." In *8½, Federico Fellini, Director*, ed. Charles Affron, 261–66. New Brunswick, N.J.: Rutgers University Press, 1987.

Miccichè, Lino, ed. *Il bell'Antonio di Mauro Bolognini: Dal romanzo al film*. Torino: Lindau, 1996.

Mignone, Mario B. *Eduardo de Filippo*. Boston: Twayne, 1984.

Milliken, Christie. "Fair to Feminism? Carnivalizing the Carnival in Fellini's *City of Women*." *Spectator* (Spring 1990): 28–45.

Mirabile, María Luisa. "The Politics of Old Age in Italy." In *The Politics of Old Age in Europe*, ed. Alan Walker and Gerhard Naegele, 110–122. Buckingham: Open University Press, 1999.

Moers, Ellen. *The Dandy: Brummell to Beerbohm*. Lincoln: University of Nebraska Press, 1960.

Mondello, Elisabetta. *La nuova italiana: La donna nella stampa e nella cultura del ventennio*. Rome: Riuniti, 1987.

Monti, Rafaele. *Bottega Fellini*, La città delle donne: *Progetto, lavorazione, film*. Rome: De Luca Ed., 1981.

Morelli, Ornella. "The International Success and Domestic Debut of Postwar Italian Fashion." In *Italian Fashion: The Origins of High Fashion and Knitwear*, ed. Gloria Bianchino, Grazietta Butazzi, Alessandra Mottola Molfino, and Arturo Carlo Quintavalle, 59–65. Milan: Electa, 1985.

Mosse, George L. *The Image of Man: The Creation of Modern Masculinity*. New York: Oxford University Press, 1998.

———. *Nationalism and Sexuality: Respectability and Abnormal Sexuality in Modern Europe*. New York: Howard Fertig, 1985.

Nardini, Gloria. *Che Bella Figura! The Power of Performance in an Italian Ladies' Club in Chicago*. Albany: SUNY Press, 1999.

Neale, Stephen. "Masculinity as Spectacle." In *Screening the Male: Exploring Masculinities in Hollywood Cinema*, ed. Steven Cohan and Ina Rae Hark, 9–20. London: Routledge, 1993.

Nerenberg, Ellen. "Tartar Control: Masculinity and *Impegno* in Buzzati's *Il deserto dei tartari*." *Italica* 74, no. 2 (Summer 1997): 217–34.

Newman, Kathleen. "'Convocar tanto mundo': Narrativising Authoritarianism and Globalisation in *De eso no se habla.*" In *An Argentinian Passion: María Luisa Bemberg and Her Films,* ed. John King, Sheila Whitaker, and Rosa Bosch, 181–92. London: Verso, 2000.

Noriega, Chon A. "Internal 'Others': Hollywood Narratives about Mexican Americans." In *Mediating Two Worlds: Cinematic Encounters in the Americas,* ed. John King, Ana M. López, and Manuel Alvarado, 52–66. London: British Film Institute, 1993.

O'Healy, Àine. "Are the Children Watching Us? The Roman Films of Francesca Archibugi." *Annali d'Italianistica* 17 (1999): 121–36.

——. "Interview with the Vamp: Deconstructing Femininity in Fellini's Final Films (*Intervista, La voce della luna*)." In *Federico Fellini: Contemporary Perspectives,* ed. Frank Burke and Marguerite R. Waller, 209–32. Toronto: University of Toronto Press, 2002.

——. "Unspeakable Bodies: Fellini's Female Grotesques." *RLA: Romance Languages Annual* 4 (1992): 325–29.

Olivieri, Angelo. *Le stelle del varietà: Rivista, avanspettacolo e cabaret dal 1936 al 1966.* Rome: Gremese, 1989.

Panaro, Alberto. "Mass-produced Valentinos: Rudolph Valentino's Doubles." In *Latin Lover: The Passionate South,* ed. Giannino Malossi, 95–113. Milan: Charta, 1996.

Pauluzzi, Fausto. "*City of Women:* Fellini's Bothersome Judgment Day among U.S. Critics." In *National Traditions in Motion Pictures: Proceedings of the Third Annual Film Conference at Kent State University April 17, 1985,* ed. Douglas Radcliff Umstead, 43–53. Kent, Ohio: Kent State University Romance Languages Department, 1985.

Pecori, Franco. *Vittorio De Sica.* Firenze: La Nuova Italia, 1980.

Perry, Ted. *Filmguide to 8½.* Bloomington: Indiana University Press, 1975.

Pezzini, Isabella. "L'ideologia virile e le sue trasgressioni: il dandy, il rebelle." In *Virilità e trasgressione,* ed. Isabella Pezzini, 9–25. Novara: Istituto Geografico De Agostini, 1992.

Piccone Stella, Simonetta. *La prima generazione: Ragazze e ragazzi nel miracolo economico italiano.* Milan: FrancoAngeli, 1993.

Piccone Stella, Simonetta, and Chiara Saraceno, eds. *Genere: La costruzione sociale del femminile e del maschile.* Bologna: Il Mulino, 1996.

Pickering-Iazzi, Robin. *Mothers of Invention: Women, Italian Fascism, and Culture.* Minneapolis: University of Minnesota Press, 1995.

——. *Politics of the Visible: Writing Women, Culture, and Fascism.* Minneapolis: University of Minnesota Press, 1997.

Pinsker, Sanford. *The Schlemiel as Metaphor: Studies in Yiddish and American Jewish Fiction.* Revised and enlarged ed. Carbondale: Southern Illinois University Press, 1991.

Pirandello, Luigi. *Il fu Mattia Pascal.* Milan: Mondadori, 1933 [1904].

——. *On Humor.* Translated by Antonio Illiano and Daniel P. Testa. Chapel Hill: University of North Carolina Press, 1974.

——. *L'umorismo.* Milan: Mondadori, 1986.

Pitkin, Donald S. "Italian Urbanscape: Intersection of Private and Public."

In *The Cultural Meaning of Urban Space*, ed. Robert Rotenberg and Gary McDonogh, 95–101. Westport, Conn.: Bergin and Garvey, 1993.

Pitt-Rivers, Julian. "Honour and Social Status." In *Honour and Shame: The Values of Mediterranean Society*, ed. J. G. Peristiany, 19–77. Chicago: University of Chicago Press, 1966.

Polhemus, Ted. *Street Style: From Catwalk to Sidewalk*. New York: Thames and Hudson, 1994.

Post, Stephen G. "Aging and Meaning: The Christian Tradition." In *Handbook of the Humanities and Aging*, ed. Thomas R. Cole, David D. Van Tassel, and Robert Kastenbaum, 127–46. New York: Springer, 1992.

Pretini, Giancarlo. *Spettacolo leggero: Dal music-hall, al varietà, alla rivista, al musical*. Udine: Trapezio, 1992.

Quintavalle, Arturo Carlo. "Fashion: The Three Cultures." In *Italian Fashion: The Origins of High Fashion and Knitwear*, ed. Gloria Bianchino, Grazietta Butazzi, Alessandra Mottola Molfino, and Arturo Carlo Quintavalle, 21–25. Milan: Electa, 1985.

Ravetto, Kriss. *The Unmasking of Fascist Aesthetics*. Minneapolis: University of Minnesota Press, 2001.

Reich, Jacqueline. "Reading, Writing, and Rebellion: Collectivity, Specularity, and Sexuality in the Italian Schoolgirl Comedy, 1934–43." In *Mothers of Invention: Women, Italian Fascism, and Culture*, ed. Robin Pickering-Iazzi, 220–51. Minnesota: University of Minnesota Press, 1995.

Reich, Jacqueline, and Piero Garofalo, eds. *Re-viewing Fascism: Italian Cinema, 1922–1943*. Bloomington: Indiana University Press, 2002.

Reyes, Luis, and Peter Rubie. *Hispanics in Hollywood: An Encyclopedia of Film and Television*. New York: Garland, 1994.

Romano, Carlo. "Anarchy Hurt the Latin Lover: Fantasy, Decline and Eternal Fascination of the Latin Lover." In *Latin Lover: The Passionate South*, ed. Giannino Malossi, 60–63. Milan: Charta, 1996.

Rowe, Kathleen. *The Unruly Woman: Gender and the Genres of Laughter*. Austin: University of Texas Press, 1995.

Rumble, Patrick. "Tornatore e L'America: Il cinema dell'anamnesi." In *Sicilia e altre storie: Il cinema di Giuseppe Tornatore*, ed. Valerio Caprara, 11–20. Naples: Edizioni Scientifiche Italiane, 1996.

Russo, Mary. "Female Grotesques: Carnival and Theory." In *Feminist Studies, Critical Studies*, ed. Teresa de Lauretis, 213–29. Bloomington: Indiana University Press, 1986.

———. *The Female Grotesque: Risk, Excess, and Modernity*. New York: Routledge, 1995.

Salsini, Laura A. *Gendered Genres: Female Experiences and Narrative Patterns in the Works of Matilde Serao*. Madison, N.J.: Fairleigh Dickinson University Press, 1999.

Salvati, Michele. *Economia e politica in Italia dal dopoguerra a oggi*. Milan: Garzanti, 1984.

Sarris, Andrew. "Pietro Germi: Idealist with No Illusions." In *Pietro Germi: The Latin Loner*, ed. Mario Sesti, 19–21. Milan: Edizioni Olivares, 1999.

Sassoon, Donald. *Contemporary Italy: Economy, Society and Politics since 1945.* 2nd ed. London: Longman, 1997.

Savio, Francesco. *Ma l'amore no: Realismo, formalismo, propaganda e telefoni bianchi nel cinema italiano di regime (1930–43).* Milan: Sonzogno, 1975.

Scala, Flaminio. *Scenarios of the Commedia dell'arte: Flaminio Scala's Il teatro dell favole rappresentative.* Translated by Henry F. Salerno. New York: Limelight, 1989.

Schneider, Jane, and Peter Schneider. *Culture and Political Economy in Western Sicily.* New York: Academic Press, 1976.

Sciascia, Leonardo. "Don Giovanni a Catania." Introduction to *Don Giovanni in Sicilia* by Vitaliano Brancati. Milan: Bompiani, 1999.

———. *Nero su nero.* Torino: Einaudi, 1979.

Serao, Matilde. *Il ventre di Napoli.* Rome: Vito Bianco Editore, 1973 [1884].

Sesti, Mario. "Pietro Germi: Life and Films of a Latin Loner." In *Pietro Germi: The Latin Loner,* ed. Mario Sesti, 22–64. Milan: Edizioni Olivares, 1999.

———. *Tutto il cinema di Pietro Germi.* Milan: Baldini and Castoldi, 1997.

———, ed. *Pietro Germi: The Latin Loner.* Milan: Edizioni Olivares, 1999.

Settembrini, Luigi. "From Haute-Couture to Prêt-à-porter." In *The Italian Metamorphosis, 1943–1968,* ed. Germano Celant, 484–94. New York: Guggenheim Museum, 1994.

———. "The Passionate South: Holiday Fun." In *Latin Lover: The Passionate South,* ed. Giannino Malossi, 64–80. Milan: Charta, 1996.

———. "La regola estrosa: Cent'anni di eleganza maschile." In *La regola estrosa: Cent'anni di eleganza maschile italiana,* ed. Giannino Malossi, 13–33. Milan: Electa, 1993.

Sgritta, Giovanni B., and Paolo Tufari. "Italy." In *Divorce in Europe,* ed. Robert Chester, with the collaboration of Gerrit Kooy. The Hague: Netherlands Interuniversity Demographic Institute, 1977.

Shahar, Shulamith. "The Old Body in Medieval Culture." In *Framing Medieval Bodies,* ed. Sarah Kay and Miri Rubin, 160–286. Manchester: Manchester University Press, 1994.

Silverman, Kaja. *Male Subjectivity at the Margins.* New York: Routledge, 1993.

Siniscalchi, Claudio. "Il primato del racconto." In *Sicilia e altre storie: Il cinema di Giuseppe Tornatore,* ed. Valerio Caprara, 21–33. Naples: Edizioni Scientifiche Italiane, 1996.

Sitney, P. Adams. *Vital Crises in Italian Cinema.* Austin: University of Texas Press, 1995.

Skinner, James M. *The Cross and the Cinema: The Legion of Decency and the National Catholic Office for Motion Pictures, 1933–1970.* Westport, Conn.: Praeger, 1993.

Smith, Paul. *Clint Eastwood: A Cultural Production.* Minneapolis: University of Minnesota Press, 1993.

Sobchack, Vivian. "Scary Women: Cinema, Surgery, and Special Effects." In *Figuring Age: Women, Bodies, Generations,* ed. Kathleen Woodward, 200–11. Bloomington: Indiana University Press, 1999.

Spackman, Barbara. "The Fascist Rhetoric of Virility." *Stanford Italian Review* 8, no. 1–2 (1990): 81–101.

———. *Fascist Virilities: Rhetoric, Ideology, and Social Fantasy in Italy*. Minneapolis: University of Minnesota Press, 1996.

———. "*Inter musam et ursam moritur:* Folengo and the Gaping 'Other' Mouth." In *Refiguring Woman: Perspectives on Gender and the Italian Renaissance*, ed. Marilyn Migiel and Juliana Schiesari, 19–34. Ithaca, N.Y.: Cornell University Press, 1991.

Sparke, Penny. "'A Home for Everybody?' Design, Ideology and the Culture of the Home in Italy, 1945–1972." In *Culture and Conflict in Postwar Italy: Essays on Mass and Popular Culture*, ed. Zygmunt Baranski and Robert Lumley, 225–41. London: Macmillan, 1990.

Spinazzola, Vittorio. *Cinema e pubblico: Lo spettacolo filmico in Italia 1945–1965*. Rome: Bulzoni, 1985.

Steele, Valerie. "Italian Fashion and America." In *The Italian Metamorphosis, 1943–1968*, ed. Germano Celant, 496–506. New York: Guggenheim Museum, 1994.

Stubbs, John C. "Fellini's Portrait of the Artist as Creative Problem Solver." *Cinema Journal* 41, no. 4 (Summer 2002): 116–31.

Studlar, Gaylyn. *This Mad Masquerade: Stardom and Masculinity in the Jazz Age*. New York: Columbia University Press, 1996.

Svevo, Italo. *La coscienza di Zeno*. Milan: Dall'Oglio, 1976 [1923]. Translated by Beryl de Zoete as *The Confessions of Zeno* (New York: Alfred A. Knopf, 1930).

Tagliabue, John. "Crowds in Rome Bid Farewell to Mastroianni, Artist of Film." *New York Times* (Dec. 23, 1996): B11.

Tester, Keith. Introduction to *The Flâneur*, ed. Keith Tester, 1–21. London: Routledge, 1994.

Theweleit, Klaus. *Male Fantasies, Volume I: Women, Floods, Bodies, History*. Translated by Steven Conway et al. Minneapolis: University of Minnesota Press, 1987.

Tofetti, Sergio. *Giuseppe Tornatore*. Torino: Lindau, 1995.

Tomasi di Lampedusa, Guiseppe. *Il gattopardo*. Milan: Feltrinelli, 1958.

Tornabuoni, Lietta. "Interview with Fellini on *City of Women*." *La stampa*, Mar. 29, 1980 (as reprinted on liner notes of DVD, 2001, New Yorker Video).

Torri, Bruno. "*Il bell'Antonio* di Mauro Bolognini." In Il bell'Antonio *di Mauro Bolognini: Dal romanzo al film*, ed. Lino Miccichè, 57–61. Torino: Lindau, 1996.

Triani, Giorgio. "Love Affairs in Romagna: The Sociology of Beach Boys." In *Latin Lover: The Passionate South*, ed. Giannino Malossi, 136–47. Milan: Charta, 1996.

Tylus, Jane. "Women at the Windows: *Commedia dell'arte* and Theatrical Practice in Early Modern Italy." *Theatre Journal* 49 (1997): 323–42.

Vanelli, Daniela. *Teatro di varietà a Livorno tra il 1880 e il 1914*. Livorno: Editrice Nuova Fortezza, 1990.

Verdicchio, Pasquale. "The Preclusion of Postcolonial Discourse in Southern

Italy." In *Revisioning Italy: National Identity and Global Culture,* ed. Beverly Allen and Mary Russo, 191–212. Minneapolis: University of Minnesota Press, 1997.

Welle, John. "Fellini's Use of Dante in *La dolce vita.*" *Studies in Medievalism* 2, no. 3 (Summer 1983), 53–66.

Willis, Sharon. *High Contrast: Race and Gender in Contemporary Hollywood Film.* Durham, N.C.: Duke University Press, 1997.

Wilson, Jason. "María Luisa Bemberg's *De eso no se habla:* From Fiction to Film, Some Notes." In *An Argentinian Passion: María Luisa Bemberg and Her Films,* ed. John King, Sheila Whitaker, and Rosa Bosch, 174–80. London: Verso, 2000.

Woodward, Kathleen. *Aging and Its Discontents: Freud and Other Fictions.* Bloomington: Indiana University Press, 1991.

———. "Youthfulness as Masquerade." *Discourse* 11, no. 1 (Fall–Winter 1988–89): 109–42.

———, ed. *Figuring Age: Women, Bodies, Generations.* Bloomington: Indiana University Press, 1999.

Zagarrio, Vito. "La regia." In Il bell'Antonio *di Mauro Bolognini: Dal romanzo al film,* ed. Lino Miccichè, 63–68. Torino: Lindau, 1996.

Index

Page numbers in italics refer to illustrations.

217

Jacqueline Reich is Associate Professor of Italian and Comparative Literature at the State University of New York at Stony Brook, where she directs the Cinema and Cultural Studies undergraduate program. She is co-editor with Piero Garofalo of *Re-viewing Fascism: Italian Cinema, 1922–1943*, also published by Indiana University Press.